ABOUT THE AUTHOR

Neil Montagnana Wallace was born in Blacktown, New South Wales, and like thousands of other kids in the Hills District he fell in love with soccer, before moving to Melbourne when he was fourteen. He later satisfied his curiosity by becoming a full-time soccer player in England's lower leagues but soon returned to Australia and continued playing in Melbourne's state and premier leagues.

He has a Business degree and has worked in a number of marketing roles, including Marketing and Events Manager at the Victorian Soccer Federation. *Our Socceroos* is his first book.

www.oursocceroos.com

our**socceroos**

Neil Montagnana Wallace

RANDOM HOUSE AUSTRALIA

Every effort has been made to identify copyright holders of material used in this book. The author and publisher would be pleased to hear from any copyright holders who have not been acknowledged. Full picture credits can be found on page 210.

Random House Australia Pty Ltd
20 Alfred Street, Milsons Point, NSW 2061
http://www.randomhouse.com.au

Sydney   New York   Toronto
London   Auckland   Johannesburg

First published by Random House Australia 2004

National Library of Australia
Cataloguing-in-Publication Entry:

Wallace, Neil Montagnana.
Our Socceroos.

ISBN 1 74051 306 1.

1. Socceroos (Soccer team). 2. Soccer – Australia.
3. Soccer players – Australia – Anecdotes. I. Title.

796.3340994

Cover and internal design by Leonard Montagnana, Woof Creative Solutions
Cover image by Scott Barbour, Getty Images.
Cover images used in strip of photographs courtesy of the players profiled.
Printed and bound by Tien Wah Press (PTE) Limited

10 9 8 7 6 5 4 3 2 1

DEDICATED TO

Gorgeous Val, for keeping me in slippers.
I am undoubtedly the luckiest love-struck
kid on the planet.

The Montagnanas for their professional and
personal generosity.

The Wallaces for being £10 Poms.

Flash for being the best boss in the world.

And, of course, to the twenty-six Socceroos
in this book for unreservedly sharing their
lives with a stranger.

TABLE OF CONTENTS

FOREWORD

Blame it on the '74 Socceroos. I was an impressionable 13-year-old when that legendary team, coached by Rale Rasic, qualified for Australia's first-ever appearance in the World Cup finals. Anybody reading this who has dared to dream can appreciate just what that event did for a football-crazy adolescent who was fantasising about fame and glory on the playing fields of the world. While my home town of Speers Point, on the shores of Lake Macquarie in regional Australia, had once seemed a whole universe away from the bright lights of the game, suddenly it was connected. Suddenly, the unattainable had been reached. The fact that Ray Baartz and Col Curran – two fabulous players who had learned the game in the same neck of the woods as my mates and me – were members of the '74 team provided additional motivation. If Baartzy and Bunny could do it, so could we! Attendances at our backyard and playground games doubled, toes were kicked out of school shoes, windows were broken, and family pets ducked for cover, as we chased a much-

scuffed ball in pursuit of the dream. That same scenario must have been replicated all over Australia as kids drew inspiration from the men in green and gold, who were destined to rub shoulders with the superstars of the world game. The extra thrust carried me right into my fifteenth year, when I found myself clutching my boots and hopes and heading for England. In the same way, a generation before, my own dad had been motivated by the exploits of the Australian great Joe Marston to make his way to the UK for a shot at a professional contract. Over the years, my time at Middlesbrough and Liverpool brought me more joy and success than an individual could hope for. My greatest regret was that I chose to never play for Australia, because I thought doing so would hinder my club career with Liverpool.

In recent years, I have been able to empathise with the European- and UK-based Australian players, as it is exceedingly difficult to put careers on hold and fly home for international duty. After I retired as a player, I lobbied for the creation of a UK base for the Socceroos and have been thrilled to see the concept, finally, has been embraced. It's made everything so much easier for the players to get together, renew their ties and advance the Socceroos' reputation as a force in world football. As a London-based Aussie, I have been glowing with national pride at the way the current generation of Socceroos have delivered so much credibility to our game.

I'm writing this shortly after watching Australia play in London and Dublin. Rather than looking like a hastily flung together national team, the Australians

played with the fluency, maturity and skill of a well-oiled Premier League side. They are a fabulous bunch of players who deserve to be seen in the same light as our finest national sporting teams.

Recognition is so important. Despite being Australia's most-played football code, our game trails the field in media coverage. This has meant that one of the greatest yarns in Australian sport – the story of the Socceroos – remains a national mystery. From the furnace of Teheran to the paddy fields of Vietnam; from the palm-lined pitches of the South Pacific to the wintry den of Hampden Park; from South Melbourne to South America, it is our greatest sporting story. When you consider the sacrifices made by those pioneering semi-professionals who played and travelled under the most hostile of conditions, you simply shake your head in awe. After all, many of them were such gifted athletes, they could have played sports guaranteed to bring more fame and wealth; but they stayed true to their code.

Nothing will ever change the fact that I didn't play for Australia. And nothing will ever change my admiration for those who did. Their stories as told in this book shed long-overdue light on the legacy they have left for those of us who love the world game.

Craig Johnston

Craig Johnston
Five English Championships with Liverpool FC
Two European Cups with Liverpool FC
Two League Cups with Liverpool FC
One FA Cup with Liverpool FC

Craig lifting the European Cup with Liverpool, 1984.

You've got to **start** somewhere...

Since 1922, over 650 men have had the honour of playing soccer for the Australian national team. Some have only played once, and an elite group of eleven have played over fifty 'A' class matches. Some have played in Olympic Games, and quite a few have experienced the heartache of failed World Cup qualifying campaigns. A small group has experienced the elation of making it to the world's biggest stage.

Not long ago, Socceroos had to work while representing their country. These days they can earn millions of dollars on the lucrative fields of international club competition. They used to nail their own studs into ankle-high boots and sweat under thick, woollen, green jumpers sporting a big gold V. Now, they wear multicoloured, multistudded, personalised, lightweight boots and high-tech, breathable fabrics. But they have all worn their hearts on their sleeves, and are united behind the hard work, passion, sacrifice and commitment required to earn the right to be called a Socceroo.

Our Socceroos provides a unique insight into the lives and careers of twenty-six Socceroo legends from the 1940s right through to today. Their personal stories show what it takes to make it to the top, and what it meant to them when they arrived.

•••

In 1922, the Australian national team played their first games as they toured New Zealand. They managed nine wins, one draw and four losses; but more importantly, they set tradition in motion. Over the next couple of decades, there were more games against New Zealand, as well as fixtures against Canada, the Dutch East Indies, China, Palestine, India, South Africa, England and a number of European club teams. Losses were quite common, but so were big crowds closely linked to a mainly British – and therefore, mainly football – heritage. When England inflicted a humiliating 17–0 defeat at the SCG in 1951, it was perhaps our darkest day, and symbolic of our status as a developing nation both on and off the field. In 2003, the Socceroos outclassed England, in England, and registered a 3–1 victory. Australia, and our national soccer team, have come a long way.

Our first major international tournament was the 1956 Melbourne Olympics. It was an era when the world's best players took part, and brought with them significant international and domestic interest. We beat Japan, but lost to India, and were unlucky not to make the quarter finals. Significantly, 102,000 people watched the Soviet Union defeat Yugoslavia 1–0 in the final at the MCG, and the pulling power of The World Game was plain to see.

The pulling power of Down Under was also obvious, and immigration was booming. The majority of new arrivals were European and they brought their ingrained love of soccer with them. Australian law makers and politicians encouraged a progressive society and, in many ways, soccer led the way.

In New South Wales in 1957 the sport's national governing body, the Australian Soccer Football Association, was challenged by a breakaway group, the Federation clubs. Their biggest issue was that newly created clubs had to begin their time in the lower leagues – which is fair enough, however there was no system of promotion and relegation, so strong and growing clubs were

Australia's 1974 World Cup heroes.

restricted in their development. Many of them had been formed and were supported by increasingly wealthy migrant groups who thought they had a lot to offer the local game. It was perhaps the first time in Australia's history that ethnic communities flexed their muscles and voted to change the system.

The conflict spread around the country. The new state Federations were not recognised by the world governing body, FIFA, which meant enterprising and opportunistic Federation clubs took the chance to bring out top players from their home countries to play in the newly formed, unauthorised competition – without forking out international transfer fees. Higher wages were paid to lure the stars here and the resultant increase in crowds generously repaid the investment. The state Federations expanded rapidly while the Association clubs were disintegrating.

Local players had to decide whether to defect to the Federation clubs that seemed to have all the momentum (and money!) and risk a life-time ban by the Association. It was a confusing, threatening time in the sport's history, but it ultimately set a platform on which the game could move forward.

In April 1960, FIFA refused to recognise the Australian Soccer Football Association because of the transfer irregularities in Federation clubs, and their lack of control over the situation. The last international game administered by the Association was held on 13 June 1959 against Hearts of Scotland, in which the Aussies crawled to a symbolic 9–0 defeat due to the bans placed on numerous players who had defected to Federation clubs. It was time for change.

In 1961, the Australian Soccer Federation was officially formed as a collective voice for the now powerful state Federations, and they lobbied FIFA for re-entry into the international soccer family. The Federation paid enough of the outstanding transfer fees for top Europeans poached during the time of the split, and in July 1963 they were acknowledged as the new governing body of soccer in Australia.

Australia's first World Cup campaign began soon after, in 1965, but ended as quickly as it started when Australia was hammered in front of huge crowds in North Korea. Players had sacrificed wages, and in some cases relationships, for that campaign, and did the same in the next major tour organised by the ASF in 1967 – a trip to Asia during the heat of the Vietnam War.

The camaraderie born from such trying conditions snowballed into the 1969 campaign for the 1970 World Cup, however, after an absurdly difficult four-month qualifying series, Australia was bundled out by Israel at the final stage. It was on that tour that a journalist named Tony Hoystead first referred to the Australian national team as 'The Socceroos' – and in spirit as well as name our national team was building an identity.

In 1974, the Socceroos graduated and made the world take notice when they made the World Cup finals (Australia's one and only appearance to date). Three years later, Australia's first national sporting competition kicked off when the National Soccer League was created, taking the domestic game to a new level. On the international scene, the late 1970s and early 1980s saw an era of 'honourable losses', before the so-called Mad Dog period in the mid- to late 1980s reinvigorated the national team. By the end of the late 1980s, the export appeal of our best Socceroos accelerated as players strived to make a lucrative living in the hotbeds of European competition. The trickle of talent leaving Australia's shores turned into a flood in the mid- to late 1990s, and created a crop of highly trained, professional players – but also raised the thorny issue of club versus country and presented difficulties in scheduling meaningful Socceroo games.

In the late 1990s, the Australian Soccer Federation was renamed Soccer Australia. Soon after, the heart-wrenching conclusion to the 1998 World Cup campaign against Iran became etched into Australian sporting history. The next time around, in 2001, Uruguay proved too good, and the Socceroos were left to ponder 'what if?' as the Australian sporting public endured yet another World Cup finals without the green and gold. Still, both qualifying games drew crowds of over 85,000 to the MCG and television audiences of millions.

Despite repeatedly being edged out of World Cup glory in recent times, and despite the debilitating politics associated with the game's administration, soccer is now the most popular sport among Australian youth, and there are numerous millionaire Aussies playing at the highest level around the world. The Socceroos have risen above the hardships, as they always have.

In mid-2003, Soccer Australia's growing list of faults led to the organisation being declared insolvent. A new board took control, and the soccer public heaved an optimistic sigh of relief. An entirely new organisation was set up to govern the game, and it was ironically named the Australian Soccer Association. The ASA immediately took over Australia's membership of FIFA – lost over forty years earlier.

•••

There have been many twists and turns, heroes and villains, laughter and tears intrinsically woven into the word 'Socceroo'. Individually, this book gives personal accounts of Australian soccer from the 1940s to today, through previously untold stories from legends of the green and gold. Collectively, it paints a picture of Australia's soccer history and its reflection of our multicultural nation.

Their stories are Australia's story.

'Their stories are Australia's story.'

Joe MARSTON MBE

Socceroo 1947–1958

The thousands of European migrants who came to Australia after World War II were united in their desire for a better life and, usually, a passion for soccer. Our social landscape changed almost overnight, and the game here boomed. But in the midst of Australia's magnetic attraction, Joe Marston took our local product back the other way.

He hasn't just played with and against some of the world's best players; he remains friends with them. They were his peers and they were his equals. He was our first international soccer star and he opened British eyes to the potential of the Australian game. Joe Marston was the pioneer for what has become a golden path for Australian players.

Joe played for five years with Preston North End in the English first division, including the 1954 FA Cup Final. An uncompromising and thoughtful defender, he was selected as the only foreigner in the English FA side of 1954, and in 2000 he was the fourth man chosen in Preston's Best 100 Players of All Time. He is one of only two Australian players to become a Member of the British Empire (MBE) in the Queen's honours (along with Johnny Warren), and is alongside Donald Bradman, Dawn Fraser, Dally Messenger, Keith Miller, Reg Gasnier, Clive Churchill, Richie Benaud and Betty Cuthbert in the Sydney Cricket Ground's Walk of Honour. He is a member of the Sport Hall of Fame and was an inaugural inductee into the Soccer Australia Hall of Fame. In spite of five years in the wilderness overseas, he played thirty-five 'A' international test matches for Australia and has also been captain and coach of the national team.

•••

Sydney's inner-city working-class suburb of Leichhardt was where it all began for the third-generation Aussie. Joe loved Leichhardt and, in a situation almost unheard of in the modern game, he spent his entire Australian career with his local club. Originally, the club was known as Leichhardt–Annandale, but in the late 1950s it became APIA Leichhardt and was run by the large Italian community that was settling in the area. He made his debut as a 17-year-old fullback in the mid-1940s and was on his way to becoming a club legend. *'I loved Lambart Park. I always wanted to play for my local club, and went on to play 410 senior games for them . . . it was when goalkeepers didn't wear numbers, and I used to wear number 1. When I came back from England, I went straight back to APIA, and I also coached them when my playing days were over.'*

Joe made his international debut in 1947 against the touring South Africans, in front of 42,000 people in Sydney. The 21-year-old played all five tests in that series and made his mark as an unflappable, reassuring force in the Aussie defence. Back then, players wore ankle-high boots and used heavy leather balls complete with thick, laced stitching. The Aussies wore long-sleeved green jumpers with a big gold V and white shorts. There wasn't any money, but there was plenty of excitement, and an ever-growing interest in the national team. Joe Marston's elite career had begun.

Our footballing pioneer arriving in 'sunny' England.

Training rain, hail and shine. Or Snow!

It was in 1949 that the seed of a challenge was sown, and it resulted in a five-year pursuit of personal improvement that took him to the pinnacle of the world's best club competition. *'There was a supporter of Leichhardt–Annandale named Percy Sewell who knew people in the game in England. He was keen to see how an Australian would fare in what was the best league in the world and suggested to our left winger he should give it a go. He [the player] was in the phone booth . . . talking to Joe Smith at Blackpool and I happened to be in the booth with him. In the end he didn't want to go, so I spoke with Blackpool instead. They didn't need a defender, but suggested Preston might be a better option.'*

Preston North End had just been relegated. They were a club of great tradition (including winning the first two league championships in 1889 and 1890) and were on the lookout for players to get them back into Division One. There were no agents back then, however Percy Sewell did what he could to help. Preston contacted Joe via telegram and quite plainly told him to get over there as soon as he could.

Joe's wife, Edith, had never left New South Wales and the young couple didn't know a soul outside Australia. For newly wed Australians in their early twenties, an experiment like this required more than the ability to kick a soccer ball. Joe's decision to go was ultimately made for football reasons, but it wasn't made alone. *'I wanted to see what it was like as a professional and how good I could be. Money wasn't the issue because I could've stayed working and playing here and earning more. In the end it was up to Edith to agree and she thought it sounded exciting. We decided it couldn't hurt to go for a year and see.'*

With determination and fortitude akin to that of the masses of migrants starting to land on Australia's shores, Joe and Edith resolved to take that same adventurous spirit back the other way. *'It all happened quite quickly in the end. I was already an Australian international and they were keen for a defender. Edith and I wanted to go by boat and enjoy ourselves, however Preston were adamant that they wanted me there as soon as possible. It was a four-day plane trip and cost £650 for two tickets. Only the elite flew then and we felt quite out of place.'*

'I wanted to see what it was like as a **professional** and **how good** I could be.'

'At half-time they tipped some whiskey on my leg as a disinfectant, gave me a mouthful as well, then put in some stitches. Out I went again.'

It was a time when the base, standard wage for a first-year professional at any English club was £7 a week during the season, and £6 a week in the off-season. It increased after you had played five senior games, but everyone basically earned the same money from club to club until the league's 'maximum wage' was abolished in 1961. Transfers were generally the exception and the players were usually from the town they played for. Close bonds were therefore formed between the fans and the players who were representing their town. Fans could go to games for next to nothing, so crowds were enormous and the atmosphere was unparalleled.

From day one in England, that spirit was obvious to the Marstons. *'When we arrived in Preston there must have been over 100 people there to welcome us. There was a lot of media and a lot of attention. The first team squad was heading up to Scotland for some games the next day, so they put Edith up in a nice hotel and the directors' wives would call on her while I was away, to make her feel welcome. We had left the Australian summer and the beach for a Northern English winter, but everyone went out of their way to help us settle.'*

The trip to Scotland was a success for Joe and after just one week they offered him a contract. The risk to fly out an unknown Australian international seemed to have worked. He was given peg seventeen in the change rooms and officially became a Preston player.

His first twenty-three games were played as a right-back in the club's reserve team. After impressing the coaching staff with his enthusiasm and defensive resilience, he made his senior debut on 21 October 1950. It wasn't an overly convincing performance, however he was given another chance when he was switched to centre-back, after the regular broke his leg in a fourth-round FA Cup tie. This time the mark Joe left was spectacular and uncompromising. The club went on to win the second division and jumped straight back into the big-time. Joe played in every game after his positional change.

'It was a good start. I had made an impression and everyone had helped us settle in. The club bought a fully furnished house that we rented from them for only 30 shillings a week and, even though there was still rationing in England [after World War II], one of the directors always managed to get us extra eggs, and another official used to be able to get extra coal.'

The 1950–51 season saw Joe form a formidable partnership with Tommy Docherty and Willie Forbes that lasted throughout the early 1950s. The three men rarely missed a game and began to tattoo themselves into the fans' affections. Regular capacity crowds of 40,000 at their Deepdale home, along with trips to Old Trafford, Highbury, Anfield and other famous first division grounds signified the answer to Joe's initial question of 'Can I do it?' Now the challenge was to stay there.

'After the '50–51 season, the club wanted to extend my contract and I agreed. I was earning the same money as the other players in England and was playing every game. I also got along well with the fans, and with the players and directors. In fact, the directors began to ask Edith when she was going to have a family. They figured it was a good way to keep me there if we had English children!'

Not only did they wear ankle-high boots and play with heavy leather balls in the 1950s, there were also no substitutes. If you were injured, you battled on as best you could or your team would be a man down. *'I remember losing three teeth one Christmas Day game. Another time, I was hit so hard in the leg with a heavy ball that the lacing and stitching left a distinct ball-shaped purple bruise for days. We got regularly cut by sliding on the icy grounds and one time I badly sliced my leg open, but it was so cold that it didn't bleed much. At half-time they tipped some whiskey on my leg as a disinfectant, gave me a mouthful as well, then put in some stitches. Out I went again.'*

A signature towering header in the snow.

Football in those days wasn't a profession for the faint-hearted, however sportsmanship was still highly regarded by players and fans alike. '*I didn't see any real violence in the time I was there. Tough tackling yes, but sportsmanship still existed. There was no diving or abusing the referee. I don't recall any violence in the crowds either, and in fact, crowds used to applaud good players from the opposing team on occasion. They loved the game and appreciated when it was done well.*'

Season 1952–53 was one of mixed emotions. The club was winning games and playing well, however the Marstons began to feel pangs for home. Nothing much was said outside their own home however, and Joe went about his business of starring for a side that was in the leading pack of the world's premier club competition. In drama that only sport seems to be able to manufacture, the league championship came down to the final round of the season. Preston did what was required of them by winning their final match, so it was left to see what Arsenal could do. The Gunners hung on to win their match too, and tied with Preston on points. '*That was the closest we came and you can't get any closer. We were on the same points, and lost the title by one goal in the end. It was a great year for the club but afterwards, I was ready for a break.*'

Joe informed the club that he and Edith were ready to go home. They didn't know if it would be for good, but after three years, they wanted to see their families and the sun. The club understood, but did not want to lose their crowd favourite. '*The mayor, the club and the fans rallied around at a function to raise money for our trip back home. They raised enough for two return airfares, as well as two tickets to watch the 1953 FA Cup final, so we said I would come back and play another two years to repay their generosity.*

'*The '53 Cup between Blackpool and Bolton was a great game and a wonderful experience to watch. It was called the "Matthews Final", after the performance of the great Sir Stanley Matthews. The singing and the spectacle was just that bit better than during the season. We were happy to just be there in the crowd, but Edith couldn't resist saying, "Wouldn't it be great to play here next year?"*'

Sending the couple to the FA Cup final on the way home was a good idea. It recharged Joe's batteries, and after a short time back in Sydney's sun he and Edith returned with renewed vigour to make the most of the next stage of the adventure. The next two years cemented Joe's place in Preston's history.

•••

That next season, Edith did get to go to another FA Cup final – and once again she didn't have to pay. Just as she had dreamt, this was the year she saw her husband take centre stage, when Preston played West Bromwich Albion in the 1954 game.

'*It was an amazing experience. [The thrill] starts as soon as you make it through the semi-finals and builds up until match day. It was so exciting to be out on that Wembley pitch, in front of so many fans having such a good time. You soak it up, but by the time the game starts the crowd and the arena fade away. You see them during lulls in the game, but in the end it was just another game.*'

Unfortunately for Joe, it was a game that Preston lost 3–2. '*It was very disappointing for the fans, and some of the players took it to heart more than others. But when we got back to Preston the next day and saw the crowds still lining the streets to welcome us home, I began to get over it.*'

Others did not get over it as quickly. The great Sir Tom Finney did not want to be captain from then on and a replacement had to be found. The players voted for the Australian, so Joe led the famous club for the 1954–55 campaign.

Preston finished twelfth behind Chelsea that season, but it is a year that will be

'I'm not an emotional person, but playing for **Australia** meant a **great deal** to me.'

remembered fondly by Joe. At the end of each season, an 'All-Star' game was organised at either Wembley (England) or Hampden Park (Scotland) between a team selected from the English leagues and a team selected from the Scottish leagues. As a measure of his success since leaving Leichhardt, Joe was selected to represent the English leagues – and he was the only non-English player in the side. *'It was a great honour and another memorable experience up at Hampden. I remember sharing a room* with the great Duncan Edwards, who was tragically killed not long after in the Manchester United plane crash. He was brilliant and also a wonderful guy. The night before the game he asked if I wanted to see a show. I thought I might as well, so out we went and had a great time – he was a star who opened all the doors. It was an honour to be the only foreigner playing in that match.'

When those final two years came to an end, Joe could not be persuaded to stay any longer. He had enjoyed five great years with the club and had played 200 first division games (including 194 in a row). He will always be fondly remembered by anyone associated with Preston North End, and he also flew the flag for Australia's development in the code. At his final home match in Preston, the Deepdale arena echoed poignantly with the strains of 'Waltzing Matilda' as the band signalled the end of Joe's English adventure.

His soccer career was far from over, though. He was looking forward to renewing his international career, as the tyranny of distance and time-consuming travel of the era had meant he couldn't play for Australia in his years away. He had only been back in Sydney for one week when he was called into the national squad once again. *'I didn't feel fit after finishing up in England, but I was happy to be involved again. I'm not an emotional person, but playing for Australia meant a great deal to me. It felt a little like making my debut all over again.'*

Imagine what it would be like if they had won! Preston's homecoming after the 1954 FA Cup final.

The 1948 Australian team that toured New Zealand. Joe is far left in the back row.

Of course, Joe was now a much more accomplished player and the experience and professionalism he brought back with him benefited the domestic game. His speed of thought and ability to read the game had greatly improved, and as a man in his late twenties, he still had plenty to offer. He went on to play thirty-five test matches for Australia, captaining his country on twenty-four of those occasions.

Unfortunately for Joe and Australia, he was not allowed to play in the 1956 Olympics because he had been a professional player, and back then the Olympics were still a bastion for amateur athletes. Who knows how his inclusion may have helped our boys to finish in that tournament, but hypotheticals are something Joe doesn't indulge in. *'There is no point in thinking "what if?" or "maybe". I was asked to captain Australia in 1950 a week before I was heading to Preston for the first*

time. It was a shame I couldn't, but my mind was made up and that was it. Some people thought I was a little mad going to England, and plenty thought I was mad coming home to Australian soccer when I did. In the end you make your decisions, and wondering if they are the right ones won't change a thing.'

Returning to Australia meant that he had to work again, so he went straight back to the brush-making business that had employed him before he left. He was happy to once again be under the Australian sun, near the beach and at the APIA club he knew so well. Life was how he had left it, and just how he wanted it.

Joe finished his playing career as a 38-year-old, lifting the championship trophy

with the APIA reserve side. It wasn't long before his experience was adapted to coaching and he became the first professional coach in Australia when he took charge of Western Suburbs in 1967. His previous coaching experience was limited but rich – he had taken charge of the national team in 1957, as well as previous experience in many senior New South Wales games. He remained with Western Suburbs until 1972, when APIA lured him back to take their helm. That lasted two years, and by 1974 he had begun a four-year stint coaching with Auburn in the NSW State League.

'There is no point in thinking "what if" or "maybe"...'

9

'Coaching and managing takes it out of you more than playing.'

Sydney Olympic then appointed Joe as coach in 1978 for the second season of the recently formed National Soccer League. He was sacked in 1979 when the team was sitting fourth and Joe began to realise that his motivation for the game was waning. *'Coaching and managing takes it out of you more than playing. You have to look after so many people and so many problems, and there are things out of your control off the pitch that end up having an influence. In total, I have had twenty-two years as a player and sixteen years as a coach. When I stopped I didn't really miss it. I still don't.'*

• • •

In a time when migration was booming in Australia, Joe and Edith became migrants in another land. Joe experienced how the worldwide community of soccer helps people assimilate and grow roots in new places. *'Because I was a soccer player, settling in England was made much easier than it otherwise would be. I did find that I began to speak with a Northern English accent after a while – mainly so that I could*

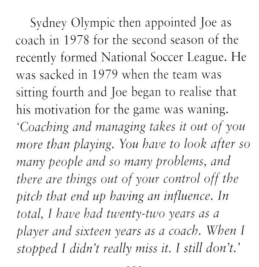

be more easily understood – and we do have a daughter who was born in England. It helped me better understand how soccer helped the new settlers in Australia. Leichhardt always seemed to have a range of nationalities and it became a centre for Italians through the '60s. It is Little Italy now and even has a great piazza. I used to take my children to the APIA functions and they saw a new culture.'

Soccer stole Joe Marston's heart at a young age because a Leichhardt neighbour, who had recently migrated from Scotland, used to lend him his football-dominated newspapers from 'back home'. Joe's growing interest was further fuelled by his time at the St Augustine Stanmore Church juniors, and if he wasn't involved in beach sprints and surfing competitions, he was playing soccer. While seemingly insignificant when compared to factors later in his career, they are two influences that by chance set in motion Australia's first – and perhaps finest – soccer export. Joe Marston is our soccer pioneer.

From top: Another muddy training session; Joe looks on, relieved, in front of the massive 1954 FA Cup final crowd; The long walk off after the 1954 FA Cup final; Preston's fanatical support.

Joe, thirty-eight, with his last piece of silverware. APIA Reserves champions.

Bob BIGNELL

Socceroo 1949–1956

Bob Bignell is the epitome of the sports-loving Aussie larrikin. He played soccer for Australia from 1949 to 1956, and captained the team in the 1956 Melbourne Olympics. But it wasn't just soccer that filled Bob's sporting treasure chest. He also attacked rugby league, tennis, cricket and athletics with the same vigour and energy that was his trademark on the soccer field. As his number of birthdays ticks over eighty, it is lawn bowls that has now become his sport of choice. *'I haven't made my name in bowls yet . . . but it won't be far away!'*

Bob was born in Wollongong in 1922 and still lives there with his wife, Alice. It is a town in which he is well-known, and an area that he loves. Wollongong and Newcastle were two hotbeds of early Australian soccer history, fuelled by the British migrants who worked in the mines and the steelworks – and Bob fits right into that mould. He left school at thirteen and spent most of his life working the coal mines in the Illawarra hills. *'Dad was English and came out here for the work opportunities. He was a decent player, too, with Bristol City. Played for England once and in a Cup final against Aston Villa.'*

Bob began his senior soccer career with Woonona Bulli (later renamed South Coast United) as a 17-year-old in the 1939 Premier League, before moving to his beloved Corrimal Rangers not long after. He also had a spell between 1944–47 at North Shore to see what it was like playing for a Sydney team, but only travelled up for games and did his training at home. The travelling soon lost its charm, and he returned to Corrimal to play out his career from 1948–62, amassing 424 first grade games. He notched up his first representative game for the Illawarra team against China as a 19-year-old in 1941.

Times were quite tough in the mining and steel towns, particularly coming out of the Great Depression in the early 1930s. *'I remember Dad coming home one day with a new pair of boots for me. Well, new-ish – he actually found them in the tip and they were old work boots that we hammered stops into. They were also size seven and I wore size five.'*

His involvement with so many sports did not win the hearts of everyone, as his wife Alice sighs. *'He always seemed to play sports that used white clothes. It was my lot to forever be cleaning white clothes!'* Bob was, naturally, more enthusiastic about the situation. *'For a couple of years I played soccer for Corrimal on Saturday and rugby for Corrimal on Sunday. I always thought rugby looked like an easy game, so I thought I had better give it a go. I was right, soccer is much harder.'*

He evidently displayed some talent at the 'easy game', as Newtown and North Sydney in the Sydney Rugby League both asked him to play for them. *'Norths offered me £7 a game – which back then was a lot of money, and plenty more than I was getting playing soccer. But Hadjuk was coming out, and I really wanted to play against them.'*

The Hadjuk to which he is referring was the famous Hadjuk Split side from Yugoslavia. And the sport, of course, was soccer. Bob always had a keen interest in the tactical side of the game and relished the chance to play against and learn from foreign opposition. This led him to put on the green and gold for soccer rather than follow a more lucrative career in other sports.

The best-looking man in Australian soccer?

'Well, new-ish – he actually found them in the tip and they were old work boots that we hammered stops into.'

Collecting one of many trophies with Corrimal.

'My first game for Australia was in 1949, against Hadjuk. They played with a new system of three at the back plus wing backs. Their players were skilful, and the team wore fancy silk shirts, no shin pads and cutaway boots. They were all about pace and skill. It didn't take me too long to figure them out though, and I soon put a few over the fence! They opened our eyes to a new way of playing, and many of the Australian club sides adopted their system, until we saw the way the Russians played in the [1956] Olympics.'

It was in the 1949 series against Hadjuk that Bob scored his only international goal, 'even though I had set up millions of others'. The Yugoslavs were disputing the referee's decision of awarding Australia a free kick just outside the box. 'Even the goalkeeper ran after the ref. I thought "hold on here...", took the opportunity from thirty yards out and stuck it into the empty net. They were furious, but bad luck. You have to be a gentleman to the referee and that's the way I played. I always called them Sir or Mister and showed them respect. I also think it helped me after some of my tackles!'

Now *that* is a soccer strip!

Throughout the early 1950s, there were plenty of touring sides that enabled the national team to play matches, and in between there was still plenty to keep Bob busy. *'I was the first to use the double-handed back-hand in tennis you know. People laugh when I say I invented it, but no one can say who used it before, so I reckon I am right!'* There were also cricket premierships and a growing interest in greyhounds; he would go on to train his own winners in the city and country.

Games against an English XI, China, Costa Rica and touring club sides all encouraged Bob's tactical imagination, helped develop the game in Australia and also kept him satisfied in the build-up to the 1956 Melbourne Olympics.

By 1954 he had earned three months long service leave from the mines. He was only at home for two weeks of that time though, due to travelling all over to play soccer. Travelling back then, of course, took a lot longer than it does today. *'Whenever I needed to take time off to play, I just did it. Some unpaid, but I had a heap of sickies, that's for sure. I could relax a bit more during my long service leave because I had the time, but I am not sure that Alice agrees.'*

The Australian team selected for the 1956 Olympics effectively had eight weeks to prepare for the tournament. The first two of those weeks were used travelling the country

playing against the other states – without a coach. *'It was only the team manager and the team, so I took on the initial coaching responsibilities. Not that coaches did much back then anyway.'* Bob, who was captain of the 1956 Olympic team, had no trouble taking on the extra responsibilities. *'They didn't pick me just because I was the best looking, you know!'*

He fondly remembers his time as skipper and refers to 'his boys' as a great bunch. *'We were like a family. We spent a lot of time together and got to know each other. We should've done better at the Olympics, but we were robbed by stupid refereeing decisions. Linesmen had to patrol the whole line in those days and they missed some offsides as a result. We should've been in the semi's at least.'*

The 1956 Olympics was the last time Bob played for Australia. It is debatable just how many times he played for his country in all games, however he played eleven test matches (as they were then called) and is immensely proud of every one of them. His last competitive game was in 1961 for Corrimal, at thirty-eight years of age.

•••

' It didn't take **me too long to** figure them out, though, and I soon put a few **over the fence!'**

Bob is the Australian furthest left, and Ron Lord is in goal.

There was glamour in the game even then.

Bob's life in soccer had seen him be a part of some major changes in the game and in Australian society. *'Before World War II, you basically only saw British people or Aussies. Immigration really grew after the war and all of a sudden there were people from everywhere, particularly in the major cities, and some of them turned out to be great soccer players, too. The crowds started to grow, the standard improved, and we were all introduced to different ways of playing. It was interesting to have them here.'*

More money started to come into the game as the growth in the population increased crowds, and as ethnic groups began to have some financial success in their adopted country. *'Late in my career, I could see how things were really changing. Good luck to the players, I say, just like I say good luck to the millionaires playing today. Take what you can get.'*

• • •

In 1982, Bob was in a horrific car crash that kept him in hospital for weeks. Many feared for his life. *'It was touch and go there for a while, and even though it affected my brain functions to some degree, I am still here.'* It could have been a tragic end to an energetic life, but he is still battling on, still watching the Wollongong Wolves, and still providing advice and tuition to his young grandson whenever he is asked.

It is often debated how players of yesteryear would fare playing in the modern leagues, but Bob doesn't have much doubt. *'The players are much quicker [now] and so is the game. But I was quick too, and I reckon I would give it a shove. The tackles are much softer today too . . . I would love to have the chance to play today.'* He then reels off a list of top-class modern players, both overseas and domestic, and how he would play against them. He still takes immense pleasure from analysing the acute details of tactics and techniques. Without a doubt 'Bobby Dazzler' would indeed give these guys a run for their money if he could still pull on the ol' ankle-high boots today.

'...good luck
to the millionaires playing today...

...Take what you can get.'

Bill HENDERSON

Socceroo 1953–1959

It is unusual for a goalkeeper to be one of the stars of a soccer team. It is even more unusual for two stars of the same squad to be goalkeepers at the same time. Australian soccer experienced it throughout the 1950s with Bill Henderson and Ron Lord. *'Ronnie and I were always good mates and, in fact, we still are. When we were fighting for the same Aussie number 1 jersey it was naturally competitive, but we were both sportspeople first and foremost and it was great to have him around.'*

Bill Henderson came from fine soccer stock. In fact, his father, Andy, played for Australia in 1923, after emigrating from Scotland in 1921. *'Dad came here in his late teens/early twenties with his brother Bob [who was a professional back home] and my grandmother. It was my grandmother's idea to come here in the hope of providing better opportunities for her kids after World War I. She was a widow and I can only imagine how tough it must have been to come here with two grown boys.'*

Bill's Uncle Bob didn't continue playing when he arrived here, however his father continued to a level that earned him an Australian debut against China in 1923. It was from the family interests in soccer that Bill and his brother Andy Jnr took up the game. *'Soccer was not popular at school or in the streets, but we didn't care. There was no other sport for us.'*

Andy Jnr played numerous first-grade games for Auburn and represented New South Wales, whereas Bill took one step further and began his own, distinguished international career. He made his international debut against China, just like his dad. Bill found out about his selection in the team against China by coincidence, when reading a newspaper his dad had asked him to buy. *'I raced back out to Dad with it and he was so proud. It was a great day and a dream come true for me and for Dad. I couldn't believe it was happening.'*

The game was in 1953, and was all the more memorable because it was played almost thirty years to the day of his father's debut against the same country. On top of that, the manager of the 1953 Chinese team also played in the 1923 game – and his son was also playing in the 1953 team against Bill! *'My debut was memorable for so many reasons, not least being the historical father-and-son ties. The game itself was a 3–3 draw at the old Sydney Showgrounds. We were winning 3–2 until the Chinese received an indirect free kick with not long to go. The shot came clean around the wall and I instinctively dived. I got my fingertips to it but it went in. Of course, it counted as a goal because I had touched it – you can't score directly from an indirect free kick, but I bloody touched it!'*

•••

The Hendersons: Andy Jnr, Andy Snr and Bill.

'She was a widow and I can only imgine **how tough** it must have been to come here **with two grown boys.**'

A flying effort – without his wollen gloves.

'We were also given uniforms we didn't have to give back for the first time in our lives.'

Around the late fifties money started to increase in the game, however the most Bill was ever paid for national team duties was £5 per game. *'Five pounds wasn't a lot, but I guess it wasn't bad to play for your country. One day, they made the mistake of paying us before the South Africa game in '55 and we came back to the change rooms to find that it had all been stolen – along with the £30 that was already in my wallet!'*

During the 1956 Melbourne Olympics, the players each received 5 shillings (approximately a dollar) a day, during the preparation and the tournament. Bill was fortunate that his job as an electrician with Hoyts Theatre allowed him time off to play for Australia at full pay. *'Hoyts were great. There were internationals in other sports working there, too, and we all got the same treatment. I had a young daughter and I couldn't have done it otherwise. Five shillings wasn't much in the build-up to the Olympics, but I didn't care. We were also given uniforms we didn't have to give back for the first time in our lives, because we were a part of the greater Australian Olympic team, and we were thrilled! The only trouble was that the actual goalkeeper top was a thick, woollen, green top with no badge. It could've been for anything . . . so Ron and I pleaded to be given an on-field top with the logo and everything. They put number 1 on the back of mine and number 2 on Ronnie's.'*

It isn't only jerseys, which are now padded (and carry badges), that have improved since Bill's day. *'Goalkeepers back then didn't wear gloves and I tell you, it is pretty difficult to catch those old, heavy, leather balls. Particularly when they took some water. I would occasionally wear woollen gloves on cold days, but they became a hazard when they got muddy.*

'I remember going to watch the Aussie boys in the 1974 World Cup in Germany and seeing the great Sepp Myer wearing specific goalkeeper gloves. I bought four pairs and brought them back to the Granville 'keepers I was coaching at the time. I'm pretty sure it was the first time there were specific goalkeeping gloves in Australia.'

One goalkeeper who was ahead of his time – whether he was wearing gloves or not – was the great Russian, Lev Yashin. Yashin was a star in the 1956 Olympics and played against an underprepared Australia in a practice game. We were annihilated 15–1. *'The goals were raining in. They were full-time army players and we were just beginning our campaign. It was like they were playing a different game altogether. Yashin was their great man and he truly was imposing. I saw him play in one game where a decent shot came in; he simply grabbed it one-handed and immediately threw it to a teammate on halfway.'*

Bill happened to see Yashin again years later at Barcelona airport, after the 1992 Olympics. He cornered him and said as best he could, *'"You, Russia. Me, Australia. 1956 Olympics, Melbourne." The great man shook my hand with a huge smile and signed a card for me. Our sport is connected by people all over the world.'*

Another great player in Bill's eyes is Gerhard Hanappi, who toured Australia in 1955 with the Austrian Rapid team. *'He was amazing, and I kind of wish I didn't play against him and just watched. I remember him shooting, and I was diving down to my left thinking I had it covered. The ball kept getting further and further away from me though, and all of a sudden it was in. It was the first time I had ever seen anyone curl or bend one of those balls. Pretty impressive! They reckon I was one of the best players on the field that day, but we still got done 6–1.'*

•••

Bill's first-grade debut had been in 1948 at the western Sydney club, Granville. *'Andy [Jnr] and I progressed all the way through the juniors together and I ended up playing 183 senior games for the club. It was a great place and, if it wasn't for the split in 1957, I probably would have stayed there forever.'*

'The split' to which Bill refers was a major point in the history and development of Australian soccer. It illustrated the growth and influence of the ethnic clubs that had

with many other players, saw the opportunities of the Federation and wanted to move. Until that time, a player was with a club for life. There were no transfers to speak of and the clubs had total control. I moved to Auburn in the Federation and ended up playing 178 games for them.'

To add another twist, Bill's 'friendly nemesis', Ron Lord was also at Auburn – but not in the same team. 'Ron had been playing at Auburn before the split, and Auburn actually split down the middle. He stayed at Auburn Association and I went to Auburn Federation. The two Aussie 'keepers at basically the same club! He didn't stay much longer, though.'

As fate would have it, Bill's decision to play for a Federation club in 1959 signalled the end of his international career because he wasn't recognised by the Australian Soccer Association (at that time accredited by FIFA). 'We all got a very abrupt and threatening official letter illustrating what our decisions could do to our careers. It did affect my international days but the club days were brilliant and, overall, I don't regret my decision. It was a watershed time and I think the game really moved forward as a result.'

The split also meant that Federation clubs could bring out players from European clubs without having to pay transfer fees, because it wasn't a competition recognised by FIFA.

developed in line with the post-World War II immigration boom: a trigger for the onset of more and more foreign players being brought to Australia's shores. In turn, the standard of play improved, crowd numbers blossomed and more money entered the local game. The downside was a bitter couple of years in the game, a lot of confused players, and Australian soccer was thrown out of the international governing body, FIFA. We were on our own.

'Put as simply as possible, the traditional "Australian" clubs up to 1956 were in the top division of the state-based competitions, under the overall control of the Australian Soccer Association. However, the clubs formed by immigrant groups arriving in the late 1940s and early 1950s were gaining strength, support and financial clout. Their teams were strong, but they had no chance of playing in the first division in each state because there was no system of promotion

and relegation. These clubs thought they could offer more to the game and organised a meeting to discuss the matter, inviting all clubs to attend.'

The first major battle ground was in New South Wales and the outcome was significant for the Australian game. 'Some existing clubs did not attend. Some said no straight out in fear of other clubs "taking over". In the end, a major breakaway group of clubs formed the NSW Soccer Federation, and played in a competition outlawed by FIFA. Other states followed. By 1959, faced with low crowds and an ever-increasing exodus of players to the Federation, the original Australian Soccer Association folded, and by 1963 the Australian Soccer Federation sought and was given Australia's FIFA accreditation.

'It was a fairly nasty time in New South Wales soccer particularly, and in some ways very confusing for the players . . . I, along

'...you are as from the twelth day of June 1957, disqualified for life from further participation in official soccer football.'

'Clubs such as Sydney Prague and Hakoah brought out first-division players from Austria, Hungary and Czechoslovakia. It really got things going and was quite advantageous to the sport here.'

•••

Nearing the end of his career in 1964, Bill was encouraged out of a proposed retirement by Polonia, a club then in the second division. They made him captain after only two games. *'We had a great year and won promotion into the first division – ironically by beating my old Association club, Granville, by one point. I was one of only four Australians at the club, and I think they made me captain because I could say "heads" or "tails" at the coin toss! The Polish terms for "yours" or "mine" were quite similar and I was always afraid of confusing them, so I just used to dive on everything.'*

Unfortunately, Bill injured his knee during a warm-up for the 1965 season and that signalled the end of his playing career. *'It was very disappointing after winning promotion with the club. They were fantastic and I would've liked to do well for them. Still, I had a good career and I have precious memories.'*

In the course of his career, Bill played thirteen tests and thirty international matches – no mean feat when you consider he was 'sharing' the role with Ron Lord in

an era when no substitutes were allowed. *'I really enjoyed every minute of my time in Australian teams, whether I was playing or not. The Olympics in Melbourne were obviously a highlight, but it was also a thrill to be in the 1955 team that played South Africa because, at that time, Dad was also the national coach.'*

•••

Goalkeepers are a superstitious lot and Bill is no different. *'I put my left sock and left boot on first, but my main thing was to rub the two little pins on the trusty green cap I wore each game, before any penalty that was taken against me. I had a good record too!'*

Bill did have a good record, and it wasn't just at saving penalties. Always a gentleman on and off the pitch, he was, and is, recognised by his peers and fans alike as a great Socceroo, and a good bloke. No matter how many penalties he saved because he rubbed the trusty pins on his 'baggy green', his career and personality have done more for the Australian game than shots stopped from twelve yards out.

Dear Sir,

Following the refusal by the Australian Soccer Football Association to grant affiliation to the Federation of Soccer Clubs, all players who engage in football under that body's control commit a serious breach of rules.

These players not only render themselves liable to life disqualification, but may also deprive themselves from any further opportunity to play in interstate or international fixtures.

You are a player who has been recognised and who must be considered for selection in Australian and N.S.W. teams to play Hungary and China this season, and also for an Australian team which is to tour the Eastern Countries and play in the Asian Soccer Tournament in November and December.

Your club remaining attached to the unconstitutional Federation is sacrificing your future soccer career, which will be of no benefit to you personally.

You are sincerely counselled to sever your connection with Federation Soccer immediately and to join a club of the N.S.W. Soccer Football Association, the only constitutional body in N.S.W.

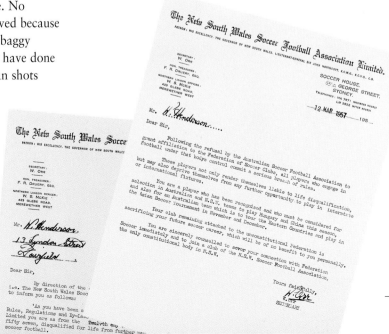

Ron LORD

Ron Lord first played for Australia in 1951 against an English touring XI. His last game for Australia was against Everton thirteen years later, in front of 51,500 fans. Along the way he amassed 399 league games, thirty-five appearances for New South Wales and, on top of many 'friendly' games for the national team, played fifteen tests for his country. He is a third-generation Australian who was good at all sports, and is, arguably, the best goalkeeper Australia has produced.

Ron Lord was a goalkeeper from the top drawer, but it could've been so different. '*I didn't ever play in goals until I was eighteen. I had injured my ankle as an on-field player with Drummoyne in the Sydney leagues, and*

I couldn't kick with it for months. I couldn't play, but went down to watch the boys. One week the second-grade goalkeeper didn't turn up. Somehow I went in, it suited me, and I guess you could say I never looked back!'

He began to take the game (and his new position) more seriously and a couple of years later was playing for Auburn in the NSW State League. Not long after that, he was selected for his first test match. '*I was really enjoying myself and playing well. I was overjoyed to then be selected for Australia against England, but it still amazes me that even by the time I was picked for Australia, I had no formal goalkeeping training. No education on technique or style. Can you imagine that today?*'

Joe Marston was playing in England throughout the early 1950s, and it was after the 1951 international series against England that Ron was asked to go over for trials as well. '*The money over there at that time was £12 a week at the most. While playing full-time appealed from the sport point of view, the money wasn't good enough to take the risk and my life here was too good.*'

Auburn maintained the services of the Australian strongman until the split between the Association and Federation clubs in 1957. '*Auburn was split down the middle. Half the guys defected to the Federation clubs, but I stayed where I was. I was enjoying myself and liked the club. I guess I*

didn't want to see it end, because everything was going so well for me personally.'

That era did end, but the good times continued anyway. Federation club Sydney Prague were determined to tie up Ron's services to secure their last line of defence in their first year in the top league in 1957. '*Prague were persuasive in 1957. At the time I was working in a small factory as a fitter and turner and my first child was just born. When I said that more money wasn't that important to me, they asked me to consider my family and what I could provide for them. Pretty smart, really, because it got me thinking.*'

Ron was still undecided but agreed to meet the Prague officials on a Friday night in a venue in Sydney's Kings Cross. '*I was a bit anxious to say the least. To make things worse, they wanted me to play for them the next day and I hadn't been able to find the Auburn secretary anywhere to let him know what was happening. Things looked pretty hairy to me when they led me upstairs to a large, dark club with minimal lighting. To their credit, though, they handled themselves fantastically over a coffee and, in the end, I became a Prague player.*' He played the very next day against, you guessed it, Auburn. '*Yes, it added to the unusual events of the week. We beat them 1–0 and I didn't have too many friends on the Auburn side of the pitch! Still, the years at Prague were some of the very best of my life.*'

'…by the time I was **picked for Australia,** I had no formal **goal keeping** training.'

Ron in one of his many New South Wales blazers.

'…I also got an opportunity to meet other cultures, and many of my Aussie friends didn't get the same chance.'

There was only one other Australian at the club, which was backed by the growing Czechoslovakian community, and that made things interesting for the Lords. 'I never had any real trouble, but I must say it was an eye-opener. It took me a while to adjust, even though they were so accommodating right from the start. The players and officials at the club would often go to coffee houses or Czech functions . . . I would usually go back home after training, but some of the functions after games were great. Looking back, I am lucky I joined Prague. Not only for the soccer – I also got an opportunity to meet other cultures, and many of my Aussie friends didn't get the same chance.'

Prague was also the first club to provide him with goalkeeping training and he lapped it up. 'I loved training. We were only there a couple of times a week, but I couldn't get enough of it. I ended up receiving a number of injuries due to all the diving around on such hard grounds, but it was worth it.'

One of the big things that struck Ron in his time with Prague was the growing professionalism of the players and the increasing crowds. 'The standard really improved in the late fifties and sixties. Top players from Europe came to play and they brought a different attitude. Leo Baumgartner was one terrific Austrian who played at a few clubs when he came here. He was on about £80 a week at one stage with Canterbury, and was a real legend. I remember when he asked if I had received my signing-on fee for the year. I replied that I hadn't because I got a fee when I first joined in '57. "What?" he asked. "You should get the signing-on every year." The Aussies were used to playing for nothing, so we didn't really know what we were dealing with. A club official once said "Don't worry about the Aussies, they don't complain," and he was about right.'

Injury is the constant shadow of sportspeople, and the combative Lord has had his fair share of time on the treatment table. 'In 1953 [while playing for Auburn] I injured my shoulder. It always felt worse after the physio massaged it, so after a couple of weeks, I had an X-ray and they found chipped bone all around the joint. No wonder the treatment hurt! At Prague [in 1957] I had to have a knee operation that could've quite easily ended my career. I've also had a depressed fracture of my cheekbone, a broken bone in my back, corked thighs and plenty of finger injuries. It's something you expect as a goalkeeper, and you just have to manage it. At least the injuries don't affect my golf swing too much these days!'

To prolong his career, Ron made his own knee guards and elbow pads to help preserve his ailing joints. Unfortunately, his athletic

Growing professionalism and increasing crowds at Prague.

The New South Wales team that would be beaten 8–1 by England in 1951.

L to R: Ron Lord (before his time with white boots), Reg Date, Bob Madden, Eric Hulme, Alan Johns, Frank Parsons, Bob Young, Bob Bignell, George Russell, Cliff Almond, Kevin O'Neill.

and uncompromising method of play meant damage was still done. *'My knees are great now . . . I have had both of them replaced, so they are almost as good as new!'* He also wore his wife Kath's woollen gloves on occasion, but in the late 1960s made some other gloves with small rubber pieces on them – a precursor to goalie gloves, which came out after the 1974 World Cup. *'I guess necessity is the mother of invention.'*

Ron remained at Prague until 1964 – the year of his last game for Australia and the year of a testimonial game put on for him by his 'adoptive family'. *'The testimonial was very emotional. I was honoured and surprised, but it just goes to show what that club and I meant to each other. It was also the first game my mother ever watched me play. She was always too nervous because I would often bump into people and got injured quite a lot.'*

Ron saw the boom that took place in Australian soccer through the 1950–60s and enthuses about the era. *'I think the first New Australian I saw playing was Milo Vesavic in the early fifties. By the late fifties, there were names like that all over the place. In the early fifties, crowds would be around* 3,000 *or so, but by the late fifties, they were usually double that, and sometimes four or five times that size.*

'I think back to when I was with Drummoyne in '48. We used to train under a street light, with bags for goals on bumpy pitches. Now, the likes of Parramatta Power have a $3 million budget and great facilities, and we have millionaires playing all over the world. I don't say that to be bitter, because I think it is a great indication of where the game has come. When [Australia] played the English XI in 1951, they beat us 17–0 in the first game. Things became a lot more respectable after that demolition, but when I watched the Socceroos beat England 3–1 in London [in 2003] I was so proud. Let's hope the game keeps progressing.'

The affable Ron speaks fondly of his times playing for Australia – particularly during the time of the 1956 Melbourne Olympics – but admits to some strange occurrences in his thirteen years with the green and gold. *'It was commonplace for the wives to have to pay to come and watch. There were big crowds and someone must have been getting the money, but Kath had to pay to come and watch. I also remember* one time when I went to watch Australia play, but I was in the crowd and not part of the game. I was waiting outside for Kath to come back from the toilet or somewhere and a gentleman came up to me, patted me on the back and said that I had a good game. Reasonable mistake I guess – but the gentleman was one of Australia's selectors! Maybe I was supposed to play less games than I did – or maybe even more!'*

Then there was the time that he and his good friend, and sparring partner for the Australian number 1 jumper, Billy Henderson, got in trouble with the Australian officials. *'Billy was in goal for the fifth test against the Austrians and as the last person to touch the ball in the game, figured he'd "go with tradition" and keep it. I was sitting on one of the balls on the sideline and I thought I'd like a memento as well. I mean, you couldn't keep anything in those days. Uniforms, tracksuits, even sweaty socks! So off we went with the two leather balls. Thing was, we were playing South China in a week and when we got to training, Tommy [Tennant, the manager and coach] said, "Two balls have gone missing from last week's game. We know who has*

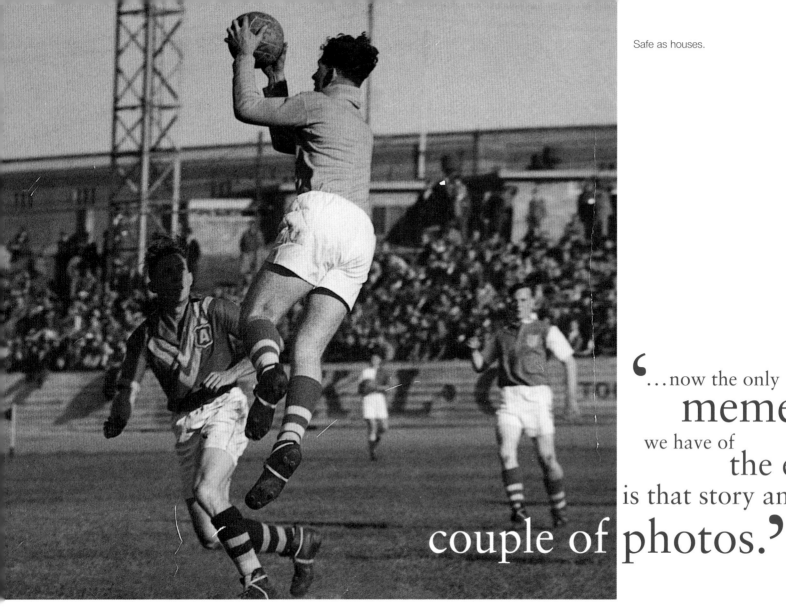

'…now the only **memento** we have of **the era** is that story and a couple of **photos.**'

them and if they aren't returned, they will never play for Australia again." We had to return them like school kids. Of course, we probably shouldn't have taken them in the first place, but now the only memento we have of the era is that story and a couple of photos.'

•••

Ron Lord was one of the first people inducted into Soccer Australia's Hall of Fame, and it is an honour that makes him

truly proud. He also had a street named after him, when the NSW Soccer Federation sold off part of their State Training Facility to profit from the urban development in Sydney's west. With or without the 1950s match ball he had to return, he is happy with what soccer has given him, and proud of what he has achieved within the game. Like many other players, he just wishes he could wind back the years and still be playing today.

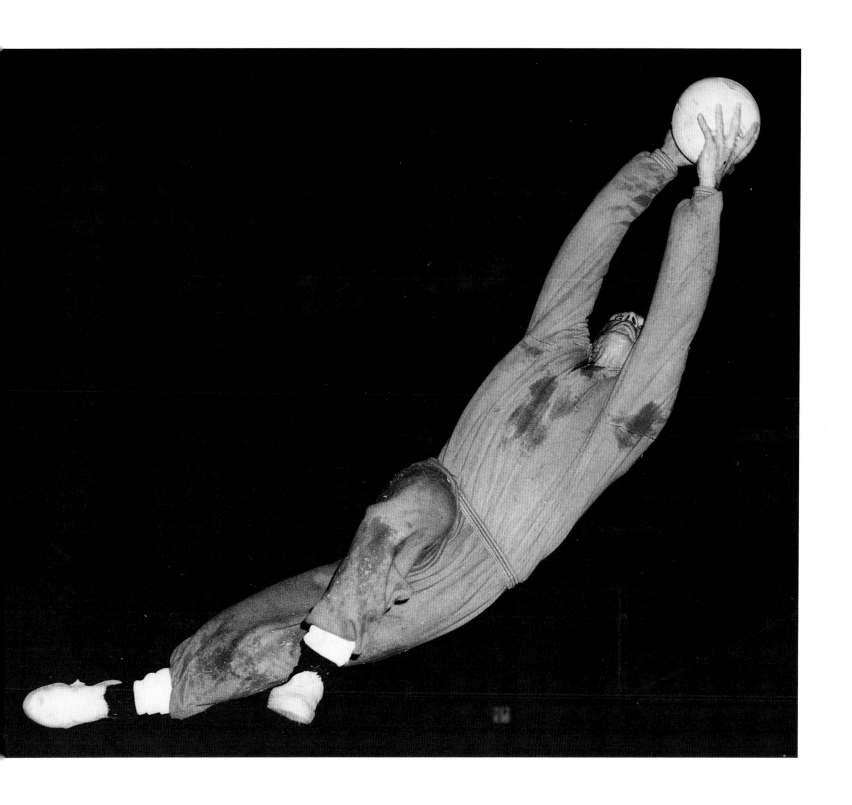

That's how it's done!

Ted SMITH

Socceroo 1954–1956

Edward Smith is definitely a 'Ted' Smith. A lifetime in the naturally conservative world of insurance and financial planning belies his warm, engaging nature. Behind the suit and tie is a broad-minded and accepting man stubbornly passionate about the equality of soccer with other sports in this country. '*I just want the game to be recognised as a sport in Australia, just like golf, tennis or cricket . . . and we are getting there.*'

Ted was born to an English mother and Australian father, who was a timbercutter.

He grew up in the inner-Melbourne suburb of North Fitzroy. Both parents had no interest in soccer – in fact, neither did anyone else around him in his early years.

'*North Fitzroy wasn't the trendy, upper-class suburb it is today. It was very much a working class area that had the finest footy and cricket traditions. Soccer was certainly never considered among most of the people in the area.*'

A naturally gifted sportsman proficient at Aussie Rules, cricket, running, basketball and golf (mainly because the more sports he played, the more time he got off classes), Ted had his first taste of the round ball as a 13-year-old. A couple of English kids were having a kick at school and somehow Ted joined them – the first of many unplanned and fortunate events that punctuated his soccer career.

The next year he joined his new friends in the Northcote High Under-14s team – one of only ten teams in that age group across the state. Ted and his friends were lucky to see two minutes of newsreel footage covering the occasional FA Cup final, but nevertheless the game had caught him.

'*I remember our class being asked by the art teacher to draw our dreams. I drew myself playing soccer for Australia and even though I was hopeless at art, the teacher still gave me a pass. I think she was impressed with my unique ambition.*'

It was not until 1949 that Ted saw his first big game. Australia played a team billed as Yugoslavia – although they were really the Hajduk Split club side. During this match, the Yugoslav goalkeeper Beara really caught his eye. '*He went on to play for the World XI and really stood out – even though he was a goalkeeper.*'

The next year, at the tender age of fifteen, Ted left school and became an employee of Sun Insurance Offices – the start of a lifelong career in the industry. '*Jobs were everywhere at the time, as the country grew and grew after World War II. In fact, I was in an ad the company placed in the program for the 1950 Australia versus England match at the MCG, to try to get more soccer kids to the company. The ad failed – but I guess it was the first exposure for Ted Smith at a major soccer game!*'

The 1956 Olympic team.

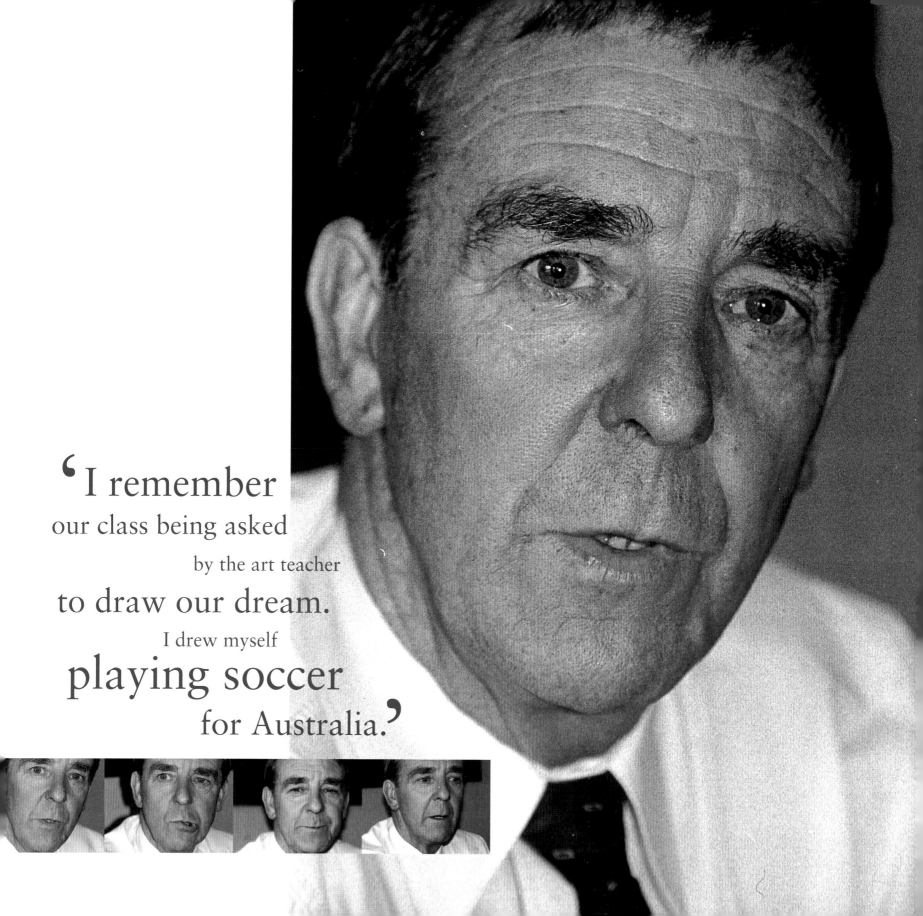

‘I remember
our class being asked
by the art teacher
to draw our dream.
I drew myself
playing soccer
for Australia.’

'...it certainly wasn't like today when cable television shows the world's best players around the clock.'

Until the 1949 and 1950 matches, most of Ted's development came through scouring any book, magazine or comic on soccer he could find. When he saw some of the world's best, like Englishman Jimmy Hagan in the 1950 match against Australia, executing what he had only read about, time stood still. *'I still remember today an exact moment when Hagan controlled the ball just like I had only seen in photos. It sounds silly, but we only ever had collections of those type of moments; it certainly wasn't like today when cable television shows the world's best players around the clock.'*

By now, Ted was playing at Preston Tech Old Boys Under-16s team. One day, a senior player got injured – and Ted was thrown in the deep end. He stayed in the second division team for the rest of that season and did enough to impress perhaps the biggest club at the time in Victoria, Moreland. Proving that the modern-day haggling over contracts is not new, Preston were adamant they were not going to lose their young star to 'the big boys'. Moreland were relieved to discover that Ted was only registered on youth forms at Preston, so they promptly arranged senior forms and snapped up the young star.

Soon after, he was asked to join the first intake of the Vic Colts, a team of young players who represent Victoria. These talented young players were provided with extra tuition under Len Young. *'Len was brought out from England to coach the coaches in Victoria, as well as take charge of the more talented kids. Things seemed to regularly fall into place for me, and in only four years of playing, I was getting some great coaching for really the first time. It was a forward-thinking decision to bring him out and he even ended up coaching Australia at the '56 Olympics.'*

One of the bigger competitions of the time was the Laidlaw Cup, a kind of 'mini world cup'. It pitted teams of various ethnic origins against one another. *'There were some fantastic crowds as the different multicultural communities supported their boys. The Aussie team had one or two boys from the first division and the rest were in second division. The English and Scottish teams were the strongest at the time and often had five or six Australian internationals playing for them, because of their heritage. It would definitely have been an upset if we ever beat them.'*

Ted first played for Australia in the Laidlaw Cup as a 16-year-old and it heightened his enthusiasm to make something of himself within the game. *'Angus Drennan and Jack Wilson were Socceroos and my mentors in the Laidlaw Cup team. They were inspirational. Another role model at the time was Joe Marston, who was playing in England.'*

During this time of youthful exuberance, Ted would often sneak out the back of his parents' home when they thought he was asleep, to go to the park. There he would practise the swerves and feints he became famous for, by 'taking on the trees'. *'I was one of the first guys to train with weights and a running coach. On top of the two nights a week with Moreland and the Colts, I would do another two weights sessions and running sessions. It was pretty unusual.'*

In 1954, the enthusiastic 18-year-old earned a call-up to the Australian team from the Vic Colts. The game was against New Zealand in South Australia. *'The outside-left got the flu and the next thing you know, I am on a plane for the first time, wearing the green and gold for the first time. I didn't get off the bench, but I enjoyed the experience and wanted more of it.'* At nineteen, he was on the bench again against South Africa and as a 20-year-old was a rough outsider to make the Olympic squad in 1956.

Current Socceroo coaches have trouble getting their best players back from Europe for games, however the distance is not a new dilemma. *'It was always difficult to make Australian teams and, due to the costs and time for travelling, it was sometimes a case of picking the majority of players from the state in which the games were played. Naturally, this could make it easier or harder for the players, depending where the games were held.'*

Travelling interstate for games was quite a big deal in those days and strong memories have stayed with Ted. *'I remember travelling through New South Wales – and in particular northern New South Wales – and seeing soccer goalposts everywhere. I was immediately jealous and impressed because that certainly wasn't the case in* *Victoria. I also recall that the Queensland and the northern New South Wales players were largely 'Aussies' like me. It was reinforced by the make-up of the national teams at the time too. The guys selected from up north were generally second-generation Australians but down south, that was the exception.'*

Moreland Soccer Club. Docherty Cup winners, 1957.

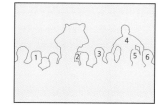

Moreland's Socceroos

1. Norm Hobson
2. Ted Smith
3. Les Goodman
4. Frank Loughran
5. Eric Heath
6. Jack Wilson

> '*Why is it that people look so fondly upon their favourite little Italian, Greek or Chinese restaurant, yet I play Wog Ball with those restaurateurs and, for some reason, our sport has never been looked upon in the same light?*'

Ted was ultimately selected to play for Australia in the 1956 Olympics and the team made a good account of itself, despite some early hiccups in the preparations. '*Soccer facilities were sparse at best, so Collingwood [AFL] Football Club was approached. Their response was, "They can train in the gutter for all we care", which was typical of the times. It was interesting for me to see Leeds United training there on their 2002 tour, because it shows how times are changing for the sport.*'

In the end, despite a 15–1 loss to the highly drilled Soviet team in their first training game, the team beat Japan (2–0) but lost to India (4–2) to get knocked out of the tournament. They were the only two games Ted's father ever saw him play. '*Some of the Indians didn't wear boots and I really think it put us off our game. Can you imagine that happening in a world tournament today?*'

Up to that point, the Australian players were still wearing ankle-high boots with steel caps over their toes and studs nailed into the soles before each game. In 1956, Ted became the first Victorian to own rubber-soled boots and was the envy of the country. '*Those boots were like heaven. I bought them second-hand off a German player at the Olympics for £5 and, even though they were too big, they were streets ahead of the alternative. Adidas had arrived in Australia!*'

After the Olympic tournament, Ted continued with Moreland until 1961 in what was a golden era for soccer in this country. '*Top-class players came from all over the world to our leagues, which really increased the standard. Quality first division players from European leagues and even full internationals like Willie Schroiff (Czechoslovakia), Con Nestoridis (Greece), Mike De Bruykere and Dick Van Alphen (Holland), Vic Jancyk (Poland), Tom Stankovic (Yugoslavia), and Karl Jaros, Herbert Ninhaus and Leo Baumgartner (Austria). All the local boys had to lift their game to compete against this new crop.*'

Coaching was also taking a more professional, insightful edge. '*People such as Manny Poulakakis, Joe Venglos, Rale Rasic, Frank Arok and Zoran Matic were all providing a fresh influence on the qualities of the Australian game. Immigration didn't just result in some great players and growing crowds; you can't forget the coaches.*'

In 1962, South Melbourne Hellas offered Ted a revolutionary payment system, as an incentive for him to join their club. '*Hellas always had good support and I thought it would give me better opportunities if I took on the challenge of a new club. Also, while we were on £5 a win at Moreland, Hellas payments were based on gate takings. Seventy per cent of the gate for a win, fifty per cent a draw and thirty per cent a loss. In one big game against Sunshine I pocketed*

£200 . . . fantastic for the players, but in reality, even then the clubs were overextending themselves.'

In a Greek-based club with numerous Greek players, the name Ted Smith stood out. '*The migrant-based clubs were obviously borne of ethnic origins. After a while though, the people in those clubs couldn't care less where you were from. If you could play, they loved you.*'

In 1964 Ted moved on to the powerful Hakoah club in what he saw as another step up in his career. He stayed for a couple of seasons, then coached the team in 1968. '*The club was backed by all sorts of businessmen from the Jewish community, but the players were largely imports from Britain. Some of the committee knew very little about the game and tried to exert authority where they probably shouldn't have, but they sure knew how to run the club and how to look after people.*'

Ted's last direct role in the game was a three-year stint as the assistant coach back at South Melbourne – including the inaugural year of the National Soccer League in 1977. '*By the time of the NSL, the locally produced talent were holding their own. Most international players coming now were big European stars coming for guest stints to draw crowds. Hellas brought out the legendary Malcolm MacDonald from England for a three-game stint. The place was abuzz but I needn't* have been so nervous when I picked him up from the airport. He was a gentleman, a great player and a wonderful boost for the club. Charlie George played for St George, Kevin Keegan for Blacktown, Alan Brasil for Wollongong, just to name a few.'

Today, Ted is a founding member of the Honours Committee that was established in 1996 to recognise high achievement in Australian soccer. He is an active link between Socceroos of many eras, and has a dream of one day seeing a Soccer Museum opened. He also genuinely believes the game is on the verge of receiving the general acceptance that is well overdue. '*It is tremendous to see so many people playing the game these days, as well as so many more that may not play but can appreciate the game for what it's worth around the world. In some ways, acceptance of the sport is already here and, to be honest, I look forward to the next few years with great excitement.*'

While Ted took his fair share of knocks for playing 'their sport' in the early days, he was spurred on by the general public's lack of acceptance of soccer at the time. '*Why is it that people look so fondly upon their favourite little Italian, Greek or Chinese restaurant, yet I play Wog Ball with those restaurateurs and, for some reason, our sport has never been looked upon in the same light?*'

Leo BAUMGARTNER

Socceroo 1964–1964

Red tape, bureaucracy and obtuse rule-setting can be a dead weight for ambition and development in any field. Ironically, the ambition of one of the most gifted soccer players to grace Australia's domestic competitions, and his subsequent influence on the development of the game here, relied on it.

Leo Baumgartner came to Australia from Vienna as a 26-year-old, highly pedigreed Austrian star. He made his name in the Austrian first division and had represented his country in junior tournaments and senior squads. He introduced to Australia a new tactical and skilful approach, ingrained by his years as a professional with Austria's biggest clubs, and directly influenced the professionalism of the game here. In 1964, he made his sole Socceroo appearance in a game against Everton.

'I came from a world of soccer. There were no cars in Vienna in the '30s and '40s when I was growing up and all the boys played in the streets and watched as many games as we could. We also played little games, using buttons as players to flick the smallest button that was the ball. It became competitive and we named all the buttons after the stars of the day from around Europe. I remember one of the group loved the great Torino of Italy and named his whole team of buttons after them. After the plane crash where the Torino side was killed in 1949, my friend put his buttons in a box and buried them and we were all told we had to go to the funeral. Soccer was a serious thing for all of us back then, but mostly it was great fun and we couldn't get enough of it.'

The Austrians were semi-finalists in the 1954 World Cup and the Austrian football association decreed that for the sake of the continued success of the national team, home-grown talent should stay at home until they reached twenty-eight years of age. Leo Baumgartner was one such talent. However, Leo Baumgartner wanted to move.

After returning from a long overseas tour representing superclub FK Austria, some financial issues began to arise in the club. Players were paid much less than they were due and Leo could no longer trust and respect the club he had idolised in his youth. Valencia in Spain, and later Sampdoria in Italy, were interested but at twenty-five years of age, his national body's rules meant he had to stay put. He could transfer to another Austrian club, however he had already had a spell at the second of the country's 'Big Two' clubs – Austria Rapid – and he wanted something different.

As an Austrian professional, Leo pleads his innocence.

'In 1957, FK Austria organised a ten-week tour of Australia and New Zealand. I was not particularly happy about leaving my wife and young daughter for so long, but what could you do? Little did I know how much that trip was to change our lives.'

The soccer aspect of the trip was not particularly eventful, however the countryside and the hospitality of the people made their mark. 'The teams we played were all very physical and athletic but there wasn't much grace. We were hustled and bustled at first, but soon began to take control on the field. The biggest thing on that trip were the white beaches, the sunshine, the space and the size of the houses. Also, the people were so hospitable and happy.'

The growing Austrian, German and Czech communities in Australia were thrilled to have the biggest club in Austria in their adopted homeland and did their best to make the visitors welcome. They took the players on car trips, to parties by the water and on ferries to the beach. Their hosts' enthusiasm about Australia was obvious and began to rub off on some of the players. 'We were enjoying Australia but I began to wish my family was with me to see the beauty. By the time we left, we felt we were leaving friends and I admit to feeling that somehow I would be back again.'

'Little did I know how much that trip was going to change our lives.'

There had been some tongue-in-cheek remarks from club officials in Sydney, that some of the players should leave and join them. The idea of leaving big-time soccer, playing in front of 60,000 fans, to move to the other side of the world and play in a country where the game was only reaching adolescence understandably did not hold much sway with the Austrian stars. Some months later, however, Leo and teammate Karl Jaros were still speaking fondly about their trip. *'We were still having some problems with FK Austria and I loosely mentioned to Karl that I wouldn't mind maybe going to Australia for a couple of years. We knew that Australia wasn't a part of FIFA and that we could sidestep the Austrian rule about not leaving until you were twenty-eight. Our masseur was with us and he wrote to a Czechoslovakian friend in Sydney. We thought it couldn't hurt. I asked [my wife] Helen if she would be interested in leaving everything behind and, to my surprise, she instantly said yes. From then on, the idea of living in Australia became very important to my family.'*

Sydney Prague was courting the two players and they quickly sent an official to Austria to get everything in order. *'We were told we would have to work in Australia as well as play, which was unusual for us. We knew there was plenty of work, though, because we knew people [non-soccer players] who had migrated there already. We were excited enough about the adventure by then that it wasn't an issue anyway. FK Austria wasn't happy about losing two players and not getting a transfer fee for them, but it was too late and we were on our way. Most people thought we were mad.'*

On 16 January 1958, the two small families made their way to Genoa, Italy, to board a liner full of migrants off to make a new life in Australia. Most of them did not know what lay ahead, but the Baumgartner and Jaros families could enjoy the trip knowing their future lay in football. *'We spent a few days training with Sampdoria while we waited for the boat. We were there by invitation of the Austrian star Ernst Occwirk and we were asked if we could stay. We couldn't because of all the rules we were avoiding. Occwirk was such a popular player in Italy that the police used to stop*

' We were told we would have to work in Australia as well as play, which was unusual for us. '

traffic to let him through. He took us to the boat and we all met the captain. From then on, we were given the best accommodation and even ate meals in the captain's quarters on occasion. It made the trip very enjoyable.'

The liner docked in Melbourne, where Prague officials met the families and transported them up to their new home in Sydney. 'Somehow our bags stayed in Melbourne for a while and we got to Sydney with next to nothing. Prague had organised a reception for us to meet the fans the next night – so one of the club officials took us to his store and let us have the clothes we wanted. All the good stuff too.'

The two families did not pay for anything for the first six months. They were given a furnished house to stay in, were provided with plenty of food by people in the club and each received a £400 signing-on fee. Life was good. *'The generosity of the people was amazing. A club official once gave my daughter Sonja £5 during a holiday to buy ice cream – a lot of money back then. It may seem a small thing, but it added up; it showed how good the people were.'*

The players knew that they would have to repay the generosity on the field, but Leo found the team placed too much reliance on their reputations and skills. *'Particularly at the start when I was unfit, it felt like my teammates were expecting too much from*

us. It took us a while to get used to the game here and after our 7–2 defeat by Hakoah in a pre-season game in front of 7,500 people, I think a few people wondered what was going to hap pen.'

Leo was not only brought out to play for Prague, he was also entrusted with the coaching responsibilities. His limited grasp of English at the time was not as big an obstacle as you would imagine, but he did have some major points to tackle. *'The team spirit was lacking and many players were used to just turning up to training when they wanted. I realised that the Australian way of living, and therefore the attitude toward the game, was different to ours. That had to gradually change if the soccer was to improve, and it did. We finished fourth that year.'*

The story of the Austrian import's year here became news in his homeland. Soon, Leo began receiving letters from other Austrian players wanting to replicate his journey. *'Tamandl, Shagi and Schwarz were all good players in Austria and wanted to come here. I pursued the [Prague] committee and in a short time I was meeting the three of them at the airport.'*

The players were billeted around and the team atmosphere began to grow. As with the majority of his Australian career, Leo saw no issues about where certain players were from and what they were doing here. *'The Australians greeted us with "Wie geht es Dir?" (How are you?) and "Auf Wiedersehen" (Goodbye), and also helped us improve our English.'*

Left: Training at his old home.
Right: Training at his new home.

39

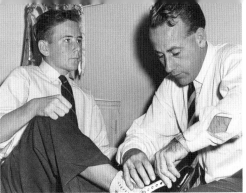

Prague won the 1959 pre-season Ampol Cup by defeating Auburn 7–0 and were set up for a great year. Performances became more and more impressive to the Australian public and there was plenty of press coverage. Attitudes were changing and standards were improving. That year, Costa Rica toured Australia and played against the NSW Federation. Leo was picked as captain. *'It was another taste of big-time soccer that I had missed in the last two years. There were big crowds and I was honoured to be playing representative soccer in my new country.'*

By June 1959, Austrian international Herbert Ninaus had also joined Prague and the club was steaming ahead. It was no real surprise that they finished on top in the 1959 competition and went on to win the rain-soaked grand final 3–2 against Joe Marston's APIA. Leo had repaid his club's generosity.

Before the start of the 1960 season, there was a committee change at Prague and some unsettling problems within the playing ranks. Leo's mentor and guardian, Mr Raymond, decided to leave the club and therefore so did Leo. *'Prague didn't pay a transfer fee for me, but they were asking for £1,000 for me to move on. It was unheard of in Australia but nothing compared to fees overseas. Hakoah were interested but I wasn't too keen on them because they seemed to be a group of individuals rather than a team. Canterbury were a young, enthusiastic side and while they weren't one of the better teams, I decided on joining coach Joe Vlasits – and I don't regret it at all.'*

Prague were still the team to beat in 1960, yet the tag of enthusiastic underdogs sat well with Canterbury all the way to the grand final in Leo's first year at the club. Their foes were inevitably Prague and while captain Baumgartner was sending positive messages to his charges, even he knew they faced a tough hurdle. *'The players were very nervous in the finals. I even had an unexpected visit from a 17-year-old Johnny Warren at my house the night before the semi-final. There were going to be 20,000 spectators at the grand final and everyone at the club was on edge.'*

At half-time, Canterbury were the shock 2–0 leaders. Prague's class brought them back to 2–2, but it was the mercurial Baumgartner that took the game by the horns, broke the deadlock and halted Prague's progress. *'It was a great goal against Ron Lord and from there we didn't look back. We played some great soccer and ran out eventual winners 5–2. It was one of the best moments of my career.'*

Around the same time, Leo had taken to managing a migrant hostel two hours south, in Unanderra. When he couldn't go to work because of soccer commitments, his wife Helen made the trip. *'It was very tiring.*

While I was down there I got to know some South Coast soccer officials and they asked me if I would like to play for them. It would certainly make my life easier . . . so even though they were down the bottom of the 1960 competition, I said yes.'

After one year at Canterbury, the entertainer was off to please a new audience. Even though South Coast were in the process of signing English star Jim Kelly, there were not many quality players to speak of and Leo began to get wary that the situation wouldn't change. *'The club was paying me good money to coach and play for the club, but after losing our first three games in '61, I could see we were in trouble. At the same time Mr Jim Bayutti from APIA was in contact with me, desperately wanting me for their club and the Italian community. After our fourth loss I explained to South Coast that I wasn't comfortable that I could turn things around and that they could probably spend their money more wisely. In the end, they were able to extract a significant fee out of APIA and were able to greatly strengthen their squad. I left for Sydney at about 1 am the next morning and resigned from the migrant hostel not long after.'*

APIA had not won a game by round five of 1961, so the round six fixture against Sydney Austral was vital for the club and their new star. Once again, Leo rose to the challenge and installed himself as an instant

'I was suspended for life.
What a humiliation...'

favourite by scoring three of APIA's goals in a 5–2 victory. *'The Italian community were a hard lot to please. They would be there in their thousands when we were winning, but hard on us when we weren't. We had a reasonable year, but just missed out on the semi-finals.'*

By 1962, Leo was appointed player–coach of the APIA team and was also given a job in the booming APIA Social Club. He was now serving the Italian community at large and was enjoying the experience. He was also appointed as coach of the NSW Federation representative team – and was approached by Sydney Croatia to coach their club in the second division. Three coaching jobs and one administrative role, on top of playing, was enough to keep Leo more than busy, but he still managed time to squeeze in success. New South Wales won the interstate competition, APIA made the semi-finals and Croatia were promoted into Division One.

In 1963, Leo had to resign as Croatia coach, as they were now in the first division and therefore in direct competition with APIA. Unfortunately, there was a bigger issue he also had to face that year. *'APIA were doing well and when an interstate game came up, [APIA President] Mr Bayutti asked Karl Jaros (who had joined APIA) and I not to play to avoid the risk of injury. The club was guaranteeing our income, so first duty was to them.'* In a precursor to the club versus country row so prevalent today, Leo resigned as captain–coach of the New South Wales team. The NSW Federation told him if he did not play, he would be banned from representative football – for life. *'After twenty-three years of playing football, in all parts of the world, having played with stars whose names were on the lips of every young boy, having proved my worth to Australian soccer, I was suspended for life. What a humiliation . . .'*

Frustration was balanced by the personal jubilation of the birth of Leo's son, Richard. As bad luck would sometimes have it, though, even that bright spot had a downside. *'The Italian fans celebrated Richard's birth with me long into the night at the Social Club. I felt on top of the world, but when I tried to drive home, I crashed into a tree and gashed my head. Two days later it split open again after heading a ball, and became infected by the chemicals used to treat the ground back then. I got severe blood poisoning and needed round-the-clock care.'*

Leo battled to make it back to fitness and play in the grand final against Jim Kelly's huge improvers at South Coast. A capacity 30,102 fans were at the sportsground to witness the clash and, after twenty minutes, South Coast had cruised to a 3–0 lead. *'Everything was going wrong for us. We played like beginners. It was horrible.'* Three was enough and the South Coast 'Kelly Gang' stole the crown. Disappointment at the loss created a few cracks at APIA and Leo began to feel that the fact he wasn't Italian was causing problems. *'The committee had two factions. One was Italian and the other wasn't. Karl and I were often told we were good footballers but that we weren't Italian. My interest was in soccer, not club politics. It was time to go.'*

Hakoah had been chasing the Austrian for years, and in 1964, they finally got him. It was also the year that Everton were touring the country and the year that the Federation saw fit to lift Leo's suspension on representative soccer. *'Karl and I were selected to play for New South Wales against Everton and were back to big-time soccer. There was over 50,000 at the Showground and we were beaten 4–1 by an obviously better side.'*

Leo was happy to be back in the representative fray, and better news was to come. *'To my excitement, Jim Kelly (now national coach) asked me after the New South Wales versus Everton game if I would*

'It was a popular place, but we went broke over it.'

play for Australia in Melbourne in the first test match. I was excited but I got injured at training in the lead-up and couldn't play. The Melbourne crowd was disappointing at that game. They booed the Australian team because there were more New South Wales players than Victorian players. I got the chance to get my Australian blazer the next week in Sydney, though, in what turned out to be my first game for Australia and my last ever representative match. Everton were a much stronger team and beat us 5–2.'

Leo would have liked to play more games for Australia, however it is not something he spends time mulling over. Things out of his control were the biggest influences in only securing one Australian appearance – not his ability as a player. 'It took five years before I was allowed to become an Australian citizen. Then there was the ban from FIFA, as well as my representative suspension from the Federation. By the time I played for Australia, it was at the end of my career.'

• • •

It did not take long before things went sour at Hakoah. Politics and in-fighting became increasingly frustrating for Leo, and he believed undue pressure was being placed on him to win games single-handedly. He left the club and intensified his interest in junior soccer by coaching with the Sutherland Shire. It was also a time when something that seemed like a good business idea sent

the family broke. 'Helen and I had set up a European restaurant. I thought with my standing in the game and the number of people I knew from all nationalities and backgrounds, it would be a success . . . but it turns out I really had too many friends. Nights would be long and boisterous and I found it difficult to charge people whose company I enjoyed and who had been good to me previously. It was a popular place, but we went broke over it.'

The Baumgartners were struggling for the first time since they arrived in Australia and Leo thought it might be better if they went home. Helen remembers the time vividly. 'Leo wanted to go home but I thought he had forgotten what it was like there. We were in paradise here and I didn't want to go back. I told him he should go by himself and see what it was like. If he was absolutely sure life would be better for us there, we would join him. Within ten days he called me and said he was coming home. Back to Australia. We won't live anywhere else.'

Helen went to work and Leo revisited some earlier training as an engineer to commence a twenty-year career with QANTAS. He also couldn't refuse a lucrative offer to pull on his boots again and join Sydney Croatia. It was 1966 and it was his sixth club as a player. 'Ethnic rivalry was very obvious at Croatia. I don't know whether it was the nationalities, or if it

really was just the people running the club that happened to be that certain nationality, but things became a bit uncomfortable for me there when we were beaten 6–1 by Yugal – a Yugoslav club that the Croatians have always had issues with.'

That year was his last in soccer boots. In the thirty years after coming home from kicking the ball under Viennese street lamps and being reprimanded for scuffing his shoes, he had regularly played in front of 60,000 people in the Austrian first division for the country's two biggest clubs, travelled with club and country to five continents and shared the field with people like Di Stefano and Puskas. He had played in the world's best stadiums and lived the life of a big-time soccer player. Some of his best memories, however, are being a part of developing Australian soccer, of winning championships and seeing the local standard improve. But most fondly of all, he remembers how good Australia and its people have been to his family.

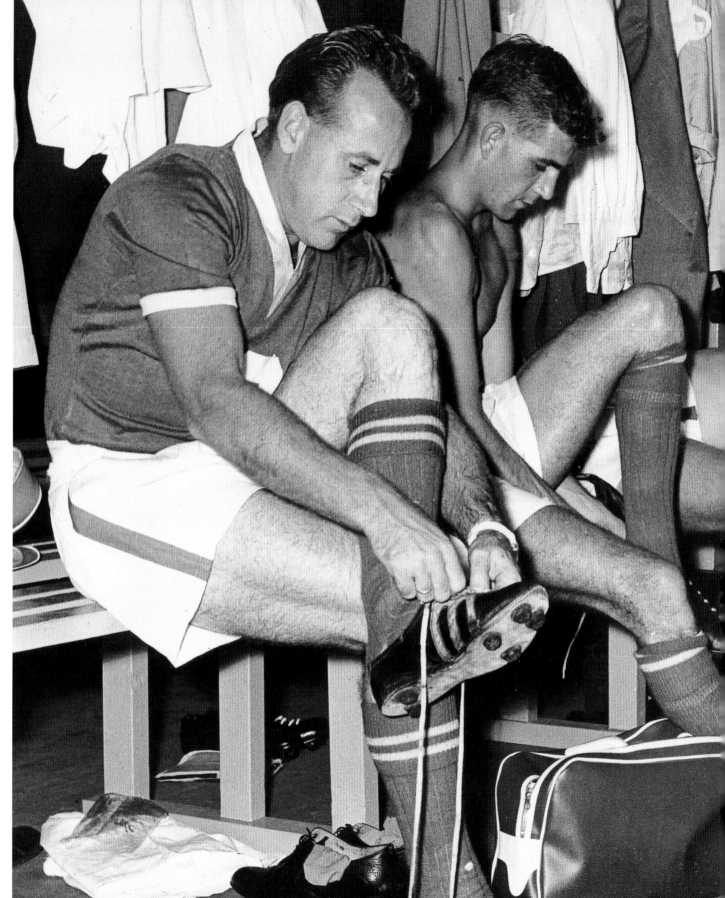

The inner sanctum.

Johnny WARREN MBE, OAM

Socceroo 1965–1974

'We should be the best in the world. We have the best of the world and have so many natural advantages.'

These are words that Johnny Warren has uttered more than once. In fact, these words are the theme of his life's work. He has pushed and pleaded, cheered and cried and always worn his heart on his sleeve for the game in the country he loves.

'To play for your country is the greatest honour, whether it is marbles or anything. When I received a telegram as a 19-year-old to say that I had been selected to play for the Australian football team, I went to the bathroom and cried my eyes out for hours. That is what it meant and that is what it should always mean.'

Since being selected by Australian coach Tiko Jelisavcic to make his debut against Cambodia in Cambodia in 1965, Johnny has notched up sixty-two appearances for the Socceroos, including forty-two 'A' internationals, and nine goals. He received an MBE in 1973 for his services to the game, an ASM (Australian Service Medal) in 2000, a Centenary Medal in 2001, an OAM (Order of Australia Medal) in 2003, joined Joe Marston in the Sport Hall of Fame in 2003 and has gone on to remain at the forefront of Australian soccer long after hanging up his boots.

Somewhat surprisingly, football wasn't always the driving force in Johnny's life. 'I played cricket and league with all the other kids, but football was always there too. It was when I went down to Melbourne to watch the 1956 Olympics that football really took over. I guess it was there that my decision to become a footballer was made.'

In 1959, Johnny's senior career began when the enthusiastic, athletic 16-year-old joined the so-called 'Canterbury Babes' in the NSW State League. Canterbury were a club determined to develop talented young players, and to make sure that Aussie kids wouldn't get 'left behind' amid the growth immigration was bringing to the local game. The situation was perfect for Johnny and he settled in quickly with his young teammates.

In 1960, the 'Babes' added the not-so-babe' Leo Baumgartner, to the team, and

they became surprise participants in that year's grand final. Johnny missed the clash against the glamour-boys at Prague due to injury, but was still thrilled to see his club run out 5–2 victors. In 1961, Canterbury again made the grand final, but lost to Hakoah. In 1962 they finished second-last after a number of talented players were lured to ethnic-based clubs that paid much bigger wages and drew much bigger crowds. As Johnny's bestselling book, *Sheilas, Wogs and Poofters*, explains, it was the end of an era. '*Canterbury's golden period came to an end when money entered the football equation. By the mid-1960s, many of the migrants who had arrived in Australia in the post-World War II immigration influx had increased the size of their disposable income, and much of this money was being spent on new migrant soccer clubs. This, in turn, meant that the old clubs began to struggle to compete.*'

At Canterbury Johnny was earning £3 a win, £2 a draw and £1 a loss, but in 1963 he was persuaded to sign with St George for £300 up-front and wages of £15 a win, £7 a draw and £3 a loss. It paid his way through university and signified the start of a twelve-year love affair with the club – a time that included nine grand finals and secured four championship victories.

Johnny became captain of St George in 1964 at the age of nineteen and he was used as the 'Aussie front' for the club. As an

A hero's welcome home after an overseas tour.

A livewire Johnny in the early days.

example of his open-minded and mature approach, Johnny was one of the first people who used hypnosis before big games in order to help overcome nerves. In fact, it was just before the 1964 grand final that Johnny got his first taste of major media exposure when his unusual techniques made the front page of *The Sydney Morning Herald*. St George was walloped 7–2 by APIA in that grand final, but Johnny continued to improve his game through a variety of mental approaches.

In the years leading up to their 1967 grand final victory, St George asserted a major influence on New South Wales soccer. In 1968, however, the good times crashed to a second-last position. The depths brought change – and introduced the enthusiasm and winning attitude of Frank Arok to Australian soccer when he was brought Down Under to become the club's full-time coach. Success returned, and Johnny revelled in the opportunity to learn in a professional environment, unique to the Australian game.

By this time, Johnny's international career was well under way. In 1965, he was part of Australia's first international tour since the Federation had been formed, when the team went to Cambodia to begin the inaugural World Cup qualification campaign. '*When we arrived in Cambodia it was like literally landing on another planet. The culture shock was incredible.*' Unaware of the health hazards, quite a few of the players fell ill

before the first match, so it was a weakened and naive Australian team that took the field in front of 60,000 fans. *'We were out of our depth and outclassed.'* At twenty-two, Johnny had been named vice captain for the tour, but was one of the players on the bench for the two qualifiers against North Korea. Australia's first 'A' international match since the ban from FIFA ended in a 6–1 rout. The next leg resulted in a 3–1 loss to make an accumulated 9–2 defeat, and it left the Aussies with no illusions as to how far behind world standard they were. Johnny's debut came shortly after those games when he took the field in a 0–0 friendly match against Cambodia.

In 1967, the national team toured Asia again – this time as public relations puppets for the ironically named 'Friendship Games' –

in the midst of the Vietnam War. A team of young players were selected by coach 'Uncle' Joe Vlasits to make the trip, in early preparation for the 1970 World Cup campaign. They were paid $50 a week for the privilege, with the added incentive that they could keep their tracksuits if they won the tournament. Victory in each of their ten games secured Australia's first international soccer trophy, and meant tracksuits all 'round for the players.

Johnny had assumed the Socceroo captain's armband by then, and led the team all the way into the 1970 World Cup qualifying campaign. Back then, only sixteen countries could compete in the finals, including the hosts. There was only one spot given to Asia, Africa and Oceania, which meant Australia was fighting against 120

other nations for one precious World Cup finals berth. We did just enough in both games against Japan and South Korea, then four weeks later played out an aggregate 1–1 draw in two games against Rhodesia (Zimbabwe) in 'neutral' Mozambique. A third game was required to break the deadlock, and the stubborn Africans were finally disposed 3–1. Next stop was the final stage, with two games against Israel. Having to play the third game against Rhodesia meant the Socceroos were already two days behind their airline schedule, and thirty-six hours in transit zigzagging around some of the world's hot-spots to make it to Israel added more height to the mountain still left to climb. Just twenty-four hours after their arrival, the Socceroos faced Israel in Tel Aviv in front of 60,000 baying fans. The

Johnny's beloved, all-conquering and star-studded St George.

'We were out of our depth and outclassed.'

Socceroos were one down after a sixteenth-minute own goal, and 'keeper Ron Corry performed heroics to keep the final score to 1–0. The return leg was at a packed Sydney sportsground ten days later, but the Aussies could only manage a 1–1 draw and therefore missed the 1970 finals after a 2–1 aggregate loss.

Four years later, Johnny became one of the famous 1974 team who wore the green and gold at the World Cup in Germany. Contrary to common belief, however, Captain Socceroo wasn't captain during the tournament, even though he had led the Socceroos for years before the tournament. In fact, it is testament to his dogged determination that he made the squad at all.

In May 1971, the star did his knee. His anterior cruciate ligament gave way under a challenge, and his energetic athleticism gave way to ten weeks prostrate in his house. On 17 May 1971, Johnny underwent the first knee reconstruction in Australia and was told there was a very real chance he would never play again. Missing the action and overcome by isolation, it was a desperate and dark time. A change of attitude was required for Johnny to dig himself out of depression. Salvation came in the form of a FIFA coaching course in

Malaysia. It was an intensive four-month full-time course that not only gave him a new understanding of the game, but took his life off hold and invigorated his attitude about returning from injury. He came back to club football with St George in 1972, determined, fit and desperate to regain his Socceroo place in the lead up to the 1974 World Cup.

The majority of the 1974 World Cup squad had been part of the 1970 qualifying series, and they vowed that the same fate would not befall them again. Johnny had added fire, fanned by his injury, and there was no stopping him. His remarkable recovery was complete in 1973 and he regained a Socceroo starting spot. He wasn't captain, but he was a Socceroo again.

Of course, the World Cup finals was a career highlight, but it also proved an ending point for his international career. Johnny played in the 2–0 loss to East Germany and picked up an injury that ruled him out of the next two games. *'The '74 World Cup was the accumulation of eight years of struggle. It had been a long road, and it was time for the next generation to wear the green and gold.'* That game ended up being Johnny's

Tough times, when crutches replaced soccer boots, 1971.

'The impact of immigration on the game and the country **is huge.**'

last international match.

Upon returning from the World Cup, St George were performing below par and Johnny was asked to make the most of his standing and qualifications to become player–coach. The Saints won twelve of Johnny's fourteen games in charge and forced their way into the grand final against their arch-rivals Hakoah. The game was locked at 2–2 at the end of normal time, so it moved into extra time. The Saints went ahead 3 2, then not long before the end of the match, Johnny took possession of the ball just inside his own half. He sped beyond a couple of defenders, and smacked the ball into the top corner of the net for one of the best goals in his career. Once his rapturous teammates let him up off the ground, Johnny seized the moment and substituted himself. That goal was the final kick of his playing days, and it not only sealed the grand final victory, it symbolised a golden full stop on the career of a player who earned respect from St George and opposing fans alike. Johnny did not watch the final minutes of the game – he took time alone in the change rooms to collect his thoughts and ponder his future. In 1975, he became the club's full-time coach and promptly took his team back to the grand final, once again returning with the silverware.

In 1976, Johnny left St George and worked privately running coaching clinics around Australia and Fiji. He was even appointed national coach of Fiji for games against Tottenham Hotspur of England. In 1977 he was lured back to senior Australian soccer for the start of the National Soccer League and he took control of the fledgling Canberra City. He enjoyed two years with the club, then did his own thing. Of course, his 'own thing' was never too far away from the game that is in his veins.

•••

It is no mistake that you will regularly hear Johnny call the game football, while most Australians refer to it as soccer. It is the world game, and the world calls it football. To Johnny, referring to the game as soccer illustrates the lower esteem in which it is held in Australia, *'and that just isn't right'*.

Johnny is a sixth-generation Australian and grew up in the Sydney suburb of Botany, where many 'new Australians' chose to settle. From a young age he was introduced to a variety of cultures and backgrounds. It is something that he relishes and enjoys discussing. *'The impact of immigration on the game and the country is huge. Early on it was the British, then the mainland Europeans. Then South Americans fled Pinochet and other dictators to come here. Vietnamese came after the Vietnam War and, more recently, Africans. And it won't be long before we see that latest wave of immigration represented in national teams.'*

His time at St George heightened his global awareness, and inadvertently introduced him to his love of South America. St George was a Hungarian-backed club, but was quick to attract quality players from all over the world to improve their standing. In fact, it was the first club to sign South Americans when they brought four Argentineans to Australia. Their arrival brought a new, skilful flavour to the traditionally aggressive, combative Australian style, and encouraged Johnny's inquisitiveness. *'Just watching the way they passed the ball was an education in itself. They could flick it, play it first time, or bend it this way and that. I had never seen anything like it and was quickly taught the importance of skill. I was shown another way of looking at the game that emphasised its beauty and style.'* The Argentineans' light-hearted and joyous attitude to life also introduced Johnny to South America, and he has had a love affair with the continent (and its football) ever since.

Multicultural Australia can be put under the spotlight through Australian soccer. There is more good than bad that has accompanied mass migration to Australia, however the cross-cultural makeup of the Socceroo teams provides clear examples of the difficulties involved in assimilating to a new land. *'I guess there was rivalry of sorts at times. I know it got to me when some of the guys were sitting in the Socceroo change*

A media stunt, or unique training methods?

rooms before internationals wondering what the results were "back home". We understand it all better now, but I guess it did create some distance [between] the Aussies and the ex-pats.'

Johnny also observed some differences in the attitudes between immigrants from various places. *'It is a generalisation, but the "real wogs" in some ways adapted better and tried to make more of things, even though they struggled with the language. The British immigrants did come to Australia for a better life, but it was often the adventure and sunshine that was the lure. It was almost like they were on holidays. Immigrants fleeing problems or hardships after war or persecution had a different attitude and really wanted to make a go of a new life here. It was no holiday, it was often a second chance at life.'*

•••

Johnny Warren was the original Captain Socceroo, and it wasn't just his prowess over the white lines that drew people's attention. He was the first soccer player – footballer – to make a mark on the Australian media, and he took his self-created responsibilities very seriously. It all began when he was writing a column for the local paper while captaining St George. His influence grew, and by the mid-1960s he was gracing TV screens to provide analysis and tips as

'Captain Socceroo'. *'I was captain of the Socceroos and I saw the job as a good opportunity to develop the game on and off the pitch. The game needed it.'*

Johnny's decision to make the most of his media opportunities had multiple benefits. On the one hand, the game needed a push in the mainstream Australian media, which Johnny thought did not pay soccer its dues. On the other hand, it provided Johnny with the chance to be involved in the game on a full-time basis, and introduced him to influential people from all over the world. *'I saw the difference I was able to make [in promoting] the game. I had to do it alone, though, and there was never a pat on the back or support from the Australian Soccer Federation. In fact, when we went to the 1974 World Cup, we were all told we were not allowed to deal directly with the media. I was writing a weekly column for* The Sydney Morning Herald *at the time, and in the end they had to contact the Federation and tell them that if I didn't write the column, there would never be another word about the game through any of their media outlets. I wrote the column.'*

His work in the media during his playing career ultimately found a spiritual home at SBS as a soccer analyst with Les Murray – and the network and the game are better for it. He currently sits on advisory soccer panels for government think-tanks and has

been an integral part of the Crawford Report, investigating the recent problems with the game's administration. He is also involved in an influential task force which has been created to revamp the NSL and this has led to the creation of a new Australian Premier League. On top of all this, Johnny remains an unofficial ambassador for football throughout his continuing international travels. The game still keeps Johnny very busy. *'I am proud of my contribution to the game since I stopped playing all those years ago. The game could do with a lot more ex-players doing their part off the field as well, and there must be a way for the game to appeal to them in that sense. Real football people will do anything for other football people, and I guess that's how I look at what I do.'*

Another battle Johnny has had to face in recent times is his health. Diagnosed with cancer in late 2002, Johnny has undergone chemotherapy and put the illness to rest midway through 2003. Unfortunately, his remission period only lasted until March 2004, when the cancer returned. In typical Captain Socceroo style, though, Johnny has assumed the responsibility of increasing the awareness of cancer by volunteering his time and using his status in the soccer community in a series of advertising campaigns for the Cancer Council of Australia.

•••

> **'** Development of this game in Australia is my life's mission. **'**

While I waited to interview Johnny in the tranquil Jamberoo pub owned by the Warren family, I sipped a beer under his signed 1974 World Cup shirt and admired the memorabilia – most of it football and all of it interesting – that adorned every available space on the walls and ceiling. Items from Johnny's beloved South America and the odd photo of Pelé. Signed copies of *Sheilas, Wogs and Poofters* were stacked behind the bar. When he arrived, it seemed everyone wanted to say g'day and wish him well. But Johnny is not only well-known in the small town in which he lives, he is perhaps our most recognisable Socceroo. He is well-known because he loves football, translated through the way he played and the way he promotes the sport now.

Not many people are lucky enough to know what they want from life, but Johnny is one. A firm handshake when our meeting concluded was punctuated by the words *'Development of this game in Australia is my life's mission'*, and it was obvious he meant it. He has said it before . . . and no doubt he'll say it again . . . and as long as he keeps saying it, Australian football will be the winner.

Captain Socceroo riding high.

Ray BAARTZ

Socceroo 1967–1974

Ray Baartz is a third-generation Australian who grew up around the steel refineries of Newcastle. Testament to the town's British background, the sports on offer in most schools over forty-five years ago were cricket in summer and soccer in winter. He had little choice *but* to chase the round ball. Not that he had a problem with that. In fact, he took to it like an angry crowd to a poor refereeing decision.

In 1962, Ray was a 15-year-old making his senior debut for Maitland in the Northern New South Wales State League. At sixteen, he was playing at one of the oldest soccer clubs in Australia – Adamstown–Rosebud. At seventeen, he was training with Manchester United, and later that year he agreed to sign a professional contract with them. At nineteen, he left the Red Devils, declined offers from other English clubs and returned to his beloved Australia. It was 1966 by then – the year he was first included in the Australian squad and signed with Sydney Hakoah for a record Australian fee of $5,600. He made his full Socceroo debut in 1967 and began accumulating his forty-eight 'A' international appearances all the way to the successful 1974 World Cup qualifying campaign. In late 1974, after the Socceroos had already qualified, he was struck in the throat in a friendly against Uruguay and was sent to hospital battling for his life. He was unconscious for two days after the freak incident and never played again. At twenty-seven years of age and at the height of his career, perhaps Australia's best ever soccer talent retired.

•••

'I was always playing soccer and cricket as a kid. There was always a group of us at the local park playing sport. We didn't have televisions then, so our life was outside, being active, and it was great. I have a brother who is ten years older than me and he would show me what to do and encourage me. In fact, he was the only coach I had for a long time. I was in state cricket teams too, and he thought I had a brighter future there. Soccer was the thing I loved the most, though, and in the end you go where your heart is.

'I went through juniors in Newcastle with [future Socceroo] Col Curran and [in 1962] we were both asked to go to Maitland seniors at age fifteen, even though we were both Adamstown boys. After a year we went back to Adamstown–Rosebud seniors. It was formed in the 1890s and is basically as old as many English clubs in England.'

Adamstown–Rosebud had the tradition, but it was also very progressive in its thinking. One of the club members had ties with the great Manchester United, and the club thought that it would be beneficial to send two young players to England for three months each year to experience top-level coaching. The idea was that, within a few years, more than half of its squad would have improved dramatically and the club would remain a force. Great in theory, but problematic from Ray's point of view. 'Doug Johns and I were the first ones to be sent over. He was nineteen and I was seventeen and to go to the other side of the planet was a big deal. We were met by Man U officials at the airport and everything seemed okay until they asked where we were staying and how long we would be there. Well . . . we told them we thought everything had been organised and that we were there for three months. They looked a bit shocked, but they must have seen our panic because thankfully they put us up in digs and paid us £3 a week for the full three months. It wasn't as if they were a small, lower division club. They could well have turned us away, but they didn't. It just wouldn't happen today.'

Big clubs have apprentices, an A and B team, a reserve team and a senior team. Doug and Ray played most of the time in the A and B teams because they were too old to be apprentices. Ray scored twice in his first game, then within two months had played for the reserves. When the three months were up, Doug went home, but Ray was summoned into the great Matt Busby's office. The Manchester United manager wanted the young Aussie. 'I didn't go over for a trial, I went to train and hopefully improve. I was pretty shy and timid over there and played with an attitude of "I hope

I don't make a fool of myself". I was lively on the field, but I didn't really have the confidence to try anything special. Still, they wanted me. I was shocked, but I was happy too. They offered £12 a week, which wasn't a lot of money because I had to pay rent out of that . . . but it was Manchester United.'

His father had passed away when Ray was thirteen and he subsequently became very close to his mother. Unfortunately, communication channels were not what they are today, and his mother did not have a telephone. Traditional post or the odd telegram was the only way to keep in contact. 'It was actually a reasonably difficult decision to stay. I had no one there I could really talk to about it and I couldn't speak to Mum either. I missed Australia, but I figured I should give it a go [in England]. I had to write to Mum and tell her I was staying for another two years. I am not sure if she thought it was good or bad news.'

The World Cup was being played in England in 1966 and there was a frenzied interest in the birthplace of the game. Manchester United had some of the best players in the world and were a brilliant, entertaining side. George Best (Northern Ireland), Dennis Law (Scotland) and Bobby Charlton (England) were the guys keeping Ray out of the senior team. 'With the guys that we had in the first team, I didn't get a look in and that was fair enough. That wasn't the reason I wanted to come home,

though. Quite simply, I missed Australia and I missed my friends. Mostly, I missed Australia's colours. It was so grey and depressing in Manchester and it hadn't really recovered from the war. People weren't happy and I could see why.'

It was in February 1966 when Ray told his boss that he wanted to go home. The response from Mr Busby was, 'But son, no one leaves Manchester United! Wait a month, then see how you feel.' The month that passed increased Ray's resolve to return,

so he turned back offers from other English clubs and put it all down to experience. Adamstown–Rosebud's three-month experiment had turned into a two-year adventure, but it had paid off. Ray could not put a foot wrong when he returned. 'I was much more confident when I got back. I was trying things and began to score a lot of goals from outside the box. I was doing things I was too scared to try in England. I'd learnt a lot over there and my career took off back here. I did wonder if I

1974 World Cup qualifying versus Iran in Teheran, 1973. Ray at his acrobatic best on the left.

should go back after a couple of months as they said I could, but I didn't ask. That's the way it is and, really, I'm glad I didn't.'

Later that year the 19-year-old was selected in the Australian squad to play Roma of Italy. He remained on the bench, but the experience strengthened his desire to represent his country. By the end of 1966, Sydney powerhouse Hakoah lured him to the 'big smoke', and once again soccer took him from home. '*It was the same for most sportspeople in Newcastle. If you wanted to progress and develop, you had to go into the bigger Sydney competitions. It was nice to get some more money, but it was all about playing at a higher level and pushing to play for Australia. I moved to Sydney, but I knew I would never settle there. I came back to Newcastle whenever I could.*

'*I spent my career from then on at Hakoah. It was a Jewish club, and they were great to play for. It was a professional place and I enjoyed my time there. A few years later, there was a benefit organised to help [former Socceroo] Joe Watson and his family in his battle against cancer. We needed to raise at least $30,000. [Current Australian Soccer Association Chairman] Frank Lowy was the Hakoah President back then and he basically stood up and said, "Here's $10,000 from me", then told two of his colleagues to do the same. Thirty thousand dollars in about ten seconds, which is a good indication of the type of people involved with that club and in the game.*'

The move to Sydney paid dividends, as Ray fired in the goals and played with trademark enthusiasm. During his first year at Hakoah, national coach Joe Venglos invited him into his team to play three games against Scotland. His debut was at the Sydney Showgrounds on 28 May 1967 in front of over 50,000 fans. From that game until his retirement, he played in every minute of every Socceroo game that he was available. '*I was so excited about wearing that shirt. I was nervous too, as I guess you should be, because it was and is a great honour.*'

That same year his old buddies at United toured Down Under to play the Socceroos. '*It was good to catch up with the guys and play against them. I enjoyed it and did well.*' So well, in fact, that when a reporter asked Matt Busby about how he thought Ray had played, the United boss replied, 'You saw how he went and you can see why I wanted to keep him.'

Ray was always a blur of energy in that Socceroo shirt.

'The whole thing was ridiculous, really, but I wouldn't change any of it for the world.'

An unsavoury incident marred one of the matches – United's Dennis Law lost his cool and headbutted Australia's Ronny Giles, who was hospitalised with a broken cheekbone. Busby and his players put their hands into their pockets and collected enough money to see that Ronny's expenses were covered. It was a gesture of goodwill that smoothed the waters, however not everyone was taken. *'There wasn't an official reception during that tour, but I knew the guys, and some of us invited them to a party in North Sydney. It was a good night and everyone was drinking and getting along. You could never see it happening with Giggs, Keane and co. today, but it was a good night. One of Ronny Giles' mates was with us and he did not let Dennis Law's headbutt go easily. You would have thought he was over it during the party, particularly when he offered Dennis a lift back into the city afterwards. Then, halfway over the Harbour Bridge, he stopped the car and told Dennis in no uncertain terms to get out. Dennis was one of the world's superstars at the time, but he was made to walk across the bridge by himself and back to the hotel through the streets of Sydney, while our mate was in a hospital bed! He probably shouldn't have done it, but it was a good laugh anyway.'*

Nineteen sixty-seven was a busy year that culminated in new coach Joe Vlasits leading the Australians on a tour of Asia, in the heat of the Vietnam War. The visit into hostile territory was a public relations exercise to help win over the South Vietnamese to the strength of the US-led forces fighting the North Vietnamese. The other teams were New Zealand, Singapore, South Korea, Malaysia, Thailand and Hong Kong. *'It was called the "Friendly Nations Cup" or something like that, but we trained and played with bombs going off all around us and with the constant support of a security team. That was about as organised as it got, though – there was monsoonal weather, the army had to help us get some decent food as a lot of the guys were trying to survive on Coke and bread, and there was no air conditioning in the hotels. We didn't have a proper training kit [uniform] and we looked a shambles. We really had no preparation for what it was like and we were there for six weeks. On top of that, we didn't get paid a cent and many guys lost their jobs while they were away. We ended up undefeated all tour, but there were a lot of young players like me and we really relied on each other. You can imagine the bond we formed in that environment. The whole thing was ridiculous, really, but I wouldn't change any of it for the world.'*

The Australians played some home internationals in 1968, then in 1969 went back to Asia to begin qualifying for the 1970 World Cup. It was an arduous and – some would say – unfair campaign, but the Socceroos came so close. *'It was terrific stuff. FIFA didn't really know what to do with nations like us – South Korea, Japan, Rhodesia [now Zimbabwe] and Israel – so they kind of lumped us together. We weren't any more organised, really, than when we went to Vietnam, and character was almost as important as ability. It was a relief to train each day because at least then we all knew what we were doing. It was very difficult for us but, once again, I wouldn't change one part of it.'*

Back then, there was only one qualifying spot from all of Asia, Africa and Oceania and just a total of sixteen teams in the World Cup. Over 120 teams fighting for one berth, yet Australia made it to the last hurdle. *'The path kept changing for us and most of the time we had no idea who we had to play next or where. We kept knocking teams off after travelling all around the world, but still we had to keep playing more. We ended up having to play three matches against Rhodesia – all in Mozambique. Then we had to get to Tel Aviv to play Israel and it was a real pain. We flew to South Africa, Portugal, Italy, then Greece before Israel. All had stop-overs and delays and we were in transit for an eternity – and then had to play the next day. We lost 1–0, then came back here and drew 1–1 when we should've won. Israel went through and after a four-month campaign, we were out.'*

'It was Tony that
coined the name
"Socceroo"...'

By name, and many say in spirit, that tour was when the 'Socceroos' were born. *'Tom Patrick from QANTAS and [journalist] Tony Hoystead travelled with the team and they really pitched in and became a part of the squad. Tony used to like the occasional drink and was fond of scotch. One day, the boys polished off one of his bottles during a day off. They refilled the bottle with tea and Tony was fuming when he found out. It was Tony who coined the name "Socceroo" and began to write his articles referring to us by that name.'*

•••

Ray married his Newcastle sweetheart Sue prior to that 1969 tour and with a new house to pay off, the time away made things very tough financially. He was a smallgoods sales rep as well as a soccer player, and when the new coach Rale Rasic decided to embark on a world tour in late 1970, Ray could not go away for so long again. *'It was tough to say no to that tour, but I just couldn't afford it. Some of the other guys were in the same boat. As it was, Rale took the opportunity to introduce some new players and it helped build the foundation for the successful '74 campaign.'*

There were some more home internationals in 1971 and 1972, and in 1973 the 1974 World Cup campaign began in earnest. *'Rale was very professional. The preparation was very demanding considering we were part-time players, but it was great when we got into camp. We knew what we had to do to qualify this time; we were paid more money by the ASF and we even had team training gear.*

'The first games were against Indonesia, New Zealand and Iraq before the team played Iran in Sydney. I think it was the first time sports psychology was used seriously. Rale brought a guy in to speak with us before we played Iran. We were more than sceptical about all that nonsense, but he began to make sense. He talked about when you play golf: if you have a hit over a bunker while you think about the bunker ... you will hit into that bunker. We all decided we needed a three-goal buffer from the home leg and took his attitude of keeping our eyes on that target. We spanked Iran in Sydney 3–0 and it was one of the best games we ever played. Of course, the psychologist became a legend!'

The away leg in Iran was a different matter. A capacity crowd of 100,000 screaming fans, and one goal down within five minutes. *'They came out flying, but even by the time they scored the second within 15–20 minutes, I was still confident.'* The final score was 2–0 but Australia progressed 3–2 on aggregate. The Islamic laws that govern the country prohibit alcohol consumption, however more than a few sneaky ones were downed at the hotel pool by the team that night.

The final step in the 1974 World Cup campaign was against South Korea. The first leg was in Sydney and the Socceroos stuttered to a 0–0 draw. *'We played poorly and even though 0–0 at home is not a good result to take into an away leg, I still don't remember being too worried.'*

They were worried when they found themselves 2–0 down in the return leg, however. *'It was a strange, robotic crowd over there. It was as if they were choreographed. Whatever it was, we found ourselves 2–0 down and battling. We then basically did what Iran did to Australia in 1997 – and came back to level at 2–2. I scored the second near the end of the game and with today's rules it would have sent us through on the away goals rule. That rule didn't exist then, though, so we had to play another game.*

The three amigos; Abonyi, Baartz and Warren.

'The decider was in Hong Kong and we ended up on the same plane as South Korea. We were laughing and feeling good, and when we saw them we felt even better. They looked down and out. They looked beaten, and I think that was actually where the game was won.'

Of course, the game was really won after a Jimmy Mackay wonder strike sealed a 1–0 victory. Australia was in the World Cup for the first time. 'You can drink in Hong Kong, and plenty of the boys did. It was a big night, and we received a terrific reception when we arrived home too.'

The Socceroos had a break and the players returned to club competition. By April 1974, two games were organised against Uruguay, another qualifier for the 1974 World Cup. It was a sound idea to play Uruguay in preparation for Australia's biggest challenge, but had the unexpected downside of resulting in an injury that eliminated, arguably, Australia's best player from the tournament. In fact, the second match of a spiteful series put a big full stop to Ray Baartz's career.

'I think Uruguay thought they were going to have it easy out here, but they had another thing coming. I mean, it was no fluke that we were in the World Cup. They have a heritage of being rough and a bit dirty, but in these games they were vicious. Of course, we didn't back off and the two

Proud Socceroos led by Peter Wilson.

games became spiteful. Game one ended 0–0 and we really wanted to take it to them in Sydney for game two.

'Three minutes before half-time in game two, I knocked a ball harmlessly clear of our box and began to follow it up field. The next thing I knew, one of them had raised his arm to stop me getting by easily – but he had done it intentionally with his full arm,

and he karate chopped me right in the throat. I couldn't breathe well, but made it to half-time to have a couple of aspros from team doctor Brian Corrigan.

'I was fired up for the second-half after that. I scored a cracker and set up the second for a 2–0 lead. With about ten minutes to go, one of their guys was disputing a corner decision and I basically told him where to go and reminded him of the score. He punched me square in the jaw and I went straight down. The boys were telling me to stay down because he'd get sent off . . . which was pretty easy because it was a fair punch! There was some push and shove and one of the Uruguayans actually punched the guy who flattened me, to draw blood so he could complain to the ref that I had punched him first! It was all quite strange, I can tell you.'

That night, Ray awoke to find he couldn't move his left arm. Thinking he had just been sleeping on it strangely, he rolled over. The 'pins and needles' he thought he had wouldn't leave him, though, and he and Sue became worried enough to ring Dr Corrigan early the next morning. 'We all went to Royal North Shore Hospital and I couldn't get out of the car because I couldn't move the left side of my body. Brian started calling for a neurosurgeon and I told him not to make a fuss. He told me to shut up and leave it to him. It was then I started getting really nervous.'

Not long after that, Ray lost consciousness. Delayed swelling in his neck – from the karate chop, not the punch – had given him a belated stroke. He haemorrhaged twice while undergoing tests and the doctors told Sue that they didn't know if he would ever come out of it. Soccer took a distant back seat. 'Of course, I didn't see all the stress because I was out of it for two days. When I came around and the situation was explained to me I was thankful to be alive. Sue was pregnant with our second child and even though I knew there would be no World Cup, and in fact no more soccer, I was happy to know I was there with my family.'

Ray was confined to hospital for two weeks. His coma lasted two days and he was partially paralysed throughout that time. Full mobility did return, however the doctors warned that the slightest impact on the same spot, or around his head, could cause haemorrhaging from which he might not recover. A tough time was made tougher when his elderly mother died on Newcastle train station after returning from time spent with Ray as he recovered in Sydney. It was a terrible month, but the game's governing body made a heartfelt gesture by still inviting him to tour Germany with the team for the World Cup. It is an indication of the standing Ray had in Australian soccer, and his teammates were thrilled to have him there. 'I was honoured to be asked to go,

Ray in hospital, 1974. The aim was to recover as quickly as possible, and get out of those glamorous PJs.

Our Socceroos with a loyal fan.

but to be honest I didn't like it. Particularly before the first game. I had never been on the bench for the Socceroos and had never even been substituted. To be there and not play . . . well, I felt like a tourist. I wanted to play but I knew I couldn't. I knew from then that when I returned, I had to get on with the rest of my life.'

Getting on with life meant opening Ray Baartz Sports Store. At the time of the injury, Ray was sponsored by Adidas and one of the staff suggested Ray should open a sports store in Newcastle with him. Three partners scraped together $3,000 each and within three months of the 1974 injury, Ray's new life was officially opened. The business is still going strong and it is an achievement that brings Ray great pride. *'Plenty of sports people were putting their names to stores but weren't really prepared to work at it. I was, and for the next two years I didn't really watch any games or get involved in soccer at all. The store was my focus after the injury and it was good to have it. It also took two years for me to begin getting over the injury mentally. I would regularly scratch my head when I was talking to people just to check my arm was still working.'*

Coaching has never really appealed to Ray, but he has helped out with his son's teams and was a co-founder of the successful Newcastle KB United in the late 1970s. *'We used to get great crowds in the NSL up here*

and a lot of support from the area. The main reason for forming that team was to provide an option for the local players and stop the talent draining out of Newcastle. None of us made a penny, but they were good times.'

Most of Ray's good times now come from his family, his business, the golf course and his beloved Hunter region. He is modestly proud of his time at the pinnacle of Australian soccer and doesn't have too much time for pondering what might have been if he hadn't been cut down in his prime. As far as he is concerned, it is more important to consider what is and what can be, instead of dwelling on what was.

'I would regularly **scratch my head...** just to check **my arm was still** working.'

Atti ABONYI

Socceroo 1967–1977

The Abonyi family huddled in a basement with their neighbours as the sounds of bombing and gunfire rattled Budapest. Atti knew life would never be the same again.

Students and workers had marched on the city square demanding the withdrawal of Soviet troops from Hungary, the formation of a multi-party political system and free elections. On 23 October 1956, Soviet troops fired on the unarmed masses in a show of arrogant strength, and immediately turned the protesters into unwitting revolutionaries. For years, the Hungarian national anthem had been banned because it contained nationalistic and religious overtones, but that day a rousing rendition in the city square had inspired Hungarians far and wide to revolt. It was a result of the spontaneous outpouring of emotion after years of Soviet repression, and the protest soon escalated into widespread violence.

Against all odds, the revolutionaries began to force the Soviets back and looked set for an unlikely victory. The Soviet authorities could only take so much insolence, however, and after two weeks of bloody fighting in the streets, they had regained control of the capital.

Twenty-five thousand freedom fighters had been injured or killed in Budapest alone, and 230 people executed. Three hundred thousand Hungarians had managed to flee the country in this short window of opportunity, as the Hungarian border guards had sided with the locals.

But the Abonyis missed that chance. Like other families who'd been hiding in basements all over the Hungarian capital, they made tentative steps back into their apartment, but apprehension was a constant companion. Few people ventured into the streets, and life was at an uneasy standstill. Atti's dad knew life could not continue this way. Something had to give. With pain etched across his face, he told his wife and young sons that he and two friends would sneak past the Soviet border guard and escape to freedom in Austria. He told them they had no choice – he would do what he could, and within two years he would get them out as well. They just had to hold on and be patient. Two years. He promised.

Atti, his 12-year-old brother and his mother were left to ponder their fate. Life was tense because of the ever-present fear that one of their neighbours in the block of commission flats could be a Soviet informer. The infernal days dragged by as the Abonyis wondered when they would be free and if Atti's father had actually made it.

'We didn't know if we would ever see him again. The borders were being closed up again by the time Dad left. Still, there was no other choice. Thousands had already left,

Left: Atti (left) and his brother just before their escape from Hungary. Right: Atti today.

'We had absolutely nothing, but our dreams had come true.'

and plenty of others were still prepared to take the risk. Some died trying, and plenty went to prison.'

Late one night, three weeks after his father's departure, Atti remembers that a knock on the door jolted him from a restless sleep.

'Of course we thought the worst, and Mum opened the door with her heart in her mouth. Then, I'll never forget this . . . it was Dad standing there with a big grin! He had snuck back in to get us!'

Atti's father had made it into Austria but couldn't bear not knowing what was happening to his family. Now that he knew the best route, he had returned to take them and several friends across the border.

'There ended up being thirteen of us. My brother and I were the only kids, and while we were obviously scared, I must admit it was all a bit exciting too. We got some transport out to a small village near the border and had all agreed that if anyone asked, we were on our way to a wedding. We met a farmer there who was also a guide and helped people escape, and we all slept in his barn for a few days waiting for the full moon to fade.'

When the moon had darkened, the guide and his thirteen escapees set off into the cold November night. They had their worldly possessions on their backs and the future in their hearts. When the guide took them as far into the forest as he was prepared to go, he was paid for his intimate knowledge of the area and returned to his 'farming' life. He told the group to head straight to the faint light far in the distance, and they plodded through the icy marshlands in silence until a threatening outline halted their progress. *'We all jumped onto the freezing ground because the figure ahead looked like a guard. We waited there for ten minutes that seemed to take forever, with only our chattering teeth breaking the silence. In the end, Dad said, "We can't wait here forever" and the guard wasn't moving. We had to keep going. When we snuck closer, we saw that it was just a tree stump! We all felt pretty stupid . . . but fortunately that's the only guard we saw the whole time. It actually gave us a laugh and eased the tension a bit.'*

The group pushed on through the darkness. The light they were heading towards got brighter and brighter, until a couple of hours later they reached a river. They plunged into the icy water and waded across. It wasn't wide, and within minutes

The *Fairsea* liner that brought the Abonyis to Australia.

they had scrambled onto dry land. Austrian land. Free land. 'We were laughing, crying, jumping, hugging, singing. Our dreams had come true. We had absolutely nothing, but our dreams had come true.'

The faint light was a Red Cross station in a monastery. The Abonyis were given a room, and they waited for their adventure to carry them as far away as possible.

•••

During this time, Australia was basking in the international glow of the Melbourne Olympics. In contrast to the situation in much of Eastern Europe, these games were known as the 'Friendly Games'. News of the sunshine, peace and harmony Down Under – and of the nation's rapid development due to immigration – spread around the world. Within three months, and without passports or possessions, the Abonyis left Europe for Melbourne as Hungarian refugees.

'I really had no idea where Australia was. We were only taught about Hungary and Russia in school. Dad knew, though, and Australia was his first choice ahead of America, Canada or other European countries. I was fascinated listening to all the other refugees' stories and where they were heading to. I began to appreciate the size of the world and I loved it. Later, I travelled overseas sixteen times with the Socceroos and I often remembered the conversations I heard back then and wondered where those people ended up.'

The Red Cross funded the Abonyis' transfer to a German port to meet 500 other refugees aboard the *Fairsea* liner. The enthusiasm and excitement was palpable as the ship ploughed away from Communist rule and on to the 'Lucky Country'. The five-week journey was punctuated with dancing, games, excellent food and plenty of good times. 'It was exciting and good fun. I had never seen the ocean, though, and being

on it for five weeks made me as sick as a dog. I remember the ship record for throwing up was eleven times in a day. People were getting third-degree burns from too much sunbaking as we got away from the European winter. Someone had told Dad that rum settles your stomach so he lined up six bottles for the journey!'

On 10 May 1957, the *Fairsea* docked in Melbourne. The Abonyis made the three-and-a-half-hour train trip north to a refugee shelter in Bonegilla. They were given a room to share and access to common bathrooms and kitchens, as well as £5 a week from the Australian Government. Within six weeks, Atti's father headed off again. Without a word of English, he and two friends went to Melbourne to look for work. Wandering down Bourke Street and admiring their new-found surroundings, they were stopped by another Hungarian who had heard the men speaking. He asked if they needed work, then took them with him. He organised jobs and rented accommodation, helped them with the language, and gave them tips on how to get by in the new country. *'It wasn't long before Dad sent for us, and we settled into a real life. Our new saviour was incredibly generous – but I don't think too unusual at the time – and that's how our life started. Within eighteen months, we were able to rent a house with another family, and within three years, we were renting our own two-bedroom house. Soon after, Dad bought a block of land outside Melbourne, next to one of his friends, for £700. A couple of years after that, both of them built exactly the same houses next door to each other and we moved in. Dad still lives there.'*

•••

Atti began playing football with a local junior club in St Kilda a year after he arrived in Australia. Around the same time, fellow Hungarian refugees formed a club that assisted the community to settle into their new surroundings. The common theme, as with most other newly arrived ethnic communities, was soccer. Melbourne Hungaria started in the lower leagues, but by 1960 had been promoted into the state league. Until then, there had only been two senior teams, but as the 'children of the revolution' grew, the club decided to create a junior arm. Atti Abonyi was one of the talented youngsters asked to join, and he quickly progressed to the senior team at just

under sixteen years of age. *'There was a real buzz around Australia at the time, and that showed around the soccer clubs. There were big crowds and plenty of atmosphere. As that generation has moved on, things have become quite different.*

'The first time I played organised soccer was in Australia. Of course, every spare minute we had in Hungary we would kick a ball made of rags stuffed into my mum's pantyhose and that's where I learnt my skills. We used to live directly behind the local senior club and peer through the fence at their training. We waited until a ball was kicked over the fence so that we could run and get it and kick it back. Anything to kick a real ball! Then, before I knew it, I was playing in organised competition on big pitches in Australia with real balls. Then, I was in front of big crowds playing for Melbourne Hungaria, Victoria and Australia. I still can't believe it.'

Melbourne Hungaria won the state league in 1967 and then secured the Australia Cup (Ampol Cup) with a 4–3 victory over Sydney's APIA, set up by an Abonyi hat-trick. He had recently made his Socceroo debut in a 2–0 loss to Scotland at Olympic Park, Melbourne, and he was thrilled to be selected by Joe Vlasits to tour Asia in 1967. It was the peak of the Vietnam War, and even though the players were paid a pittance, only Pat Hughes (the captain) declined the trip. And so it was that a bunch of naive, enthusiastic Aussies entered the lion's den. *'We still have a laugh now about having a lot of memories but no money. They were actually exciting times and we went with great spirit. Vietnam was the poorest country I've seen, with the worst conditions, but we were still in heaven because we were playing for Australia. It's funny that the worst times seem to give the best memories – anyone can stay in five-star*

'…anyone can stay in
five-star luxury around the world,
but not everybody can play soccer in a
war zone not knowing what is safe to eat,
and training on a concrete hot-box hotel roof…'

once. Atti played every minute of the games against East Germany (0–2), West Germany (0–3) and Chile (0–0), and while the team worked incredibly hard and deserved to be on the world's biggest stage, he knew their real standing. *'I was driving to work in 1973 when I heard the draw read out on the radio. I'll admit to being pretty intimidated when I heard it, but it didn't last long. Everyone expected us to get thrashed but, to be honest, I was just happy to be there. There were only sixteen teams and we were part-timers, for crying out loud. England didn't even make it, and players like George Best have never been to a World Cup. It was pretty surreal; I mean, what rights did we have to be there, really?'*

Atti doesn't relive the experience too often, but when he does, explaining the thrill is quite simple. *'It's the World Cup. I mean, it's the ultimate. Those two words say it all. World Cup. We did more than brilliantly over there and all the sacrifices were worthwhile.*

'We were paid $5,000 minus tax for the thirteen games in qualifying plus the three games in the finals. We even had to fight to get that much and had actually threatened not to go, but we needed something. I lost two jobs in my career – it was virtually a case of lose your job or lose your place in the team. It wasn't a tough decision most of the time, though, and plenty of people lost jobs or ruined relationships. I think it was a

luxury around the world, but not everybody can play soccer in a war zone not knowing what is safe to eat, and training on a concrete hot-box hotel roof because it is the safest place.'

It was during this tour that Atti was introduced to Socceroo and St George captain Johnny Warren. *'When I was told I'd be his roommate I thought I'd definitely made the big-time!'* Johnny and Atti became close friends and, as time passed, the idea of moving to St George to join 'Captain Socceroo' began to take seed. Melbourne and Sydney had the best competitions, in direct relationship to the numbers of

immigrants who had settled there. In fact, in the late 1960s, Sydney had arguably the strongest competition and St George was one of the 'big three' clubs – along with APIA and Hakoah. The fact that it was also Hungarian was an added bonus. In 1969, Atti was finally persuaded north and began a highly successful and enjoyable eight-year period with the club. That same year was also Atti's first World Cup qualifying campaign, and while ultimately unsuccessful it set the platform for the very successful 1974 campaign.

It is a well-discussed fact that Australia has only made it to the World Cup finals *case of the less you get, the more you give and it was the spirit that kept us doing it. Sometimes, the more you get, the more you want, but we didn't have that luxury.'*

Atti's dad flew to Germany for the 1974 finals, and organised a trip for his son back to Hungary after the tournament. They travelled their old escape route in reverse and visited old friends. Atti saw how much his life had moved on and developed a heightened respect for Australia and his father's fortitude. It was also around this time that he decided to retire from the national team, at the age of twenty-eight and after the high of the World Cup finals. *'Unfortunately, the game didn't really kick on like we thought it would. It's probably best explained by the fact that the Federation said they would present us all with a medal to celebrate the achievements of everyone involved [in the World Cup], but we never got it. Instead, a fan took about a year to make copper plaques of each player with a team photo on the back. They are so well done, and I don't even know who the guy is. All the players signed them, and it is the only memento I have hanging on my walls at home. The fans were ready, but the ASF perhaps wasn't.'*

Atti's unbridled enthusiasm for the game wouldn't rest and his self-imposed international retirement was short-lived. In 1976, he accepted Brian Green's pleas for him to rejoin the Socceroos. It was the last game of Brian's short-lived spell as Socceroo coach, but the new incumbent, Jimmy Shoulder, made sure Atti remained in the team. Jimmy took him on the Socceroos' tour of England, Israel and Asia later that year in preparation for the 1977 round of World Cup qualifiers. The Socceroos' failure to repeat the success of 1974 signalled the real end to Atti's Socceroo days. *'When we lost in Tehran to Iran in '77, I knew that was really it. I knew I didn't have another four years in me at that level, but it was disappointing to end on such a bad note. We had an easier path that time, and still didn't make it.'*

Nineteen seventy-seven was also the year that Atti began life at a new club. It was the first year of the national league and St George was expected to do well. His old World Cup teammate Manfred Schaefer had been given the coaching responsibilities, and one of his first tasks was to try and keep Atti at the club. *'The national league was going to mean extra demands on the players, so I thought it was fair to get more money. In the end, they said no, and I thought it was time to look after my family. I transferred to Sydney Croatia and earned more money in three years there than in eight years at St George.'*

Sydney Croatia was not permitted into the national league because they didn't want to remove the direct reference to Croatia in their name. Within a couple of years they would be awarded entry, but the final three years of Atti's playing career took place in the NSW State League. *'We were still regularly getting 8,000–10,000 crowds because of the Croatian community. They couldn't leave the club out forever.'*

Sydney Croatia is where Atti's coaching career began. He was player–coach in 1978 and 1979, before he retired from playing and moved to another state league club, Melita Eagles, as coach. In 1981 and 1982 he accepted a full-time position with Riverwood in the state league, then entered the NSL fray as coach of Canberra City. He had kept a house in Sydney, though, so when Sydney Croatia asked him to come back to the club and coach them when they made it into the national league, he jumped at the chance. It didn't last long, however, and he was sacked halfway through the season. He took charge of Rockdale for season 1985 in the state league, which he looks back on as a mistake. By then, he knew that nothing could compare with the joy of playing and he found that club politics were stifling his passion for the game. He took a break, but was lured back by Frank Arok and St George Budapest. *'I was Frank's assistant in the '87 and '88 NSL seasons and I loved being back at St George. By late 1988, though, I decided to move away from the game and went north to Coffs Harbour. I didn't want to end up prostituting myself around Sydney, but could*

I was chasing balls

for these guys,

and now I was playing

with them.'

see that it would happen out of habit of being involved. After thirty years in the game, it was time for something else, and Coffs was the answer.'

•••

Within five years of his arrival in Australia, Atti had made his Victorian State League debut as a skinny, skilful 16-year-old. At seventeen, he had played for the Victorian seniors, and ten years after landing on Australia's shores as a refugee Atti Abonyi had played for his adopted country. He went on to make eighty-nine appearances for Australia (including sixty-one 'A' internationals) and score thirty-six times. He played every minute of the 1974 World Cup finals and has more fond memories from soccer than he ever dared dream. 'From age twelve to fourteen, I was a ball boy at Olympic Park. I was only supposed to do it for a month, but I loved it. I couldn't sleep for days when I knew big teams were coming to play. I would see them in the change rooms and be a part of all the excitement. I just loved the game so much that I couldn't get enough of it. I never thought that I wanted to be like those players, though, because I guess that seemed too unbelievable. When I was seventeen, I

played for Victoria at Olympic Park in front of big crowds and I wondered what I was doing on the inside of the pitch kicking the balls instead of collecting them for the players. When I made my Socceroo debut against Scotland [also at Olympic Park] I just couldn't believe I was there. Not so much because of my background, because by then I definitely felt Australian, but because just a few years before I was chasing balls for these guys, and now I was playing with them. Wondering what I was doing there was the over-riding memory of my debut.'

For someone with a career as successful as Atti's, it is difficult to remember every incident in detail. He does remember the great players, though, as well as the wonderful teams, the eye-opening tours and the friendships. But most of all, he glows when remembering the joy of the game. 'To be honest, I probably have fonder memories as a kid than as an international. Everything was innocent, and you only cared about looking forward to the next game. I never dreamed of playing for Australia, unlike many people who say they do, and I didn't think of making money or being famous. I purely loved the game. In fact, I don't think anyone loved the game more. It was bliss.'

When Atti was a kid in Hungary, he looked forward to the luxury of the orange he would be given each Christmas. Later, he could have as many oranges as he wanted during the numerous half-time breaks in his career. He had to escape his homeland under the cover of darkness, then later on toured the world sixteen times representing the country that accepted him as a refugee. He had never eaten a banana until he arrived in Australia and, in a somewhat symbolic twist, now lives near the Big Banana on the New South Wales north coast. He was involved with elite-level soccer for thirty years, but now enjoys swinging his golf clubs in paradise rather than dealing with the politics and stress of coaching. It's been a fulfilling career, but more importantly, a cherished life. 'I've been more than lucky. I mean, when I look back on where I am from and what has happened since, I still can't believe it. I earned some money in soccer, but didn't make any money . . . but the game has given me the gift of friendships, memories and experiences. Australia has given me a whole new life, so there can never be any regrets.'

A hungarian refugee meets a boxing kangaroo at the 1974 World Cup.

Harry WILLIAMS

Socceroo 1970–1977

Harry Williams grew up in the St George area of Sydney and played in St George district junior teams. There was a logical path to the powerhouse senior team of the 1960–70s but as it happened, he went to play second grade at Western Suburbs on the recommendation of a scout. Joe Marston was coach of the Western Suburbs senior team, and Harry probably would've stayed at the club if he hadn't faced logistical issues. *'I had to travel from St George and I didn't have a car. I was studying and I just thought it would be easier to be at a club closer to home. I was enjoying the soccer [at Western Suburbs], and I didn't move clubs because it was a career decision or because I was asked. In fact, I had to ask St George if I could transfer to them.'*

Harry's rise to prominence was swift. In fact, it was foot-to-the-floor greased lightning. While he was playing as a left-winger in reserve grade for the continually successful and powerful St George Budapest, the club's senior left-back got injured. There were six games to go in season 1970 and with a slight adjustment to his game Harry was drafted into the vacant spot. Left-back and Harry Williams hit it off instantly and in those six games he could do no wrong. In fact, he did so much right that he was selected to go on a world tour with the national team later that year.

'My debut was a low-key game against a provincial side from Macau, but it was still a very special feeling to pull on the green and gold shirt. It is a huge honour to play for your country, and I was made to feel very welcome by [coach] Rale Rasic and the squad.'

The unflappable and articulate Williams was also excited about the prospect of travelling to play the game he loved. *'The most I had ever travelled before that trip was on the ferry over to Manly. Then, all of a sudden I was on a plane with the national soccer team going to places like Hong Kong, China, Israel, Iran, England and Ireland. Iran in particular was one of the most challenging places. There were armed guards everywhere, 50,000 men – no women – in the crowd, and thirty-foot-high fences around the ground. We were away for eight weeks and, in many ways, it was really the start of the unity and preparation required for the '74 World Cup.'*

Harry's debut may have been low-key, however there were plenty of tense occasions on the way to amassing his forty-four games for the green and gold – including the Holy Grail. He wasn't one to let nerves get to him, though. *'Some players would throw up, and some would pace up and down. Of course, there were the jokers who kept things light-hearted, but I just kept to myself to allow me to focus on the game ahead. It all started for me as soon as I awoke on match day. I followed the same routine and quietly went about my business, whether it was playing for St George or playing in the World Cup for Australia. Plenty of the guys felt the added pressure of millions of people watching us in the World Cup on television, but collectively we were confident; we knew we deserved to be there. We also had plenty of support from neutrals or supporters of countries that didn't make it, like England, so it perhaps wasn't as bad as it could've been.'*

Harry remained on the bench against West Germany and East Germany in the 1974 World Cup finals, but played in the rain-soaked 0–0 draw against Chile. *'It was great to get on the field in the World Cup but I wasn't too disappointed to not play the first two games. The whole squad felt a part of the action and we were a close group. A family. We were all in it together whether on the field or on the bench. It is emotionally and physically demanding sitting on the bench because when you play you just get on with it. Being on the bench makes things very tense because you are riding every moment. I think it is just as tiring as playing!'*

Playing in a World Cup is obviously one of Harry's career highlights and whatever happens, he and the other members of the squad can always say that they mixed it with the best and made the world take notice. *'You have to remember that only sixteen teams qualified for that tournament – not like today when there are thirty-two.*

The media rankings actually had us finishing eleventh overall due to our goalless draw in the pouring rain against Chile. It was strange being treated like stars over there while we were virtual unknowns back home, but I enjoyed it. People in the streets of Germany knew who we were, and people were waiting for autographs after every training session. In the grand scheme, though, I am not bothered by being relatively unknown here even though it was good for a time over there. In the end, it is just a sport and I am not sure that people should just be remembered for being good at a sport.'

Good performances in world tournaments put players in the shop window for big European clubs, and world tournaments don't get any bigger than the World Cup. 'Some players certainly saw the World Cup as a chance to possibly impress enough to make a move over there after the tournament. In the end, only Noddy [Adrian Alston] was signed up, even though there were plenty of rumours and discussions about others. I would've seriously considered playing in the big leagues, but nothing really eventuated, so back home we came. These days there are special programs, training camps and relationships set up with European clubs that provide kids with such good opportunities if they want them. Australian players are sought after and a lot more doors are opened. The development infrastructure of the game and the coaching can still do with continued development, and of course we can learn from other sports. However, there is still a lot more opportunity for young players today, and I say good luck to them.'

•••

'The whole squad felt a part of the action and we were a close group. A family.'

Harry was the first – and, to date, is the only – Aboriginal Socceroo. It is an often overlooked fact that fills him with great pride. He is proud to be an indigenous Australian, but is quick to add that his background was never an issue. It was all about the football, and his heritage was never more than an interesting aside. No different, really, to the players arriving in Australia with a variety of ethnic backgrounds. 'No one went about congratulating me because I was an Aboriginal playing soccer. There were jokes and banter with the other players, just like there was with guys from other backgrounds, but that was it. Things like Noddy asking me to smile in the dark so that they could see me . . . so I'd remind him that he was only a £10 Pom, then ask him when he last had a bath. No one took offence because this is a big part of Aussie humour, and everyone would take a gentle dig at each other, just to get a laugh. It was

a part of the atmosphere in the squad in the early '70s. It was a big family where the players were the kids, and Rale played the father figure. In fact, he still does.'

With so much of the Australian game and Australian society influenced by migrant groups, Harry's indigenous roots provide another insight. 'I actually always felt at home with the migrant communities. We found common ground through the round ball, and the shared interest built up a great understanding. We were all soccer players, and it didn't matter where we were from. Soccer is a great leveller for that all over the world.'

The reason Harry is the only indigenous Socceroo is not easily explained. 'The opportunity for indigenous Australians to play soccer was probably more limited. Most Aboriginal communities were introduced to league, union, AFL, boxing and to some degree basketball. I was

exposed to soccer by a friend across the street at six years of age. For me, it was just a question of circumstance. It just happened. Maybe it was fate, or maybe it was chance. In hindsight, maybe it could be called luck.'

•••

Harry found plenty of success on pitches around the world, but it is life off-field that fits most neatly into his memories. The pranks played in hotels, the laughter at each other's expense and the bonds formed during tours of inhospitable parts of the globe. Shared experiences of success, failure and sacrifice throughout the early 1970s created a team spirit that helped the Socceroos to the 1974 World Cup finals. 'Max Tolsen, Bunny Curren, Baartzy and Noddy probably led the way, but everyone got involved. The Poms in the team used to sing "Swing Low Sweet Chariot" or "The Northern Lights of Aberdeen", and the Aussies would come back with "The Road To Gundegai". On the rare occasions when the players catch up now, it is those things we laugh about.

'The atmosphere was totally different after the World Cup. It was an abrupt end when we came back. It's like travelling – when you come back you see things through new eyes because of new experiences. We had been involved with the game at the highest level . . . then it stopped. The atmosphere in later Socceroo camps was different, mainly due to the change in player

'We were all soccer players and it didn't matter where we were from.'

personnel. It's like when you walk into someone's house, and it can feel like a home straightaway – but when you walk into another place it has a different feel about it. The chairs, tables, walls and roof are all there, but one feels totally different to the other. The '70–74 squad was home; it was family.'

Harry was only of slight build, but he was fast and athletic and used those traits to play the game just as the coaches demanded. He did the simple things well and didn't let his concentration slip. *'I did what I was asked during the games. Particularly when defending, you had to have discipline or it could be disastrous. At training, though, there were times I couldn't resist and tried all sorts of tricks. One night Atti Abonyi started calling me "Fancy Nancy" and that's how I was often known with the players.'*

After his international debut in 1970, 'Fancy' remained in every Australian squad until his final game in Melbourne in 1977. It was one year later that his successful time at St George also ended, and he moved to the ACT to join Canberra City in the NSL. The Saints had won three NSW State League grand finals and three runners-up medals during Harry's time. They were sixth in the NSL's first season (1977), behind inaugural winners Sydney City (previously known as Hakoah Eastern Suburbs). *'St George was a great club and we were very successful. It was very progressive in the way that it was run and the way the game was approached. I think it was the first club to use sports psychologists and concentrate on nutrition. The players were pretty sceptical at first, but our success soon changed that. After seven years there, though, it was time for a change and I came to Canberra. It was great in the early years of the NSL, and we would get some good crowds at Bruce Stadium.'*

Harry remained with Canberra City until 1984, when he joined another ACT club, Monaro. *'We won the state league in '84 and then I was back into the national league for the '85 and '86 seasons. I ended up playing my last game in the ACT State League with Monaro in 1990 as a 39-year-old. I sometimes think I could've played longer, but I lost the commitment for working as hard as a 39-year-old needs to, so I called it quits.'*

Since then he has watched some games, but has not played again. *'I didn't really fancy playing in the lower leagues, so when my time was done I figured there was no point hanging on. The decrease in commitment was quite a relief, actually.'*

Making it to the top in any field requires dedication and sacrifice – whether there are special training programs and links to the best opportunities in the world like there are today, or not. The situation is magnified in soccer due to the travel required and the associated time away from home and work. *'I lost a couple of jobs due to the travel and overseas tours. I found work again reasonably easily, but it wasn't the best way to live. I also lost a marriage, so playing for Australia had some major costs.'*

His working life settled as his playing commitments decreased and Harry placed more attention on a number of roles within Aboriginal Affairs and ATSIC (the Aboriginal and Torres Strait Islander Commission), working on social, economic and justice development. He is currently developing policy and programs for Corrective Services in the ACT – so his move to the capital to play soccer all those years ago has provided much more longevity than ever expected. His work also introduced Harry to the late Charlie Perkins, and he was impressed by the Aboriginal politician and activist. *'Charlie loved to talk and was always on the go. He was a very good soccer player as well as politician, and did some great things for indigenous Australians. I am not exactly sure how I started doing the work I do, but while it is demanding, it can also be very rewarding and I enjoy it.'*

Some sportspeople collect mementos to commemorate their sacrifices, and others don't think about it until years later. Harry falls into the second category, and while at times he wishes he did keep some things, he is not one to place too much emphasis on days gone by. *'I don't have many photos and I haven't kept shirts or other things. I guess at times I think it would be nice if I had, so I can leave a legacy for my kids, but it is the memories I have that I treasure most. Those days were back then and it is not something that an old shirt or a photo is ever going to change.'*

Harry does miss the excitement of the pre-game build-up. He feels a bit numb when watching games these days because he doesn't get that same sensation sitting in the crowd; the game doesn't seem the same. He misses preparing for a match from the moment he woke, of quietly going about his business throughout the day, and the mounting tension when he arrived in the change rooms. Feeling nervous about what lay ahead – excited nervous, not scared nervous. The sensation of adrenalin being released when the first whistle blew. The tension that lifted after his first touch of the ball. In his quiet moments, it is these feelings Harry considers, and they provide more satisfaction than any shirt or photo that could be hanging on his wall.

'…playing for Australia had some **major costs.**'

Not this time, Harry!

Jimmy ROONEY

Socceroo 1971–1981

Jimmy Rooney came to Australia in 1968 'for a laugh'. He wasn't enjoying playing part-time for the second division Scottish club Montrose, which he had moved to after not getting any breaks as a teenager with the English club Peterborough. Then one day he received a letter from an Australian soccer club that had discovered he was on the transfer list. A little confused about what it meant, yet with a growing twinge of excitement at the possibilities, he showed some other friends who were also on the outer with their clubs. All of a sudden, the 21-year-old and three mates had packed their bags and commenced an epic journey.

The enterprising club that sent the letter was Melbourne's Essendon Lions, and the exercise cost them a mere £10 in immigration fees. Jimmy bought out his own contract from Montrose before jumping on one of the boats leaving for Australia's sunny shores. Four weeks and plenty of partying later, he set foot Down Under a 'free man'.

'It was so exciting to be coming to Australia on such an adventure. Fortunately Essendon were a great club and they really helped me to settle. They were Ukrainian at the time and were a wonderful group of people. They also really knew how to drink and taught us lads a thing or two!'

Jimmy is from the old school of Scottish professionals and he fitted right in to his new surroundings. *'I have always said that you train as hard as you drink. I am a hard trainer and I have always made sure to enjoy life and to enjoy my football. Even on the boat out here, we would train in the morning and before parties in the evening. Socialising after games is not only great for team bonding, it gives you the chance to play the game over and over again with your teammates, and it is a great learning environment.'*

The breaks that hadn't come in his native Britain began to eventuate in Australia, and with his reborn enthusiasm and ever-widening smile, he was playing well. He quite quickly noticed, however, that the Socceroo sides seemed to mainly be composed of New South Wales players, and after discussions with the man who was soon to become his mentor and future World Cup coach, Rale Rasic, a decision to move north took shape. *'I have always wanted to play at the highest level possible. At the time, Sydney seemed to be where all the action was, and therefore the place I should be.'*

'**I have always said that you train as hard as you drink…**'

Joe Venglos had coached Australia in 1967 and recommended Jimmy to Sydney Prague – even though he was leaving for a new role in Czechoslovakia. Wally Tamandl replaced Venglos and agreed with the recommendation. So, after two years with the Lions, Jimmy moved north to Sydney for a then-record $6,000. *'The transfer fee was a lot of money back then and good luck to Essendon for getting what they could. They opened a new door for me and I wished them all the best.'*

Things started quite well in Jimmy's first year at the club. He was selected in the New South Wales team and once again settled quickly into his new surroundings due to the efforts of his new colleagues. *'Prague were a Czechoslovakian club and, at the time, the Czech clubs in Australia were bringing out plenty of Czech and Austrian first division players. They knew how to make people from all over feel welcome and it was great to be among another new group . . . I played in midfield with Raul Blanco, who they had brought out from South America, and we became great friends. We still are.'*

By the end of the 1970 season, Rale Rasic had started as coach of the national team and was about to take his new charges on tour in Asia. Jimmy was not selected, so he planned a trip back home to the UK for the first time. Rale made him aware that he was in his future plans, however, and it was then that Jimmy started to consider playing for his new home. *'Out of the squad that Rale took to Asia in 1970, eight took the field in the '74 World Cup. It indicates his forward planning . . . and begins to illustrate how it was no fluke that we got there.'*

Even though he was considering a long-term future in Australia as he boarded the boat to Scotland, the World Cup was far from Jimmy's mind. He was looking forward to seeing his family and friends – and to the four weeks afloat living the high life. *'That trip home showed me that I did miss home, but it also showed me the opportunities I had back here. I came back refreshed, enthusiastic and dedicated and things began to happen.'*

The 1971 season with Prague was a good one for Jimmy. As well as winning some personal accolades and awards, he made his Australian debut against an English FA XI at the Sydney Football Ground. His reaction to the honour was considered, and probably a fair representation of the feelings of the millions

of immigrants who have made a new life in Australia. '*I was proud to pull on the jersey, but to be honest, probably not as proud as if I had stayed in Scotland and pulled on the Scottish jersey. I had only been in Australia three years and I guess in some ways was still viewing it as "the big adventure" rather than a permanent home. In saying that, patriotism grows on you and every year I am here I am more in love with Australia. I always wanted to play at the highest level I could and that is what playing for Australia represented . . . every time I played for Australia, I loved Australia more.*' Later that year the Socceroos had another Asian tour. This time Jimmy travelled with the team,

and began accumulating his multitude of national team appearances for Australia.

In 1972, Jimmy got an insight into Sydney's Italian community when he signed for APIA–Leichhardt. '*I can't remember the transfer fee, but it was something like seven APIA players to Prague for me. Somehow, that seems a lot more significant than money.*'

APIA were one of the strongest sides in the league and in keeping with Jimmy's philosophy of playing at the highest level possible, it was another logical move. '*Prague were a great club, however they were quite small and often battled. I ended*

up leaving to have five fantastic years at APIA where the club won honours, I won some personal awards and I played for Australia many more times. Once again, the people were great and I was certainly happy with the decision.'

Under Joe Marston at APIA, Jimmy also began to develop an interest in coaching. '*I became quite interested in the coaching side of the game at a relatively young age. I have been quite heavily involved in coaching since I finished playing and really enjoy it. If I won some money, I would set up an academy for young Aussies and not charge them a thing to develop their game.*'

At the 1974 World Cup.

'...patriotism

grows on you and every year I am here

I am more in love with

Australia.'

There was still a lot more playing to do before coaching took over, however, and his five years at APIA came to an end at the dawn of a new era for Australian soccer. *'The national league was starting in 1977 and APIA did not want to enter, even though we were one of the strongest clubs going around. They saw they could get some money for me by selling me to an NSL club, but I didn't want to go. I was club captain and I loved it there.'*

In the end he did go and of all things was sold to APIA's neighbours and Italian community rivals, Marconi. The day Jimmy signed was the day the players voted him to be captain – a humbling sign of Australian soccer's growing respect for him. *'I have always enjoyed captaining sides. I like to lead by example, to encourage the youngsters . . . and of course make sure the lazy older pros are pulling their weight!'*

By 1979, Jimmy was keen to get back to where it all started – Melbourne. It was made possible by signing for Heidelberg, a team full of great players and ambition with a strong supporter base. The club was formed and backed by many of Melbourne's Greek community – just like South Melbourne Hellas, who actually offered three times as much money to Marconi for Jimmy to move there, as well as improved personal terms. *'It was pretty unusual because, even though Marconi would get more for me if I went to South, [Marconi*

Chairman] Tony Labbozzetta let me take my pick. I have never chosen a club because of money. I was impressed by the strength of passionate support at Heidelberg, and I was friends with some of the players. We used to get big crowds and plenty of atmosphere, and it was the right move.'

Jimmy played his last game for Australia in 1981 against Ireland, as captain under Rudi Gutendorf. He later transferred to Croydon in the Victorian State League where he finished his competitive career. *'I always said I would retire when I was at the top. It's a nice sentiment, but I've found it impossible. I have been playing in "legends" games and in thirds leagues and don't want to stop. I reckon you'll still see me buzzing around when I am eighty.'*

In his career, Jimmy has met people from around the globe, and has enjoyed the company of them all. *'I can honestly say that the people at every club I have been at have been great. It has never been an issue for me whether I was playing for Ukrainians, Italians, Czechs or Greeks and at the time I don't think it mattered to them. There were imports from all over the place, and we were there to play football and to create a good life in Australia. For the fans and for ourselves.'*

•••

An Australian legend greets an international legend.

Jimmy finished his career as the fifth-most-capped Socceroo. *'The official records show ninety-nine Socceroo games but it is 100. One of the newspapers looked into it and they also think so.'* Whether it is ninety-nine or 100, it has become obvious that, even though he has kept a Scottish twang and visits Scotland every year, Jimmy Rooney is very much Australian.

After playing fifty-seven 'A' internationals, and pulling on the Socceroo shirt 100 (or ninety-nine!) times, each game tends to blend into each other. Jimmy is not the kind of person who remembers precise details of matches he has played in, however some salient points in his career do come to the surface. One was when Australia played against his home-town club, Dundee. *'It was quite special playing against Dundee and I guess a measure of where that decision in 1968 had taken me. It was nice for the family but, while they wanted me to do well, they definitely wanted Dundee to beat us Aussies!'*

Another was when the Socceroos took on Pelé's Santos of Brazil and Jimmy scored a goal Pelé described as one of the best he has ever seen. Then of course there was the run into the 1974 World Cup finals. A 3–0 victory at home to Iran set up a nervous return leg in Tehran in front of over 100,000 screaming home fans. *'I was on the bench from the start and we happened to be 2–0 after twenty-five minutes or so. It was forty*

degrees and I really felt for the guys out there. With twenty minutes to go, Rale [Rasic] sent me on with instructions to keep the ball. A 2–0 loss would see us through. I was running with the ball all over the place . . . across the pitch and back again . . . down to the corners and back again. Anything we could do to waste time. In the end we held on and I don't think I have ever been so enjoyably drunk as I was after the game in the hotel. The waiter was non-stop back and forth to Jimmy Mackay and I by the pool.'

That win set up the showdown with South Korea for a place in the finals. The Socceroos were down 2–0 early on, however this time clawed their way back to 2–2. The game that would decide the series was in Hong Kong. Of course, the Socceroos won from the famous Jimmy Mackay piledriver, after a Jimmy Rooney layoff. 'We didn't get so drunk this time. We were roommates and just lay on our beds saying "What a goal" over and over. And over. We were going to the World Cup finals.'

Jimmy played every minute of Australia's three games in the World Cup and the 'little general' (so called because of his stature and influence during games) earned some impressive international reviews. 'We played East Germany on their own soil and we were supposed to get thumped. The 2–0 result flattered them and we did very well. We were beaten 3–0 by West Germany in

World Cup battle against East Germany.

the next game and to be fair, they battered us. Nil–nil against Chile got us a point. We actually were a bloody good side – regardless of the fact that we were part-timers. We were up against people like Beckenbauer and Müller and we did not care. Rale had us prepared and confident. We deserved to be at that level because we worked hard and earned it.'

•••

Jimmy is pleased with the development of Australian soccer and the recent successes of Australian soccer players. '*When we were playing, everyone looked up to the imports too much, like we were so much better by reputation. Today, the players from overseas have a much tougher time of it coming here, because the Australian kids believe in themselves more, have more ability and a tougher attitude. These days, Aussies can take on the world.*'

He also looks forward to the day that the Socceroos qualify again for the World Cup. '*It disappoints me when I hear people say that the '74 players don't want current teams to qualify so that we can remain the only ones. We should have been the first to qualify, not the only. Jimmy Mackay was as* hard as nails and he cried openly when the Socceroos were knocked out by Iran at the MCG in 1997. The game and the country have come a long way and I want to see us up there again.'

As we finished our conversation at Jimmy's local pub in a Melbourne suburb, he obliged me by signing my trusty Boxing Kangaroo flag. At this point, a guy in a business suit sitting next to us looked over his glasses, then nudged his mate. They knew Jimmy must be someone, but couldn't place him. Jimmy didn't see them but I get the feeling he wouldn't have cared. He is happy with his place in Australian soccer history, and that his 90-year-old uncle is proud to drink under his signed World Cup Socceroo shirt hanging at his old junior club in Dundee. Over thirty years since coming out to Australia 'for a laugh', Jimmy Rooney is still laughing.

'These days **Aussies** can take on the **world**.'

Jimmy TANSEY

Socceroo 1976–1981

A bitter rain sweeps across an obscure football ground in northern England, in early 1974. It is the initial rounds of the FA Cup – the not-so-glamorous end of the romantic competition, where the minnows are weeded out before the 'big boys' join the fray. The FA Cup is the FA Cup, though, and any progression for a part-time club to the next round deserves celebration. Particularly when you scored one, set up another and performed in keeping with more illustrious circumstances. Add to the mix a couple of pints in the clubrooms (that someone else has bought for you) and it is heady enough times for any 20-year-old to take on the world.

Then a stranger interjects and asks you if you would like to sign for a club in Australia. You realise the stranger is serious when he explains that the game is really being pushed down there, and that there could be worse places to live. On top of the world and naively prepared for anything, Down Under holds some appeal.

The stranger calls a few days later and you confess it has been on your mind. A couple of answered questions later, you decide that you actually want to go. I mean, why not . . . ?

Jimmy Tansey, future Socceroo and National Sports Marketing Manager of Adidas, was on his way to a new home.

'I didn't think he'd call again but he did. And even after he did, I thought the whole process would take a while. After I had said yes, though, he called back the next day and said, "Your plane leaves on Thursday. Have fun." So that was it. Three of us were on the plane to the other end of the planet.'

The enterprising club that had signed Jimmy and two of his teammates through their English agent was Prahran Slavia in Melbourne. They set the three new boys up in a St Kilda hotel and tried to make them feel at home. *'St Kilda was not the trendy bar and café society it is today. Far from it, actually. Still, it is near the sand, sea and sun and it could have been worse.'*

For three young guys whose only experience outside England had been two-week boozy soccer trips to Spain, Australia opened their eyes. *'I remember early on, one*

Sunday around noon, one of the lads and I wanted a beer. We had played the night before and had the day off so we thought we'd relax. The trouble was, none of the pubs were open at that time – unlike back home. We were told by one guy that we should go down the street to a restaurant, order pizzas and get beers with it. Trouble was, we had never heard of this "pizza" before. Still, we went down to the restaurant and ordered two beers. We were again told we needed to order pizza as well so we nervously added, "Okay, pizza as well," still without the foggiest idea what the hell they were. He said, "What sort?" and pointed to a big blackboard with all sorts of words like "anchovies", "salami", "Calabrese". We

'Then a stranger interjects and asks you if you would like to sign for a club in Australia…'

Early days in the Australian sun.

took a punt and nervously ordered something and wanted those beers more than ever! The guy had also suggested we get a jug of beer because it was cheaper, so that's what we did. When he put it on the table, my mate's eyes lit up. "I was told these Aussies can drink, but this is a bit much," he said before picking it up with two hands and drinking straight from it just as the waiter came over with two glasses for us to pour the beer into!'

Within a few weeks, the three Liverpool lads had rented an apartment in the leafy beach suburb of Elsternwick, began playing and training, and found work, while also discovering chicken schnitzel to add to their pizza experience. 'I loved schnitzel. I had never heard of it before, let alone tasted it, and ended up having it three or four times a week at the Elsternwick Hotel for $1.80 – including all the salad I wanted. Life was good.'

His experiences at Slavia were also culturally unique – though not in a way you would first imagine. 'There were a lot of British players around who had been brought out here like I was and a lot of them lived in the same area. I spent most of my time with the British guys. In fact, when I was in Liverpool I only knew two Scottish people. I came here and met more of them than I knew what to do with.'

The first year in Australia, surrounded by so many other new arrivals, was relaxed and carefree, and it suited Jimmy's personality to a T. 'There was plenty of work around, we were near the beach, the soccer was competitive, there were trips up north and life was easy. Then, the Victorian team started playing some quality teams from around the world and I started to look at my life here more seriously. I woke up to the possibilities in Australia about eighteen months into the adventure, and I really began to work hard.'

The change in attitude resulted in more-polished performances and he began to regularly attract accolades. Jimmy started playing for Victoria against some good international club sides, then in late 1975 he made his Australian debut in a 2–1 loss against Russia at Melbourne's Olympic Park. 'I am prouder of my achievements now than I was then. Actually, I have been proud of my achievements since I "woke up" to Australia in 1975, and to play for what I knew then was my new home was very satisfying.'

'...we had **never heard** of this "**pizza**" before.'

1977, leading up to the 1978 World Cup qualifying series, when I was told my three years were up. So we went to the High Commission in Suva so that everything could be sorted out. The locals even put on a bit of a ceremony and it was like I was a minor celebrity. I officially became Australian in Fiji.'

Historically, state representative games provided a good start for aspiring young players and new arrivals to the country. They were also big occasions for the soccer community. Before the start of the national league in 1977, playing for Australia was usually a result of playing well for your state and Jimmy's progress followed that path. *'State games were definitely a springboard to national selection. There were regularly 15,000-plus crowds, and I remember 20,000 people in the pouring rain at Olympic Park when Victoria played AEK Athens. There was still plenty of interest in state games in 1978 and 1979, but it slowly started to drop off after that as the national league grew.'*

One of Victoria's matches that Jimmy played in was against the star-studded New York Cosmos in 1979. The newly formed American domestic competition was throwing money about with the aim of luring top quality European players, who would in turn attract big crowds to games. It worked. *'Olympic Park was full against Cosmos . . . They had some world-class players. I remember the score was 2–2 until*

At the culmination of the 1976 season, Jimmy won the Player of the Year award with Prahran Slavia and was starring on the Victorian state team. In 1977 he left Prahran to join Fitzroy Alexander (later renamed Heidelberg), a big club backed by many in Victoria's Greek community. *'It was the start of the NSL and we used to get some good crowds. It was not uncommon to get 20,000 at Olympic Park when we played Hellas. I was at the club for seven or eight years. I captained them and even coached them later on, so I'd say they got their value out of me.'*

Australian soccer gave Jimmy the chance to experience new things and be exposed to new cultures, whether playing here or touring with the Victorian or national teams. *'I remember the '76–77 tour of China. I would often go outside the hotel and just watch . . . The place and the people were just so different and I was amazed. Some players would just stay in the hotel, but I always liked to have a look around.'*

Jimmy knew that Australia was for him within a couple of years in the country and knew that when his visa expired, he would naturalise and become 'dinky-di'. Non-citizens could play for Australia – but only in non-official and friendly games. As an Australian 'real' games would become an option. *'We were actually on tour in Fiji in*

a couple of minutes to go, before [Dutch international] Neeskens picked up the ball about thirty-five yards out and on an angle. I closed him down as quickly as I could, and remember saying "Hit it, hit it," as I did. It was supposed to put him off, but he must have liked the idea because he struck it beautifully and it went in off the post for them to win 3–2. To rub it in he said, "Well, I did hit it," as he walked past me after the celebration. I could do nothing but admire it. Beckenbauer was brilliant on that tour as well. He kept things so simple, but his touch was amazing.'

•••

Jimmy rode high throughout the late 1970s and early 1980s, but in 1982 he had to swallow the bitter pill that many sportsmen face. A crunching tackle buckled the knee on his sweet left leg, the pain reinforced by a full knee reconstruction and three months in a cast from hip to foot. He didn't play for Australia again. *'They were dark times. I went from playing and working in labouring jobs earning decent money to zero overnight. No movement and no money. My wife and I had just bought a house and the insurance money was slow coming. We scraped by, but it wasn't easy.'*

Faced with a fragile leg that wouldn't straighten after the cast came off, Jimmy was able to go back to work but was unsure how his playing career would be affected. *'I was working on the building site for the Victorian Arts Centre and there was a large portion of the Greek community working that site. They wanted me back playing – whether they supported Alexander or Hellas – and moulded a concrete shoe that I used to put on during breaks to exercise my leg. When it rained and they were inside playing cards, I would be with them doing leg raises. I was back in ten months, when the doctor said it would be twelve.'*

Things were never quite the same, though, and after another couple of seasons, Heidelberg sold him to Footscray J.U.S.T. He stayed one year with the Yugoslav club, then dropped down a league to Croydon, a British community-based club. *'I really enjoyed myself at Croydon. The intensity had dropped a notch and it was fun.'*

It dropped even more as his career wound down and fun became the name of the game once more. He joined Sandringham, another British club in the lower leagues of Victoria. *'I remember the first game of the season, when we were all in the change rooms and the coach set off on his fiery team talk. Not long into it, one of the boys said, "Shit, I've left the washing on the line and my missus is away. I have to sort it out." Away he went to make some calls. I have never laughed so much as when at that club. The camaraderie was excellent, and they are some of my better memories in the game.'*

Some players struggle to retire because the game is so much a part of them. Jimmy knew when it was time to quit. What's more, he has never looked back – which is fortunate because he still has a tribunal hearing pending if he wants to play again. *'I was sent off in my last game. I was too slow and brought down a young kid with a clumsy challenge as he bore down on goal.'*

‘The **camaraderie** was excellent, and they are some of my better memories of the game.’

'I was **sent off** in my **last game.** '

No malice, I just couldn't get there. The kid got up and let me know that I used to play with his dad. George Wallace at the VSF said I had an appointment at the tribunal over the red card but I told him not to worry, because that was me done. I just knew it was over.'

In fact, Jimmy has played only twenty minutes of soccer in the last twenty years, when he pulled the boots on for a friend's testimonial. His injured knee still causes him trouble, but his daily regime of rising at 5.30 am to hit the gym before work has kept him in fine physical shape. It is a discipline learnt from years at the top and it serves him well throughout all areas of his life. '*I am representing one of the world's biggest sporting companies and it just wouldn't be right to puff on cigarettes and have a big beer gut. Particularly when I am giving advice to young athletes. I try to do the right things.'*

When Jimmy looks back on his career, a few names tend to surface in his memories. People who influenced his career and helped him make the most of his adopted homeland. '*Johnny Sanchez was my coach in the early days at Slavia, and he was the one who helped me realise the opportunities for me [in Australia] back in '75. Len McKendry was coach at Heidelberg as well as a number of Victorian teams, and he was a huge influence on my game. Ronny Smith was another. He was assistant Socceroo coach when I was in the team, and also looked after the AIS program. I am grateful to so many people, but those three had the biggest influence on my career.'*

•••

As Jimmy's playing career wound down, his business career ramped up. He may not be able to kick any more, but he is still heavily involved with the game through his senior position at Adidas. He was responsible for signing Harry Kewell to the three stripes and negotiated the longstanding arrangements between Adidas and Soccer Australia. He has been to three World Cups, three Olympic Games, European Championships and countless Australian matches in an official capacity. He meets the top people in all sports and travels the world to develop the organisation he is obviously proud to have been associated with for almost twenty years. His career path is built on the same philosophy of hard work and dedication that took him to the top of his playing career. '*I started in the Adidas warehouse when I was playing at Croydon. It was set hours of nine-to-five and I was finally off the building sites. After a couple of years I saw the job I really wanted within the organisation and I just went for it. It is not all the glamour it sounds, but I do love what I do.'*

A clearance against England one day, working on a building site the next.

So, with his business cap on, how have things changed in Australian soccer? *'The sleeping giant is now awakening. It's really been since the Japan–Korea World Cup, and when we beat England in 2003. Sales of top-level equipment here are still going strong and I am getting proposals from all sorts of marketing companies, and from dads saying I should sponsor their young superstar, who is apparently going to play for Man United one day. There are clinics all over the country and our world reputation is really growing. The lead-up to the 2006 World Cup is exciting – both commercially and emotionally. I want Australia to win for a number of reasons.'*

Jimmy is commercially involved with numerous sportspeople, however he has only ever put his hand up to recommend one soccer player. *'It was not long after I presented Mark Viduka with an NSL Golden Boot on behalf of Adidas that I wrote off to [ex-Liverpool legend and then-Blackburn Rovers Manager] Kenny Dalglish to let him know about Mark's talent. I got a reply letter of "We'll keep an eye on him. Thanks," and was a bit disappointed. It was only a couple of years later that Celtic signed Mark for around $7 million and I felt vindicated and a little amused. Kenny Daglish had just arrived there as manager and made the purchase.'*

With all his success in various fields, Jimmy remains humble and maintains a healthy perspective. *'Australia played an England XI out here in the seventies with the likes of Bobby Charlton in their side – so yes, I have played against some great players and great teams. But, the day after I shared ninety minutes with Bobby Charlton I had to get on a tram early in the morning back to the building site. He didn't.'*

He might not be Bobby Charlton, but he is quietly proud of where he has come from and what he has done. At eighteen years of age, he was told he wasn't good enough by the then-European Champion, Liverpool Football Club. *'I was shattered and thought I was never going to be a footballer. In hindsight I probably set my standards a bit high – I mean the best club in Europe didn't want me and I thought my career was over. At least I was told I was crap by the great Bill Shankly!'* Of course, his career was not over . . . forty-four games for the Socceroos and a suitcase full of magnificent memories that, even today, Jimmy Tansey is managing to pack more and more top-level sport inside of. It is a script that, at times, even Jimmy struggles to believe.

'...the day after I shared ninety minutes with Bobby Charlton I had to get on a tram early in the morning back to the building site. He didn't.'

Gary COLE

Socceroo 1978–1984

'Three games stick out in my memory: my debut against Greece in 1978 at Olympic Park [Melbourne], the game against England at the SCG in 1980, and that bloody loss to New Zealand in the '82 World Cup qualifiers. My first season in Australia playing in the Vic Metro fourth division reserves competition was also pretty memorable . . .'

Gary Cole came to Australia on his fifteenth birthday in 1971. He was a pale, bright-eyed Londoner who didn't really know what to make of the family adventure – he had some adjusting to do. *'When we arrived it was thirty-eight degrees at 7.30 in the morning. Australia was mid-drought at that stage and everything was brown. I remember asking if this country had grass. We were over the weight limit with our baggage because we were coming here to live and brought everything. We'd had to put on a couple of coats so they didn't have to go in the bags, and I walked through customs into thirty-eight degrees with a mohair suit and an overcoat on. I quickly peeled everything off as soon as I could and I ended up walking around the airport in mohair trousers and a white chest looking like an ice cream.'*

The Cole family traipsed out to one of Melbourne's beach-side suburbs to set up a home. Getting lost walking to the beach the second day and making it home burnt to a crisp strengthened the reservations Gary already had about Australia. *'Not long before we arrived, the Westgate Bridge [in Melbourne] had collapsed and a couple of people were killed by snakes. I enjoyed life in London and was wary about where I was going to. Dad was so enthusiastic, though, and knew there would be a better life for us here.'*

Stan Cole worked as a skin flesher in London. It is an important role in the fur trade and although it sounds gruesome, it put food on the table and shoes on the feet of his two kids. He had considered a move Down Under for a while, but only talked about it at work. One day, a fellow pelter showed him an ad in the paper asking for people just like him in Australia. It was time to act. *'Dad came home and said, "Right, we're off." Off to where, we wondered. We didn't really know where Australia was, and had no idea how bloody far away it was. Still, Dad could see the opportunity and adventure and while I didn't like it here initially, it soon became home.'*

When Gary went to school, it wasn't long before he made friends and went to the beach to get burnt again. He could see some positives about Australia, but he missed the life he had on the streets of London. Melbourne just didn't have the bustling, big-city existence he was accustomed to. His dad decided if young Gary played soccer it would help him settle, and it became the link between his new life and the old.

'I played in youth competitions in London and, like every kid, dreamed of a life as a professional footballer . . . although I didn't really know what that meant. I always loved the game, so Dad thought I might as well get into it again. He took me down to South Yarra and we both played in the reserves for the Metro fourth division. I was a big kid, but I was pretty soft, and that year with pretty basic players toughened me up. There were a lot of Poms at the club, and the social aspect helped the family. There wasn't much future in staying there playing with Dad, though.'

Bill Curran, a Scottish expat, ran the Victorian representative set-up at that time and organised trials for the Under-16s Victorian team. Gary wandered down at his father's prompting, and made the side. Soccer was helping him settle, but now it was taking on extra importance. Bill Curran suggested he get out of the fourth division pronto, and arranged trials for him at Prahran Slavia in the state league. It didn't work out there, but when the family moved east of Melbourne shortly after, Ringwood Wilhemmina were keen to sign him to their state league squad. It was pre-NSL days and the standard was high. *'Ringwood's ground was magnificent. Great surface and stand and they got some good crowds from the Dutch community. They offered me $20 a week and I asked where to sign. I was still a kid and was pretty excited about the whole thing.'*

Gary's the one hogging the trophy.

Just before his eighteenth birthday, and after only three years in Australia, he came off the bench to play for the senior Victorian side against Ferencvaros of Hungary. *'I didn't play for long, but I couldn't help but think what the hell was I doing there. The state team used to get big crowds pre-NSL days, and I was playing against a big club from Europe!'*

By 1976, ex-Socceroo goalkeeper Jack Reilly was coach at Fitzroy Alexander and asked if Gary would join them. They were a big club with some great players, and it was a good move for the young striker – particularly when the club became Heidelberg United Alexander and joined the fledgling NSL in 1977. *'We all thought the NSL was going to be bigger than Texas and it was exciting times for soccer. The VSF wasn't too happy about clubs leaving their state competition to join a national competition, and as I remember it, they were pretty threatening to them. Mooroolbark were the first Victorian club to throw their hat in the ring and Heidelberg followed soon after. The players were happy they did because we were excited about the possibilities, and even had in the backs of our minds that it could lead to becoming full-time professionals.'*

The majority of the stars at the time were imported players from Britain, and most of the high-profile coaches were from the Ol' Dart too. No Socceroos were playing

overseas and the Aussie standard was high. *'There were a lot of Poms in the game then. I guess we were seen as being from a country that knew football and it was the English first division that you saw on TV. Some of the guys who came out here to play made life-long friends with other players in the same boat as them. There was a real community of soccer players in those days, probably because everyone needed each other.'*

...

'I ended up walking around the airport in mohair trousers and a white chest looking like an ice cream.'

'...you have to **be prepared** to make sacrifices if you want to succeed.'

One of Gary's many goals for Heidelberg.

'The anthem was something special **and I was so proud** to be out there representing **my adopted country.** '

Strikers live or die by the goals they score, and Gary quickly became a crowd favourite at Heidelberg because he did just that. He was the first NSL player to score fifty goals, bagged the fastest ever NSL hat-trick (three goals in eleven minutes) and was the league's top scorer in 1980 and 1981. He played for the Socceroos forty times and returned twenty goals – seven of which were scored against Fiji in what was a world record, until Archie Thompson's thirteen-goal haul against American Samoa in 2001. In a total of 240 NSL appearances, he netted 109 times, mostly with the 'Bergers.

'We won the title against arch-rivals Sydney City 4–0 in 1980. It was a great day in my NSL career. I scored a hat-trick and was voted Man of the Match. Helps win the hearts of the supporters!'

Gary knew his limitations as a player, and was willing to work hard to overcome them. It takes sacrifice and dedication to make it to the top, and more skilful players than Gary didn't have those qualities. *'My first touch wasn't the best, but I worked hard to make it better. I was always willing to do extra physical work too, and my pace was a big weapon. I knew from an early age that I couldn't go out drinking with friends if I wanted to make something of my soccer career. It annoys me when people say certain players have the skill to be great players when you know they spend too much time partying and not looking after themselves.*

Talent and $1.50 will get you a cup of coffee . . . you have to be prepared to make sacrifices if you want to succeed.'

With all of the foreign imports floating around soccer grounds at the time, it was fortunate that you didn't officially need to be an Australian citizen to play friendlies for Australia. But only Australian citizens could play in 'A' internationals recognised by FIFA, so to ensure he had every chance of selection for the Under-23s national side in 1975, Gary obeyed the formalities of becoming Australian. *'My naturalisation ceremony wasn't emotional because there were so many people around in the Melbourne Town Hall. It was when I had the Aussie shirt on that it really meant something. There were a lot of imports playing for Australia at the time, and many of them may have felt more honoured to play for Australia than the guys who had been here for generations because they appreciated the opportunities Australia had given them.'*

With the success of the famous 1974 World Cup Socceroos, the Australian public thought that, after getting to the World's Greatest Show once, it stood to reason that we would be there again the next time. It wasn't to be, however, and after final-stage losses to Kuwait, then Iran in the failed 1978 qualifying campaign, the coach Jimmy Shoulder decided it was time to blood new talent. *'Even though the team failed to*

What's that . . . rain in Melbourne?! Slogging it out for Victoria.

qualify in '78, there had already been games organised against Greece not long after. Jimmy [Shoulder] decided it was time to get some new players involved, and I was picked for my debut in the first game in Melbourne. There was a full house at Olympic Park in my home town and I was on from the start. The anthem was something special and I was so proud to be out there representing my adopted country. I played for Heidelberg, a Greek club, and Melbourne has a massive Greek community. There was more support for Greece than us – it was like we were playing away. It felt that way quite a bit in those days. We lost 2–1, but I scored a nice goal and was quite happy. It was the era of "honourable losses" for Australia.'

Rudi Gutendorf took over the Socceroo coaching reins from Jimmy Shoulder after that game, and selected Gary for the 1979 tour of China and Taiwan. Most of the time, the team were on planes or buses or in hotel rooms, however they were still able to sample some unique experiences. 'We were the first Australian sporting team to visit what was then still a deeply communist China. We were taken to the Great Wall and some of the other sightseeing spots, but the thing that really stood out was the lack of colour. Everyone wore grey or dark green and had dark hair. There was no advertising and very few cars, and it was a real eye opener. We were quite a bit taller than the average,

Go on . . . give us a kiss! Rooney and Cole after a 2–1 defeat by England in 1980 in which Gary scored.

'We walked off as if we had won the World Cup.'

and also stood out in our yellow tracksuits. The food was appalling, too. We just couldn't stomach most of it and had cans of soft drink and cake most of the time. The milk had bits floating in it and didn't smell the best either. I went off milk on that trip and have rarely had it since.'

There were a number of Socceroo games in 1980 that were used as preparation for the tilt at the 1982 World Cup finals. The big one for the ex-Londoner was the clash against England in Sydney. *'It was a great experience to play against England B in England, but the Socceroos didn't grab much attention when overseas those days. It was a cold, wet, English day as well, without much of a crowd. Playing them here was a different story, though, and definitely a highlight for me. There was a full house in Sydney and we were playing against guys we saw all of the time on TV. It was a good game, and we gave them a real fright. We lost 2–1 – another honourable loss – and I scored a penalty. We walked off as if we had won the World Cup.*

'My dad was particularly proud. He is a soccer nut, but we had to make some sacrifices to get him up from Melbourne for that game. When I was a kid in London, I had found a bike lying around. It was a fantastic bike that all my friends wanted, and it was just sitting there. I took it home, but Dad said I had to take it to the police. I reluctantly did, but in three months it

wasn't collected, so I got to keep it. Anyway, we brought it with us to Australia and it was hardly ever used as I got older. We sold it before that England game so that Dad could afford to get a bus ticket up to the game and get into the ground to see me play against his old homeland.'

'Honourable losses' aren't good enough in World Cup qualification, and another one of Gary's memorable Socceroo occasions was one of devastation. Knocked out of the qualification series against New Zealand, of all things. *'We had drawn 3–3 in Auckland after being behind a few times, then had to win in Sydney. We were atrocious that day and very flat. I came on just after half-time and had to be out there when the final whistle went. Two–nil and knocked out by New Zealand. It was the worst experience of my career.*

'Gutendorf came out as a well-credentialed expert from Germany. He was a strange man and had some very odd techniques. A week before the must-win game against New Zealand, he picked his team. All week, we played full-scale games with that starting eleven against the six subs who were left, topped up with the fat masseur, the gear steward . . . or anyone who happened to be walking by. Obviously it doesn't make for the intense preparation needed for such an important game, when you are playing against opposition like that. After the loss, the senior players got together

and agreed something had to be done. So [captain] Murray Barnes went to [ASF President] Sir Arthur George and explained the players believed that to have any chance of qualifying for the finals, Rudi had to go.' New Zealand went on to qualify for the 1982 World Cup in Spain and Gary couldn't watch. It was the first time Australia had lost to New Zealand at home for twenty-seven years, and the fact remains that New Zealand has played in a World Cup more recently than Australia. It signalled the end for the coach, and the start of plenty of soul-searching for Australian soccer. Another coach of German heritage who grew up in Australia, Les Scheinflug, took charge almost immediately.

The number of games played by the Socceroos decreased through 1982, and Gary refocused his efforts on the NSL. By 1983, however, he knew that it was time for a change. His old mate Peter Ollerton was coaching Heidelberg's fierce rivals, Preston Makedonia, and persuaded him to move. He signed for season 1984 and immediately struggled. *'It was the one time in my career that I wasn't able to score goals. I couldn't even score at training and the crowd got on my back a bit. Consequently, it was the year I also played my last game for Australia. I slowly turned it around, though, and stayed with Preston until 1986.'*

Season 1986 was his last in the NSL, although he wasn't expecting it to be. *'I was*

just thirty and still fit, but Preston wanted me to re-sign for about half the money and I told them to stick it. I felt they put a transfer fee on my head that no one could pay. At the same time, Ronny Smith spoke to me about applying for the job as his assistant coach [at the AIS]. I had recently completed my level three coaching course and as a trained teacher, I knew that coaching was something that was in me. I thought I might as well apply. I mean, there aren't many full-time coaching jobs in Australia, and I felt Preston were shutting me out anyway.'

Gary got the job, and moved to Canberra with his family to start a new life. He was there for four years and it proved a magnificent grounding for a coach with growing ambitions. In 1989, Frank Arok was national coach and asked Gary if he would be his assistant, as well as AIS assistant. Gary jumped at the chance of being involved with the Socceroos once

again and enjoyed his short spell – until Frank left in 1990. *'It was great to be involved with the national team again. Frank and the Federation President, Ian Brusasco, actually spoke to me about the youth team coaching position and I was excited about the prospects. Not long after, the President left. My national coaching opportunities disappeared.'*

In 1990, Gary left the AIS, but stayed in Canberra to work with the Australian Sports Commission to help set up sports and participation programs. It paid well and was less demanding than coaching at the AIS, and he enjoyed his time away from the game. *'I left soccer for a while and basically gained a family. I could spend time with my wife and young kids and it was fantastic.'*

Not long after, he was visiting Melbourne and bumped into some of the old Heidelberg committee in a restaurant. Sometimes opportunities can come when you least

expect them, and this was one of those times. *'They spoke to me about coaching in the NSL, and I admitted I was interested – but not while they had a coach. It wasn't long before they actually got rid of their coach, and offered me the job for season '91–92. I was looking forward to getting involved with the game again.'*

Gary moved back to Melbourne for the role, and spent plenty of time on the Hume Highway between Heidelberg and Canberra, where his family still lived. His first NSL coaching job nearly didn't happen because of one of those trips. *'I hit a semi head-on and almost died. I was in a little Mazda RX7 and it could've fit into a shoe box afterwards. Luckily, the first person on the scene was a nurse and the second a policeman. I went to hospital and ended up having my face reconstructed, on top of some other surgery and treatment for broken bones. The brake pedal actually ended up going through my hammy and I was very lucky to be alive.'*

Part way through his second season as an NSL coach he made the only decision he regrets in his career. After a string of bad results and feeling that he just couldn't get through to the players, he resigned. *'It was an emotional decision after a loss, and I regret it.'*

He left the game again and began to build a career managing leisure centres. After three years, he was lured back to coaching in the 1996 Victorian Premier League, and took to the challenge with relish, winning the championship in that first year. He is still plying his skills at that level while continuing to build his leisure management career, and is enjoying the game once again. He is serious and considered about the impact of good coaching, and it is something that he believes needs greater attention in Australia. *'There is not enough of a mentoring system for coaches in Australia and it is something I know a lot of people would greatly benefit from.'*

' It was the **worst experience** of my career. '

From a 15-year-old struggling to come to terms with his new home on the other side of the world, to a middle-aged Aussie still getting tingles on the back of his neck whenever he hears his adopted home's national anthem, Gary Cole has come a long way. Not just in distance from his homeland, but also in the development of his life as one of Australia's most prolific goal-scoring Socceroos.

Let me at it! Playing against England in 1980.

Eddie KRNCEVIC

Socceroo 1979–1990

Eddie Krncevic speaks six languages, he was the first foreigner to play in the Yugoslav first division, and the first Australian to make it big in mainland Europe. While carving a fourteen-year professional playing career in Europe, he scored seventeen goals for Australia in thirty-five games and picked up numerous personal awards. He has a FIFA coaching diploma and coached three clubs in the NSL. Oh, and he is also a qualified hairdresser!

Eddie's parents arrived in Melbourne in 1959 after being detained in an Italian refugee camp for trying to escape communist Yugoslavia. After a few months in the camp, they were told they were going to Australia. They didn't even know where Australia was.

In 1960 they settled in Geelong, south of Melbourne, after a short time in an Albury refugee camp on the New South Wales border. Eddie was born soon after. *'There was a large ethnic community down there and we all played soccer in the streets. I remember making the one-and-a-half-hour trip to Melbourne as a 6-year-old playing with Corio Under-10s. I didn't get a touch the whole game, but I knew even then I wanted to make something of soccer. I almost didn't get the chance, though, because Mum and Dad didn't know I had gone and they were looking for me all day. There was serious trouble waiting for me when I got back.'*

In 1968, the family moved to the inner-Melbourne suburb of Carlton and Eddie joined Melbourne Croatia juniors. It was a logical fit, due to his heritage, and he enjoyed his time there. *'I was scoring goals left, right and centre. I found it very easy. The senior team wasn't allowed in the national league because of various political* reasons, and were playing in the state league as Essendon Croatia when I made my debut at fifteen. I was getting $50 a week.'

He was one of many players who showed great talent from a young age, but was one of few to translate that talent into ongoing success. He played in all of the Victorian junior state teams, but in those days, there wasn't a Joeys or Young Socceroos team to take his junior progress further. The highest level was the Australian Schoolboys team and, while he may have been a talented player, he initially missed out on the squad. *'I left school after year nine. I was astute and did well, but I just didn't want to be told what to do. I saw the careers counsellor, and when he wasn't looking I basically closed my eyes, then stuck my finger in the careers book on "Hairdresser". That's what I left to become and in fact, that is what I did become. Bobby McLaughlan was the coach of the Schoolboys team at the time and he told me I couldn't be selected because I wasn't at school. So, when I was around year twelve age and still training to be a hairdresser, I went back to school so that I could be in that team. The thing was, I went back into year ten so that I could be with my cousin. I had a bit of fun for a few months, played for the Schoolboys, then left again.'*

Eddie is the third kid from the left at the back.
Alan Davidson is third from the left, front row.

'I have travelled ever since and I always will.'

Eddie broke his leg playing for Essendon just before the Schoolboys team went on a short overseas tour. He still travelled with them, though, and enjoyed the experience of life beyond Australia's shores. His first appearance for the Schoolboys was finally made in Whyalla, on the border of Victoria and South Australia. '*I remember pulling on the Australian shirt in 1978 and it still gives me goosebumps. I did well and things went from there.*'

Later that year Marconi of Sydney signed the 18-year-old. The move north reaped instant dividends when the club were crowned champions and he was named the Under-21 Player of the Year. In 1979 he toured with the inaugural Young Socceroos to New Zealand and then Paraguay under coach Rudi Gutendorf. The team failed to qualify for the Youth World Cup, but it was the first experience of big crowds for most of the players. It was other elements of the trip that affected him most, though. '*Paraguay was only just coming out of decades of army rule and dictatorship. It was nowhere near as developed as Australia and the people lived so differently. It really opened my eyes to other cultures. I have travelled ever since and I always will.*'

It was also in 1979 that Eddie made his full Socceroo debut. '*We played a friendly against New Zealand and lost 1–0. Of course, it is great when you represent your country. There is no greater honour. There were eight Marconi players in the squad, and I remember there being an issue before the game because the Socceroos were sponsored by Adidas and everyone but me wore Adidas boots. I was sponsored by Puma and wanted to wear Puma boots.*' Game one, and the young Krncevic was already building a reputation for standing up for what he thought was right. It is a trait that has raised a few hackles over time, but one he won't compromise.

'*I was also in the Socceroo squad soon after the New Zealand match, for games against China and Taiwan, and from there became a more regular starter. Still, I was only nineteen and I carried the bags for the older boys. You wouldn't see that today, but I didn't mind. They were the guys I looked up to and they taught me a lot.*'

By 1980, Eddie was playing so well for Marconi that he was one of the first picked for the Socceroo World Tour late in the year. The trip satisfied Eddie's thirst for new places, and heightened his desire to play regularly in Europe. He played well throughout most of the tour and started to get some attention in the European media. Perhaps too much attention, however, when he met his extended family in Croatia for the first time. '*Partway through the tour, a last-minute game against Dinamo Zagreb was organised. I had some uncles come to watch the game and I met them afterwards. They took me out to their village to meet the rest of my family. We drove for hours in the snow and I met my grandparents. I wanted to sleep, but people kept coming in to say hello and there was far too much food. I was exhausted by the time I got back to the squad the next day, but it was good to see where I had come from.*'

The next day, he was told that the Dinamo Zagreb committee wanted to meet with him. '*I had played well in the Zagreb game, and I guess my Croatian name also drew their attention. They were interested in seeing more of me and I knew we would keep in touch.*'

The tour continued and the Socceroo spirit of the early 1980s was formed. The team developed a closeness that only time together can forge, and a tenacity that saw the team succeed in many of their games. When the squad returned to Australia, Eddie built on the confidence he gained from

A fourteen-year European career.

'...65,000 fans started chanting "kangaroo" to put me on.'

international matches and the maturity gained from world travel. He was scoring goals for fun, and was the name on everyone's lips.

In 1981, it was Dinamo Zagreb's time for a world tour. *'It was in January when Zagreb came out here. We played them in Canberra and I did pretty well. The same committee members that I had met the year before were still there, and they asked me to join them right after the Canberra game to continue their tour with them. Tony Labbozzetta was the Marconi boss at the time and he said no. He wanted me to stay for the NSL season. I was frustrated, but I went over later that season for trials – and didn't come back for fourteen years.'*

So, responsibilities with Marconi complete in late 1981, Eddie returned to Yugoslavia to reacquaint himself with Dinamo Zagreb. He was met by his extended family once again, and while they knew he was there to create a future with Dinamo, they had different plans. *'My family were Hadjuk Split fans and great rivals of Dinamo Zagreb. In fact, one of my cousins was involved with Split and he organised some trials for me. I immediately felt out of my depth when I trained with them. The touches and the skill were so much better than in Australia. I wasn't too comfortable there to be honest, but to my surprise they offered me a contract. I didn't tell them no, I just didn't tell them anything.*

I just left, went over to Zagreb, and immediately felt more comfortable. That's where I wanted to play.'

Dinamo Zagreb had finally got their man. Eddie agreed to a four-year contract worth zero dollars in transfers and zero dollars in wages. His lucrative European odyssey had begun! *'Yugoslavia was still a socialist country then, so the players didn't get paid. They didn't pay a transfer fee to Marconi and I played there on a temporary visa. They put me up in an apartment and looked after my food, but there was no money. My signing-on fee was a hairdressing salon. I couldn't believe it. They knew I was a trained hairdresser and the theory was that fans of the club would all want to get their hair cut at my salon. I guess it was a good way around not getting wages . . . but I never did get that salon.*

'I was the first foreigner to play in the Yugoslav first division, which at that time was of a very high standard because Yugoslav players weren't allowed to leave the country. I was on the bench for the first few games, then at one home game, the 65,000 fans started chanting "kangaroo" to put me on. The coach threw me on and I was over the moon. I was only twenty-one, and I couldn't have been happier.'

Determination is a critical success factor in any sportsperson's career, and Eddie had it in spades. He hadn't travelled across the globe to earn no money and not make a go

of it. He would often go for extra training runs through the forest with weights around his ankles, sometimes starting at 4 am to beat the summer heat. He was a man possessed. The arrival of his soon-to-be wife helped complete the adventure. *'I had met Maggie in Australia before I left. We had only known each other for three months, but within about six months of me being away, she came over. We had no money and were really struggling, but it didn't matter because we were so much in love.'*

Near the end of a successful second year at Zagreb, Eddie and Maggie decided to marry. Never backward in coming forward, Eddie decided that seeing as he was earning nothing, the club should pay for the ceremony. He asked for US$6,000 to cover the wedding they wanted, but the club refused. Upset, Eddie threatened to leave, but the coach jumped in and told him he would cover the costs himself. *'Two or three days after he said he'd help us, he ripped into me at a team meeting and said how wrong it was that I had asked for money. That I was living in a socialist country and it was the wrong thing to do. Particularly US dollars. I was so embarrassed and angry.'* A toned-down wedding went ahead, but the romance of a wedding night had to succumb to professional demands. The club would not give him the night off and he had to go to a game. *'I only ended up on the bench and I was so pissed off. Not the best start to married life, I can tell you.'* It was a

The Kangaroo climbs high in Croatia, Eddie's debut for Dinamo Zagreb.

'I was in bed for almost **three weeks and** lost seven kilograms.'

sequence of events that put an end to Eddie's Yugoslav soccer career. It was time to earn some money.

Partway through 1982, Italian Serie A club Pisa began to show serious interest when they discovered the boy Krncevic playing in Yugoslavia was actually an Australian citizen and could move abroad. Eddie spoke with the President, but nothing concrete eventuated. At the end of that season, Eddie and Maggie took a holiday to Italy and Eddie thought they might as well have a look at Pisa. *'We loved it there, and one day I walked up to the ground unannounced and asked for the President. He came down to see us, then we ended up staying at his house for three weeks. He was incredibly generous and we had a great time. They wanted to sign me, but at the end of that year they got relegated. At that time, Italian clubs could have three foreigners in Serie A, but were not allowed to sign any new ones if they got relegated. If their foreigners left, then bad luck. We were shattered and had to stay in Zagreb.'*

Meanwhile, a new German coach had taken over Zagreb for the upcoming season, and it was obvious he was not going to get the best out of Krncevic. Two-and-a-half years into his four-year contract, the coach did the right thing by organising a transfer to the German second division club MSV Duisburg. Eddie didn't receive his hairdressing salon as stipulated in his contract, which meant he could leave Zagreb for free and was in a strong position to negotiate a good wage from Duisberg. The Krncevic bank balance finally crept above zero, but he spent much of his time in an unaccustomed midfield position and struggled with the German way of life. *'It was hard work. I was earning a little bit of money, which was nice, but I was struggling with the language and didn't really crack the team environment. I only stayed six months, but at least it got me out of Yugoslavia.'*

By now, Eddie had an agent working for him and the first thing he did was organise a trial at Cercle Brugge in Belgium. *'The trial was no better than okay. Afterwards I felt like they just left me and didn't let me know how I went. I thought they were dogs, actually, but they ended up wanting to talk terms. I didn't care about them at that point, so we pushed it and asked for more than we thought I was worth . . . and they accepted. As soon as Maggie and I moved there, it was an instant relief. Brugge is a great place and we settled immediately.'*

The transfer fee of $150,000 put a bit of public pressure on Eddie's shoulders, but he had initially only agreed to play for six months and complete season 1984–85. It was a new lease of life. *'I was Man of the Match on my debut and began playing consistently well. The club took to me and when I re-signed for another year I pocketed a hefty sign-on fee.'*

By season 1985–86 Eddie had become a big-name player in Belgium and, therefore, the big clubs came knocking. Anderlecht and Club Brugge are the two biggest and it was Anderlecht that won his signature in June 1986. He enjoyed the big stadium and big support. 'It took a while to get going, but when I did I was flying. My old coach from Cercle Brugge then came to the club and I was suddenly scoring from everywhere.' The club won the championship in 1986–87 and the penniless days in Yugoslavia were fast becoming a distant memory.

Near the start of season 1988–89, however, Eddie's blossoming career hit a wall in the form of hepatitis A. 'It really knocked me about. I was in bed for almost three weeks and lost seven kilograms. It was the lowest point of my career overseas, but I gradually regained my enthusiasm as my fitness returned. I became confident again and even more motivated to do well.'

The illness came during the negotiations for a future contract. Not the best timing and Anderlecht were understandably unsure what to do. The confident Krncevic had a plan though, and by now he knew what he was worth. 'I told them I needed a bigger signing-on fee because I was going to be the league's top scorer that season and that they needed me. I got the bigger fee and I became top scorer. Everyone was happy.'

By the end of that season, Eddie thought it was time for a change. He had achieved all he could in four seasons with Anderlecht and needed another challenge. On top of that, the club was slowing up with its payments. 'They owed me some money, which I ended up getting, but I had a good offer from Mulhouse in France and decided to take it. I got $300,000 upfront . . . Just before my first game for Mulhouse, I had not been paid another $300,000 I was owed and I said I wouldn't play unless I got it. They gave it to me, but there were some problems at the club. We didn't have a good year and we gradually fell out of the top league.

'Payments in France were structured differently to Belgium. In Belgium, things were heavily weighted to performance bonuses with a reasonably low base-wage. In France, wages were high but performance bonuses were low. We would be coming home from games on the plane in France and the players would drink champagne and eat bread and cheese with basically the same feeling, whether we won or not. It was an easier life in France because there wasn't the same competitive stress.'

His next move was back to Belgium, where in 1991 he joined Standard Liege. Unfortunately, his passion for playing began to diminish at this point and strapping on his boots became no more than a job. His performances suffered and at just over thirty years of age, he should've been doing more.

Eddie's bread and butter.

'I didn't play very well but still had a good reputation. After a while, though, I fell out with the club and wanted to leave . . . I ended up playing with the reserves and was becoming quite cynical. I would go to training in my Merc and some of the players used to make fun of me because of it. I didn't care because they were the ones talking about it while I was the one driving it . . . and I told them so.'

It was during this time that Eddie studied for his FIFA coaching qualifications. By then he could speak Croatian and English due to his heritage, he'd learnt Italian at Marconi, Flemish from his time in Belgium, and a little German he picked up in his six months with MSV Duisburg. He had learnt French while at Mulhouse and developed it further during his FIFA studies. *'I seem to be able to pick up languages easily and it is one of the benefits of travel. I actually wrote a book in French for the coaching badge and used it regularly when I came back to Australia to coach. It was a bit of work having to translate it back to English for the players though!'*

It was out of the frying pan and into the fire when Standard Liege finally let Eddie go. The next stop was Aalst in the Belgian second division for season 1993–94. They were quickly promoted, but there were ongoing problems. *'The coach knew his football, but he couldn't relate to the players. One day we had a sports*

Another day, another dollar; Sticking one away for Anderlecht.

psychologist come to training to help us out and when he asked the players what they thought of the situation, no one said anything. I was pissed off because I knew no one was happy with what was happening, so I finally told him and told the coach. The coach told me to sit down, but the psychologist overruled him. Still, none of the players backed me. The next day we had a meeting without the coach, and only then did all the players speak up. I guess it shows how scared people are to get dropped from professional teams, but I was bloody upset with them for not doing what was right.'

By the time Eddie was thirty-five and an old hand in the Belgian big-time, his next stop at Charleroi provided the shot in the arm he needed after his Aalst experiences. After a couple of years of professional grind, he was once again training hard and was setting an example for the younger players at the club. Besides the bout of hepatitis A earlier in his career, Eddie had basically remained injury-free until six months into his eighth European club. *'I copped a corky on my thigh when someone ran into me. I thought I'd get over it, but it turned out there was some serious damage and they would have to operate. I was just starting to be motivated by the game again, but my initial reaction was that I would just retire and avoid the surgery. But they said I needed the surgery anyway, and told me I would be out for twelve weeks. That got me fired up, and I returned to the first team in*

under eight weeks and was pretty proud of the work I had done to get there.'

The episode had got Eddie thinking about the future. He had two young children at school in the French-speaking Charleroi district of Belgium, but as crime and tensions on the street began to rise, Australia entered his mind more regularly. *'I really wanted to come back to Australia and coach. I just got the feeling that Europe was becoming less safe for a family, so Maggie and I decided to come home. We had been away so long and made a great life for ourselves in Europe, but Australia was still home.'*

In February 1996, Eddie broke his contract with Charleroi and landed in Melbourne. *'As we flew into the airport, I remember thinking, "What the hell have I done?" It was so desolate and boring compared to approaching European airports. Still, once we got into Melbourne we were happy.'*

The plan was to get straight into coaching an NSL club, however it didn't quite work that way. His reputation had preceded his arrival, and the evergreen Frank Arok persuaded Eddie to play for him for a year at Gippsland Falcons – a two-hour drive from the family home. *'Frank accused me once or twice that year of not really wanting to play, but there was no way I would've travelled so far three or four times a week if I wasn't keen. There were some great,*

honest people at that club and I enjoyed myself. It was also a good reintroduction to the NSL and gave me a good chance to have a look at a few players.'

In 1997, Carlton SC was formed. It was an exciting new proposition for the NSL because the club was structured on a full-time, professional model and held no longstanding ethnic ties. It was a 'club for mainstream soccer supporters', and Eddie was asked to be coach. He wore his Versace suits to press conferences and slicked his hair on the sidelines. He brought a new pizazz to the competition, and also success. *'We only had four guys at our first training session. We gradually got our new signings and built the place up, but it was a scary start. We made the grand final that year, though, and we were pretty proud. Unfortunately the club didn't handle it too well, and [Club President] Lou Sticca said afterwards that the success of the club was because of management rather than the players and coaches. It was the beginning of the end.'*

Eddie took charge in year two as well, but it wasn't as inspiring. Dwindling crowds and spiralling wages meant it was only a couple more seasons before the club fizzed into a bankrupt memory. In 1999 he became coach at his old stamping ground, Marconi, and remained in Sydney until he was lured home by South Melbourne in 2002.

' I regret **not playing for Australia** as many times as I could've, but...I wouldn't change my career for it. '

His time with the Melbourne institution saw Eddie blood some bright young talent, but it was also a time marred by unresolved controversy surrounding money associated with the transfer of a player overseas. Eddie left the club disillusioned. *'There is so much politics involved with coaching. You don't think about it as a player, but as a coach you have to deal with so much crap you shouldn't have to deal with. I needed a break from it.'*

A break did not mean he was ready to make the most of his hairdressing qualifications just yet, though. He set up a player management business and is currently using his wealth of international experience and European contacts to help the next batch of young Aussie players make it overseas. *'Eurogoal aims to help young players get overseas, because that's where young players want to go. Of course, we also help them when they are over there so that they can just concentrate on playing, but we don't work with just anyone. If the first question a player asks is how much money they can earn, then we aren't interested. The first thing should be wanting to make it to the highest level you can – the money will look after itself.'*

●●●

To get to the top takes sacrifice, and one of Eddie's greatest regrets was not playing more times for the green and gold. His last Socceroo game was in the 1990 World Cup qualifiers against Israel, and the game before that was seven years earlier. Forging a career in a foreign land left him out of sight and out of mind. *'I was asked back [from Europe] in 1986 to start the World Cup qualifiers against Fiji. I was playing in the Belgium Cup semi-final so said that I couldn't come, but would love to play future games. [Coach] Frank Arok said publicly, "Who is he to pick and choose?" and I was only asked back once after that. Even after Eddie Thomson had taken over. These days it happens all the time and it is managed better. I regret not playing for Australia as many times as I could've, but it wasn't my choice, and in the end I wouldn't change my career for it.'*

It was said that the four-minute mile could never be broken until Roger Bannister slipped through the mythical barrier in 1954. Thousands of athletes have done it since. Eddie Krncevic was one of the first Aussies to imagine a footballing life beyond our shores, and he was the first in the modern era to prove it could be done. These days, hundreds of Australian professionals play overseas and thousands more know that they can be next.

Alan DAVIDSON

Socceroo 1980–1991

'Who's that Chinese kid?' was a question Alan Davidson heard a lot. He actually descends from a Japanese Samurai family, but to most, Chinese was close enough. The minority status of Asian kids in Australia through the 1960s and 1970s meant plenty of ridicule for Alan – but an Asian kid playing soccer also drew attention of a positive kind.

'Throughout my whole time in juniors and youth soccer, there was not one other Asian kid. My brother and I had to put up with a lot because we are Japanese and we spent a lot of our childhood back-to-back with each other, fighting our way out of trouble. But being different had its benefits at soccer because it helped me stand out to selectors.'

Standing out is something that Alan Davidson does well. He is passionate, disciplined and determined, and he does not accept anything but the best in whatever he does. The same applies to his family and to the people he surrounds himself with. A large proportion of his driven, thoughtful approach to life can be attributed to the immense importance he places on being raised as a proud Japanese–Australian.

'Mum and Dad met in Japan in the fifties after World War II, when Dad was there with Australian troops as part of the occupied forces. There was a huge amount of resistance to them being together because, after the war, the Japanese were so ashamed of what had happened. They also despised the Western forces for dropping the atomic bomb, and some of my family were killed in Hiroshima. Honour and respect are very important in Japanese society, and my mum's family thought she was turning her back on that. The family were not going to accept the marriage, until the family elder said that if Mum was willing to withstand all the pressure to be with Dad, then she must love him, and the family would approve. He had the final say, so she left with Dad to come back to Australia and become his wife.

'That wasn't the end of it though, because when they got back to Australia, they had to go through more drama. The Australian side of the family did not approve of my dad marrying a Japanese girl because of everything Australians went through fighting in Japan. They were outraged. One of my uncles was actually a prisoner of war in Changi for three years, where most people only lasted three months because the conditions were so bad. Of course, the family thought he would have the final word on not approving the marriage after all he had been through, but when he spoke he said, "The war is over and we should start getting over it too. They obviously love each other, and I wish them all the best." He then went on to say that no one was to tell her that he was in Changi, because it could've caused too many problems. Mum broke down and cried when she found out at my uncle's funeral years and years later.'

From an early age, the Davidson boys were encouraged to be the best. They were told that it was an honour to have Japanese blood and that their direct links to the Samurai family of Yamada made them special. It was an upbringing that cultivated Alan's single-minded dedication to achieve success. 'For years I couldn't figure out why all the other kids wanted to fight with us. I mean, we were special because we had Japanese blood – didn't they know that? Looking back I realise that Mum and Dad were preparing us to be strong because they knew what we would have to go through in our youth. They had gone through plenty of racial hardship to enjoy their life in Australia, and knew that we would have to be tough as well.'

Being young wasn't all hardship for the Davidson boys, however. Athletic pursuits were always a positive outlet, and Alan captained the school Aussie Rules team and excelled in most sports. The thing was, most of the friends he made were Greek and the most natural thing for a Greek kid in Australia to do was play soccer. Alan's first steps into the sport that would be his career were – to be polite – tentative. 'I was crap. I started playing at school when I was about nine and I didn't have a clue what I was doing. I scored an own goal in my first game

and spent most of that year on the bench because I was the worst player. For some reason, I still loved the game though, and I practised and practised. I used to knock on all the kids' doors after school to see if they would come and play with me. Even if they didn't want to (I was pretty bad) I would have a kick by myself. The wall in the park became my best friend, rain, hail or shine. By the next year, I was one of the best players and everyone wanted to play with me in the park. The next year, a lot of my friends joined our local club, Altona City. I am still friends with them today.'

Alan played with Altona City from Under-11s to Under-16s and then broke into the state league senior team before his seventeenth birthday. He was also in all the Victorian state teams from Under-13s to Under-18s, but couldn't play in the Australian Schoolboys team because he left school at fifteen. 'I left to do an electrical apprenticeship. I had a scholarship for school and it broke my parents' hearts when I left, but I wanted to be a soccer player by then and school seemed to be getting in the way.'

'...because we are **Japanese** and we spent a lot of our childhood **back-to-back** with each other, **fighting our way out of trouble.** '

'I had to knock on the NSL clubs' doors after that Young Socceroos tour and tell them who I was. Melbourne J.U.S.T didn't want me and Heidelberg didn't want to pay me, but were happy to tie me to a long-term contract. Finally, South [Melbourne] were interested after I trialled there, and they signed me. I only trained with the youth team afterwards though, and I was devastated. After three weeks I asked the senior coach what was going on, and I began to train with them. I made the match squad a couple of weeks later and was on the bench for the first few games. In the third game of the season I played for five minutes in the midfield position I was used to. In the fourth game, our left-back got injured early on, so I jumped off the bench and told the coach I could play left-back. I had never played there before.'

That game was against South's Greek rivals, Heidelberg, at Olympic Park, and Alan was named Man of the Match. In fact, he started and starred in the next ten games as left-back, and by the end of 1980, he was selected by Socceroo coach Rudi Gutendorf to join his squad on a world tour. The Young Socceroo had graduated.

'You don't get many opportunities in this game so you have to take them when you can. I ended up playing for Australia as a right-back after playing for South Melbourne as a left-back, and spending my junior days in midfield. I didn't care where

Alan's performances in the national championships and the Victorian State League earned him a position in the first-ever Young Socceroos. While on the qualifying tour for the 1979 Youth World Cup he had to sit an exam for his electrician apprenticeship, but the thing he learnt most about wasn't in text books. 'It was a real education when we were in South America to see how many people lived so poorly.

I had never considered poverty before, then it was all around me. It made me much more patriotic towards Australia, because I realised how good our country is.'

The Young Socceroos failed at their first attempt to make the Youth World Cup, but Alan played well. It would seem logical that an NSL team would want to sign him when he returned. It wasn't that simple, however.

'You don't get many opportunities in this game so you have to take them when you can.'

I played, I was just so hungry for success and wanted to be on that park.'

By the time Alan returned from the tour and began preparations for the 1980 NSL season, he was the target of a number of clubs, and he knew it. Never lacking in confidence, he asked the captain at South, Stuart Baxter, how much he got paid. The next day, Alan was asked to the office of President Sam Papasavas, armed with the knowledge of what he was worth. He took his dad, but also took control. '*I told them that I wanted a house and they laughed. I told my dad to get up and we left. After two months, they told me they had the deposit for the house and I signed for two years. The next year, the house was paid off.'*

Alan continued to impress at South Melbourne and became a regular in Australian teams. By the end of his two-year contract, he renegotiated another deal that improved his wages, and also included a clause that he could never be transferred for more than $15,000. The next contract stipulated he couldn't be sold for more than $30,000.

'*When I joined South I didn't even have a suit and tie. I used to go to games in thongs and shorts. Sam Papasavas took me aside and bought me everything I needed. He told me I had to start looking the part if I wanted to be the part. That club helped me grow into a man in many ways. In fact, I owe everything to the Greeks and they are still my friends. I still live by the lessons the people at that club taught me.'*

By 1983, Alan was playing regularly for the Socceroos. When the Socceroos played England, he was the best player in the series, and even the media in England began to take notice. Arsenal showed some interest in signing the 22-year-old, but Bayern Munich were the ones that got to him first. '*Bayern are obviously a massive club and I was there for six weeks. They had three change rooms for training. One for the youth team, one for the first team and one for the internationals. I was in the international room as equals with guys I had only seen on television as superstars. Bayern wanted me, and I certainly wanted to stay.'*

Professional soccer is rarely straightforward, though, and Alan had to make a big decision. Actually, for someone as patriotic and success-driven as Alan, it was a massive decision. '*You could only have two foreigners in the German leagues back then. Bayern said they wanted to sign me and put me straight into the first team squad, but the catch was that I would have to take out German citizenship. I love being Australian. What was I supposed to do? It was Bayern Munich! I rang Dad and he basically said it was my decision, but also said that he knew plenty of people who had suffered and even died to be Australian. What he said*

confirmed what, deep down, I already knew, but didn't want to believe at the time. It was heartbreaking to see an opportunity like that drift by, but being Australian is the most important thing.'*

It was the off-season in Australia, and Arsenal were still interested, so Alan figured he might as well head to London instead of going home. Two weeks later, he had a call from Brighton and Hove Albion. To cover his bases, he went to the English seaside for more trials. A fortnight later, he was back at Arsenal and not long after that, the Gunners offered him a contract. '*Everything was ready to go at Arsenal, but life is full of obstacles and I couldn't get a work permit. South Melbourne also wanted me back because I had already missed the start of season, but I wanted to stay as long as I could while we tried to sort out the red tape. In the end, the red tape won and I had to come back. I was devastated.'*

South Melbourne won the championship in 1984, and in the same year, the Socceroos played a tournament against Nottingham Forest, Juventus, Iraklis, Glasgow Rangers and Manchester United. The two players of the tournament were Bonjak of Juventus and Davidson of Australia. Afterwards, it was Nottingham Forest's turn to chase the Australian's signature. They were crafty enough to get a work permit first and this time, it looked as though Alan might finally get his break into the big-time. He was able

'You are the only one to have earned your wages this week. Get ready for Man United next week.'

to negotiate excellent personal terms, because Forest only had to pay the mere $30,000 as stipulated in his South Melbourne contract. *'This time I agreed to terms before I left. I went over not having to trial and was straight into the first team squad for a club playing in England's top league. It was a dream about to come true, but my first week there was a shocker. It was freezing and wet and the grounds were full of mud. I couldn't pass a ball three metres. For the first time ever, my confidence dropped and I began to play mind games with myself. It was tough being away from home, and I began to feel a lot of pressure.*

'After a week's training, they moved us onto an Astroturf pitch to get away from the mud. It was the first time I met [manager] Brian Clough because he had been away. As I walked onto the bus past him, he said, "Who are you?" I was shattered. My new boss didn't even know who I was! The mind games went into overdrive, and I figured if I didn't train the house down, I might as well go home. Fortunately everything I did that session came off – even things I didn't mean. When we got back on the bus to go home, the boss called me down to his couch at the front and said, "You

are marking John Barnes when we play Watford this weekend." Talk about the highs and lows.'

Alan's confidence was back and he was looking forward to stepping out as a first division player. However, even being in the big-time doesn't make you immune to the slapstick that life enjoys serving up. *'I was getting changed close to the change room door at Watford and as I bent over, someone came in and opened the door into my head. I was knocked flat on my backside and when I looked up, it was some bloke in a top hat and big glasses. Clough said, "Are you trying to kill my Aussie before he even starts?" and it was then I realised the guy in the top hat was Elton John. He was the chairman of Watford and was married to an Australian. He started chatting to me while I was on the floor. I was so embarrassed. Other than that, I remember the game itself going at a million miles an hour. I was nervous and excited and even though we lost 2–1, I was happy to have got it over with. After the game, Brian Clough tore shreds off everybody, but when it came to me, he pointed a finger right in my face and said, "You are the only one to have earned your wages this week. Get ready for Man United next week." I was pretty happy with that.'*

There were 35,000 people jammed into the City Ground when Alan made his home debut against Manchester United. The

experience was surreal for the naive new kid. *'The crowd were all singing as we walked out. They chanted everybody's name, but they did mine first because it was my home debut. I had no idea what to do or what was going on. One of the other players had to tell me to clap them, then they would move on. I was glad when the whistle blew to start the game, because I could focus on the ball. It was strange to think that it was me out there.'*

Forest went into the half-time break 2–0 down, and Clough's old-style management techniques were about to get a workout. If Alan was glad to hear the whistle to start the game, he soon wished he didn't hear the one that signified half-time. *'Clough was steaming. He is an intimidating man, and he grabbed me by the throat and had me up against the wall telling me I was a crap signing and that if I wanted to stay in the first division, I had better do something special. We were face-to-face and there was spit everywhere. My toes were dangling and my legs were jelly. All I could think of was "Don't cry, don't cry." Then one of the other players said something and he dropped me to the floor. He began throwing tea around the room and I just wanted to be anywhere but there. To my horror, I was still in the team for the second half. There was no way I wanted to go back out there, but I was too scared not to. I gave it everything, and we ended up winning 3–2 in the last*

On the move at Forest.

So proud of that Socceroo shirt; versus England, 1983.

minute. Clough walked past afterwards and said, "That's what I pay you for."'

Brian Clough had a reputation for unconventional techniques, arrogance and intimidation. He is also one of the world's most successful managers of all time and it was his astute understanding of the game, and the people within it, that got him there. He knew Alan wasn't happy. *'I used to regularly get notes on my locker to go and see the boss. He would ask me why I didn't smile and if I was doing okay. I always answered in yes's and no's and that was it. The fact is, I was scared of him. The only times I enjoyed myself over there were when we were playing or training. I was a long way from home with no friends and it was empty and lonely. There aren't many friendships in the game, which made it harder. There are teammates, but not many friendships, and the distinction between the two is important. I went over as a 23-year-old who thought he was a man, but players over there have lived in such a competitive environment from the age of sixteen; they have become tough and street-wise. I soon learnt that I was a naive boy in comparison, and that it was up to me to become a mentally tough man.*

'Clough actually asked me if I would do him the honour of joining his family for Christmas that year. I really didn't want to, but couldn't find a way to say no. Most of the senior players had never even seen his

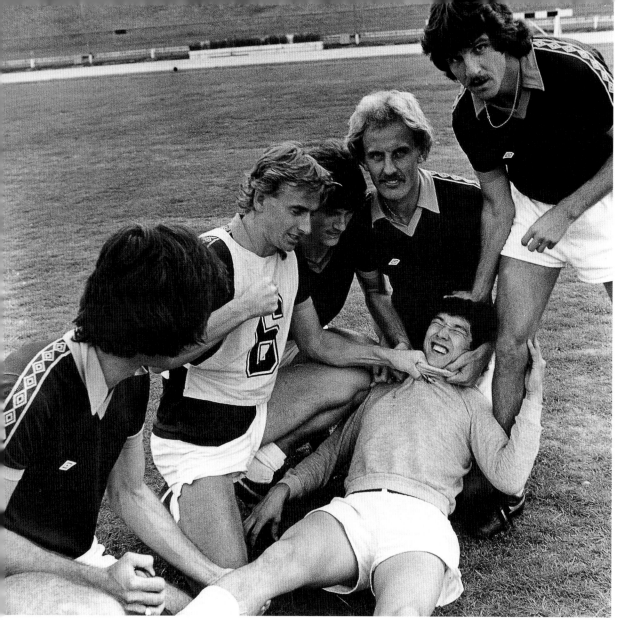

and had done well for the club. And this was the thanks I got when I was in trouble. I knew professional football was cold, but this was over the top. He ended up admitting it was wrong, then got me the best neurosurgeon in Britain. I was put on medication which I still take, and was able to keep playing. Forest kept me.'

Alan did well in the next gruelling pre-season and was in great form until another cruel football blow blindsided him. *'We were playing Everton in a friendly just before the season. Someone slid into my back with their knee and broke three vertebrae. I had a cast over my whole torso for three months and couldn't move. It was too much for me.'*

There are times in every person's life when they indulge in serious introspection. Footballers have a lot of spare time, and Alan spent too much of it dwelling on why someone living the life of boyhood dreams wasn't actually happy. Three months in a body cast wasn't going to make the mental challenges any easier, but the unenviable situation ultimately provided some clarity. Alan gave the game away at the age of twenty-five. He had done what he had always wanted to do, but injury and maturity had given him a new perspective on life. *'I used to think money and achievement were everything. That attitude got me to the English first division, but I began to realise it wasn't necessarily right. Until you*

house and I was going for Christmas dinner! He was a different, much more relaxed man in that environment, but I was still on edge. He offered me a drink and when I said no, he laughed. I mean, it was English soccer in the eighties and everyone drank. He told me to get a drink and again I said, "I don't drink, boss." He looked at me intently, then said, "Well done son. There's lemonade in the fridge."'

•••

Just beyond the halfway mark of the season, Alan collapsed against Sheffield Wednesday. Tests discovered brain tissue damage that was a form of epilepsy, and the club doctors said he shouldn't play again. Alan went to see Clough and his world rattled when he said he wanted to terminate Alan's contract. *'I couldn't believe it. It was the only time I ever stood up to him. I told him that I had come to the other side of the world to play for him. I had left family and friends behind*

are not happy, you don't realise how important happiness is – and I wanted mine back. I came home and opened a restaurant in the city.'

Among family and friends in home-town Melbourne, the smile that eluded Brian Clough returned. And after eighteen months without soccer, his passion for the game also crept back. *'The 1988 Seoul Olympics were coming up and I wanted to play. Melbourne Knights signed me for the 1987 season and I had to work hard to get fit and prove the critics, who thought I was finished, wrong. I played with a back brace for the year and it took almost that whole season for my match instinct and desire to return. I did think at times that I should just give up for good, but I rediscovered my joy for the game and made it into the 1988 team. I am now an Olympian.'*

Alan was selected as the best Australian in that tournament, but he thought he should retire on a high – until Frank Arok persuaded him to stay on for the next World Cup campaign. Once again, the Socceroos failed to qualify, and the devastation was enough to put a full stop to Alan's international career. It may have been a premature end for a 28-year-old at his peak, but he still managed to play seventy-seven times for the green and gold and is one of a small, prestigious group of Australians to have played fifty 'A' internationals. *'The most emotional time being a Socceroo was*

when the anthem was played. It brought tears to my eyes every time and sometimes it still does. It was a turbulent time with the Socceroos in the eighties, but I am proud of every moment.'

The 1980s were known as the 'Mad Dog' era of the Socceroos. Frank Arok selected a group of people with a mean streak who didn't care for reputations. Short fuses and passionate personalities resulted in a couple of occasions where arguments turned into

physical altercations and signified serious team trouble. Arok tried to channel that mentality into a method of playing that would force the soccer world to pay attention to our national team, and in many ways it worked.

The perceived differences between the large number of British immigrants playing for Australia in this era and those born in Australia caused disharmony with some players, and in many ways it reflects the difficulties of our developing nation. *'It used to annoy me when we might be watching Australia play England in the cricket and some of the Socceroos would be cheering for England. I couldn't understand it. They were Australian now.'*

Alan continued to play for the Melbourne Knights, and was an integral part of the 1991 and 1992 championship winning teams. In 1991 he was also lured out of international retirement by Eddie Thomson. He was given the captain's armband, and accumulated his seventy-seventh Socceroo appearance against Czechoslovakia. *'Eddie asked me to return for the beginning of the World Cup campaign, but after that I knew I needed a different challenge. I played Czechoslovakia in my first and last games, and ended up being involved in four World Cup campaigns.'* At the end of 1992, Len Ashurst called him from Malaysia on the recommendation of ex-Knights coach Ken Worden, to see if he wanted to play for

Another Malaysian trophy.

Pahang. After serious deliberation, he decided to take a punt. *'I was married to Effie by then with one child, Jason, but we thought we would go for a six-month adventure. We ended up staying for six years, had our second son, Jamie, there and absolutely loved it. The Malaysian King (who was also Sultan of Pahang) ran the club with the Crown Prince and we lived very well. They hadn't won a trophy in ten years and the King just wanted at least one that first year. There were five on offer and we ended up winning all five. I guess that helped win him over!'*

Malaysian football may not have the same aura as the English first division, but this time Alan was with family and he had already proven himself. His customary high standards were set, but he was bought as an experienced professional and therefore didn't have to battle to make a name. The standard of living his family was provided with also didn't hurt. *'The club gave us a seven bedroom house with servants and anything we wanted. After a while, we decided we wanted something smaller and more homely, so I asked the Prince if we could move. He couldn't understand why, but asked me to show them what we wanted. I took his aide to a street on the beach where there were some nice places and pointed out one in particular as a good example. The next thing you know, he was knocking on the door and went inside. He came out minutes later and said, "It's yours". I was gobsmacked –*

I didn't mean to kick people out of their house! He told me the deal was done and I could shift in two days.

'The Prince used to come and watch training in his helicopter. Fair enough if you have one, I guess, but he used to actually hover above training to watch – you couldn't ask for a better view. I remember winning a particular game and afterwards, I took my shirt off because I was hot. Almost instantly a group of people came around me and told me to put it back on because it was disrespectful to the Princess sitting in the crowd. Later in the change rooms, we got word that the King was coming down. Everyone stood to attention and I was like a fish out of water. He congratulated us, then called the captain forward. There was bowing, then the King said, "Well done. How much?" The captain muttered "$5,000", and the next thing you know, all the players had $5,000 in their hands as a bonus. Effie had a go at me for being late out of the change rooms, but she didn't mind when I gave her the cash!'

The Malaysians love a trophy, and all told, Alan won sixteen of them with Pahang. Actually, it was really seventeen if you count his stellar performance in the region's Under-7s outfit. *'I got a Royal invitation to be at the club for the Crown Prince's son's birthday. I assumed there'd be some cake and some photos and signatures, and that would be it. On the way in, though, there was a lot of traffic and when I got to the*

ground there was a lot of noise. I began to wonder what was going on, particularly when I got inside and saw that the stands were full. Forty thousand kids had been given tickets. I was ushered into the change rooms where all the match kit was laid out. It took me a while to realise it wasn't all one big joke, but apparently the Prince's Under-7s team could never beat their arch-rivals and the birthday boy wanted to make sure it happened that day. There were four first-team players there for his team – all internationals, including the Malaysian captain. We walked out of the tunnel to the national anthem like it was a real game. Proper officials, security and everything. It was so embarrassing – I was three times their size! The Prince wasn't the best, but he had to score, so we were putting them on a platter for him. He finally put one away off his knee and was celebrating like he had won the World Cup. At the end of the game, I wanted to get out of there, but I had to hang around. The young Prince walked us up to get the trophy from the King. It was so big he almost fell over when he lifted it to the crowd. We got the best-quality medal I have ever received. I am glad my kids didn't come along, because there is no way I was going to be able to compete with a birthday party like that for them!'

Six years in Malaysia was enough and in 1998 the Davidsons returned to Australia for their children's education. Alan played for one more year as a 38-year-old with the

'The Prince used to come and watch training in his helicopter.'

Melbourne Knights, but had lost his desire for the game. *'It's all about the quality of life. You have to do what you love and be driven to high standards. If you want to make it in soccer though, you have to do more than love it. You have to be addicted to it.'*

Alan's addiction has shifted to his children. He enjoys setting them high standards and doing what he can to help mould their future. He is bringing them up with the mixture of the Davidsons' Australian patriotism, the Yamadas' Samurai spirit and with the Greek influence that began at South Melbourne and has continued in his marriage with Effie. He is also throwing in the lessons he has learnt travelling the world with the Socceroos, steeling himself in the English top-flight and living like royalty in Malaysia. It is only possible to pass on the lessons of experience once you have lived them, and as far as Alan Davidson is concerned, that is the best outcome of his distinguished career.

Alan was awarded with the AMP Medal (the highest honour for a foreign player in Malaysia), but the adoration of the fanatical Pahang supporters was far more obvious.

Charlie YANKOS OAM

Socceroo 1983–1990

Charlie Yankos is determined to do things his way. Not by snubbing his nose at authority, but by ensuring at all times that his terms are not compromised. It is a simple philosophy from a man who relishes the complexities of human nature and the opportunities to learn from all walks of life. It would not be surprising if his business card read 'Don't die wondering'.

'I was given the opportunity to play in South Australia for West Adelaide Hellas partway through my career, but at the time I was building a business career in Victoria with the TAB while playing for Heidelberg in the NSL. I remember an older, easily forgettable sort of guy at work saying that I would always get other opportunities in business, but opportunities for Australians to play top-level sport are rare. It could be something that I would regret if I didn't give it a go. I'd hardly spoken to the guy before then, but he was right. I don't ever want to say that I had a chance and didn't do anything about it. Good advice can come from unlikely sources.'

Living by that philosophy, Charlie went on to have a Socceroo career spanning seven years, from 1983 to 1990, and became one of the top twenty Socceroo goalscorers – a remarkable statistic when you consider he spent his entire career as a defender. As well as notching up eighty-nine Socceroo appearances, Charlie experienced life as a European professional when he signed for the Greek club PAOK in 1989. He became one of our longest-serving Socceroo captains, and his business career has since gone from strength to strength. The TAB's Mr Forgettable was right.

Charlie's historic roots are in northern Greece. Travelling alone, his father, Tom, moved to Australia in the 1950s when he was fifteen and met up with his uncle, who was running a farm west of Melbourne. Within a year, his immediate family joined him. They didn't find it too difficult to settle because they mixed in the Greek–Macedonian community, and it was through those connections that Charlie's father met his future wife, Maria. Charlie was born in Carlton, Melbourne, in May 1961.

His parents did not have a background in sport, but were strong from a life working the land. Charlie took an interest in the round ball from an early age, but did not play for a team until he was twelve. *'There was a group of boys in the area that I grew up in after Mum and Dad moved from the farm. We played soccer in the local park constantly. All sorts of games that developed us as players without us knowing it. Alan Davidson was just one guy who grew up in*

Frank Farina, Dave Mitchell and Charlie Yankos.

Check out the pose of the kid on the ground! Charlie in the *real* glory days with Polonia Maribyrnong.

the same area, and even though he was the year above me, we used to play one-on-one for hours. The street lights would come on and we would just keep going. I would often get in trouble for getting home late because I would totally lose track of time. One time I put a ball through the local kindergarten window and we all ran. Of course, the ball had my bloody name on it so, in the end, trouble found me anyway.'

The school soccer competition in the area became strong because of all the extra 'training' in the park, and after a while Charlie and his friends joined Polonia Maribyrnong and were introduced to their first real coach, at the age of thirteen. *'Father Richard Gamanski was my first coach and he was fantastic. He taught us all so much about soccer and about life. I still remember how well he would strike a ball – his timing was perfect. My parents, uncles, aunties and cousins would come to games and have a picnic and social occasion. It was their chance to catch up, but it also gave us great support and created a good atmosphere at the club. It was a Polish club, and they treated all of us superbly. They were good times.'*

Playing in the park, Father Gamanski's coaching and the atmosphere created by his family combined to help Charlie's Polonia team win everything before them. For season 1976, at the age of sixteen, six of the boys, including Charlie, were snapped up by

Fitzroy Alexander in the Victorian State League. A year later, the NSL was formed and Fitzroy was renamed Heidelberg. All of a sudden Charlie was involved with the country's first national sporting competition. *'We all signed what we thought were one-year contracts, but they turned out to be three-year deals with a three-year option. Six years! I stayed eight seasons anyway, but all the other guys I started with left. We were on $30 a win, $20 a draw and $10 a loss if we played in the first team, but we spent a couple of years in the reserves. No wonder they quit!'*

He only played two senior games in the first two years, but he had a grander, private goal of playing for Australia and he was learning a lot from the experienced players around him. *'Jimmy Rooney would often pick me up from the train station and we would talk about soccer and life, and I know now how valuable that was for my development. Before a Cup game against arch-rival South Melbourne Hellas, my roommate happened to be Jimmy Tansey, who said to me "Never give a sucker a break. When your chance comes, take it." It was Socceroos like that giving me advice and encouragement that helped me keep at it.'*

Charlie's commitment was displayed by the one-and-a-half-hour trip on two buses and two trains that took him to training three times a week after school - and the fact that he still made sure to get there early for some extra practice. *'I wanted to be a Socceroo and, to me, the sacrifices I was making didn't feel like sacrifices. I would arrive at training thirty minutes early and test myself with penalties and free kicks – always trying to do better and better. It is a habit I kept throughout my entire career and probably the reason I scored so many of the type of goals I did.'*

Charlie first wore Australia's green and gold in the 1978 Schoolboys tour of Canada and the USA. He had played in all the Victorian junior teams from the age of thirteen, (having only started competitively at twelve), and the Schoolboys team was a logical step to make. The tour was his first

' I wanted to be a Socceroo and, to me, the **sacrifices** I was making didn't feel like sacrifices.**'**

time overseas, and he enjoyed every minute. *'We landed at Los Angeles airport and felt so small. The airport, the city . . . everything about that place is massive and I was glad I was travelling with a team. In Vancouver, the players were billeted out to Canadian families and it was a great experience to be away from home at seventeen. The soccer was good, but the main thing from that tour was the importance of camaraderie and the cultural experience of travelling and meeting new people.'*

The Schoolboys tour and his growing commitment to Heidelberg in the NSL coincided with his year twelve studies, and Charlie knew they didn't gel. *'I knew I'd fail if I went for the exams that year. So the year after the Schoolboys and pushing for the Heidelberg first team, I decided to go back and do year twelve again. The delay turned out to be a good decision because I did well and managed to pass.'*

Charlie later gained a Bachelor of Arts degree in Urban Studies, and supplemented his soccer income by working in sales and management at a local gym. Not only did working in a gym keep him fit, but the sales and marketing experience provided a good foundation for his future career away from soccer. It also meant he was mixing with another group of people away from the game. *'I was mixing with soccer people, uni people, my family and the people at the gym. It was important to have that variety because people are all so different and you can learn from all of them.'*

This open-minded and relaxed approach to different cultures and priority systems meant that he occasionally clashed with his traditional Greek parents. *'I became a bit of a black sheep in the family because I often didn't go to the christenings and weddings and I definitely didn't fast at the appropriate times with the Orthodox Church. I'll eat what I want – particularly when I have a game the next day. In some ways, Mum and Dad brought beliefs with them when they came out, but haven't moved on since, whereas Australian kids have definitely moved on, and so have the Greek kids in Greece.'*

On the flip side was the fact that he was playing for Heidelberg, a club formed by migrants from the same part of Greece as his family. Becoming an Australian international was also a continued source of pride for his family. *'There were three or four Greek boys in the Heidelberg team and the fans did treat us a little differently to the others, as if we were more like them – even though I couldn't speak Greek. Mum and Dad loved the idea of me playing for "their" Greek community, but I found all that stuff was garbage. I was just playing for a good club in the NSL.'*

He loves a tackle! Versus England, 1983.

'...overseas clubs were beginning to look **pretty favourably** at the Aussies.'

Charlie made his socceroo debut in 1983 against England in Sydney. Not a bad place to start. *'Les Scheinflug was the coach back then, but actually decided to go to the Youth World Cup rather than take the team in the series against England. Frank Arok took over and brought in some players that he liked, including me. We drew the first game 0–0 in Sydney, lost the next 1–0 in Brisbane, then drew 1–1 in Melbourne. There were good crowds and England had a good team. It was a pretty big occasion to make a debut.'* Scheinflug reclaimed control of the team for a tour of Singapore after the England series, but it was his last act as coach. Arok assumed full control for the rest of the 1980s and Charlie became a mainstay from then on.

By 1986, Charlie had notched up eight successful years at Heidelberg and was playing regularly as captain of the Socceroos. He was about to be married to his long-term Aussie girlfriend, and it was time for a change of scenery. *'The day before my wedding, I flew to Adelaide to sign contracts with West Adelaide. They did offer more money, but I was just at a stage where I felt I needed a change. We needed to start fresh and to be our own people.'*

It was a time when the NSL was split into Northern and Southern divisions, however,

after one season, the leagues merged into one and West Adelaide was left behind. Of course, the Australian captain was not going to be left in the South Australian State League and the offers came flowing. The club that won the race was APIA. *'Rale Rasic was coach and the President, Joe Prestia, came to pick me up to take me to a meeting. Of course, we had a big Italian dinner with the committee and talked about life, then later on shook hands on a deal. The next day I left for an overseas tour with the Socceroos and hadn't signed anything. I called Joe while I was away to check everything was okay and he told me they had already bought me from West Adelaide. I said that I hadn't signed yet and he just said they trusted that I would. Bought on a handshake. I kept my word and signed for them. We won the championship that year.'*

Charlie enjoyed two years in Sydney, but by the late 1980s, playing overseas was becoming an increasingly viable career path. APIA started to experience difficulties on and off the pitch and by the end of the 1989 season, Charlie felt that it was time to move on. Next stop, the Greek first division. *'The Socceroos had some good performances in the mid- to late eighties and overseas clubs were beginning to look pretty favourably at the Aussies. John Margaritis was one of Frank Arok's many assistants and he had*

some contacts in Greece. PAOK wanted me, so John and I went over to meet them. Their President was "the man" and he drove us around town in his Mercedes with his entourage behind. He took us to a nightclub and, when we arrived, the crowd parted as we went down the front. He had a table that was permanently reserved for him. They were smoking cigars and downing all the top-drawer drinks, but I just had some mineral water and kept quiet. It was all show, but it ended up being a test for me as well. The President was seeing what sort of character I was. At the end of the night, I offended him by offering to pay, but he told me later he could see I was serious about playing in Greece and that I wasn't a troublemaker. The fact that I couldn't speak Greek that well probably helped me keep reserved in the nightclub . . . but I am not sure the President knew that. I also found out that the nightclub bill was $10,000 paid in cash, so I was glad he was offended enough that I didn't have to pay!'

PAOK gave Charlie one week to pack and get back to Europe. The day after he arrived, he had to leave his hotel and head into the local village for a training camp, because the city of Salonika had been brought to a standstill by heavy snow. It was a good chance for the new kid to get to know his teammates, but because he went

'I used to sneak out of Greek school as a kid to play soccer.'

over as a proven player, he didn't have to battle too hard for respect. PAOK already had their quota of foreign players, but Charlie had dual citizenship and the Socceroo captain was actually signed as a Greek national. It was a convenient situation for player and club, but one that would ultimately see his premature return to Australia's sunny shores. *'I was there as a Greek, but could hardly speak a word. I mean, I used to sneak out of Greek school as a kid to play soccer. I didn't bother learning Greek at home either because I spent my school days with heaps of non-Greek kids. I did pick some up pretty quickly in Greece though, because it was cheaper to eat out than cook at home and you soon start mixing. I do remember ordering donkey instead of prawns once though.'*

One word he soon learnt was 'Vuno', the nickname the crowd quickly gave him due to his strong physical presence and solid performances. *'It took me a little while to figure out what they were calling me, but it basically means mountain or volcano. I played pretty well right from the start, and the team was doing okay. I even settled well off the ground, although the local players sometimes gave the new foreigners a bit of a hard time.'*

The playboy President who had signed 'Vuno' left the club about nine games after Charlie's arrival, however, and it signalled

troubled times ahead for the Aussie skipper. The new President signed a new coach and the foreigners, including Charlie, were pushed aside. *'The new coach's nickname was "Crazy". His team talks would sometimes take an hour-and-a-half, where he would talk about the Spartans and wars and*

the pride of being Greek. It was all done in Greek and the foreigners were left out, but I picked up enough to know that I didn't want to know. We used to have bets about how long each talk would take. The new President wanted to renegotiate my contract, but I said no.'

While all of this was happening, Charlie wanted to return for the 1990 World Cup qualifiers as he always said he would. It was a red rag to a bull for PAOK, but Charlie didn't care. Six international trips in four weeks is testament to his ambition. *'I flew cattle-class up to thirty-six hours every time. I thought I could handle it, but it took its toll and my performances began to suffer. I basically wanted to do whatever was needed to play for Australia.'*

Payments from PAOK became delayed or non-existent, and things became increasinly complicated. Decision time. *'I was assured by the first President that I wouldn't have to do National Service, but I wasn't so sure with the new guy. One other player had tried to transfer out under him, and within weeks he was wearing army boots. I was approaching my six months [the time expatriate Greeks are allowed in the country before becoming eligible for service] so I had to make a decision. I came home with no regrets.'*

Charlie's elite soccer career was winding down. Australia failed to qualify for the 1990 World Cup in Italy and he realised it

'Vuno' in PAOK colours.

would be a major struggle to be competitive by the time the next campaign came around. Consequently, he sacrificed his place in the Socceroos after that qualifying series. *'Life is lived in chapters. My life used to be driven by soccer, but I could see it was time to close that chapter and I became driven by my management and business career, as well as the desire to spend as much time as possible with my daughters, Kaitlin and Taylor. I retired from the Socceroos [in 1990] on my terms and went without fanfare after a general media release and quiet chat with Eddie Thomson [the appointed caretaker national coach]. Every now and then I can re-open whatever chapter of my life I like and I look back on them fondly. In the end though, it is more important to look forward.'*

Even though a new chapter was opening wide, Charlie couldn't write the previous one off completely. His priorities had changed, but the game was still in his blood, and he completed the 1989 NSL season with Blacktown City. The next year, he accepted the opportunity to work in a major shopping centre in Wollongong. He moved to the South Coast of New South Wales, and started a four-year stint with the Wollongong Wolves in the NSL. Finally, injuries took their toll and his work and soccer priorities became increasingly polarised. In 1994, he snapped the soccer chapters closed.

'I keep pretty quiet about my soccer career, but I enjoy being able to look back on it when I want to. I wanted to play for Australia from when I was a kid, but I didn't tell anyone about it. It was my dream. Because of that, every time I walked out for Australia was a special and proud moment – particularly when I was captain. We had a mixture of heartache and great times, but overall that Mad Dog Socceroo period of the eighties under Frank [Arok] was fantastic.'

The Mad Dog Socceroos were full of interesting characters who had a fierce desire to drag Australia's soccer reputation to a higher plane. There were often personality clashes, but the encounters were usually kept on the training ground. As captain, they were times that kept Charlie busy. *'The training sessions were absolutely full on. Players were fighting for places in the team and wouldn't hold back. It was survival of the fittest where, if you aren't hard, you die. It was aggressive and would usually simmer just below boiling point. Occasionally, it would tip over the edge and things would get very interesting. Most times the aggro was left behind when we finished training,* but sometimes it carried on after as well, and I guess I had to play peacekeeper a few times. Frank would often tell the team that we all wanted the same thing in the end. We didn't have to be friends, but we had to play together and that was the important thing.'

The term 'Mad Dog' Socceroo was introduced by the Israeli media before the 1985 World Cup qualifier in Tel Aviv. *'We had one of our intense training sessions before that game, even though the lights happened to go out. We continued under some street lights and could hardly see. We were still kicking lumps out of each other, though, and the Israeli media thought we were crazy. They asked Frank about the physical training methods and he just said, "Wait until you see what will happen in the game tomorrow." All the media reports basically ran with the story that we were just there to kick them off the park. Of course, it was mind games and we won 2–1. From then, the era under Arok became the "Mad Dog" period.'*

There was method to the madness, however, and as captain, Charlie was

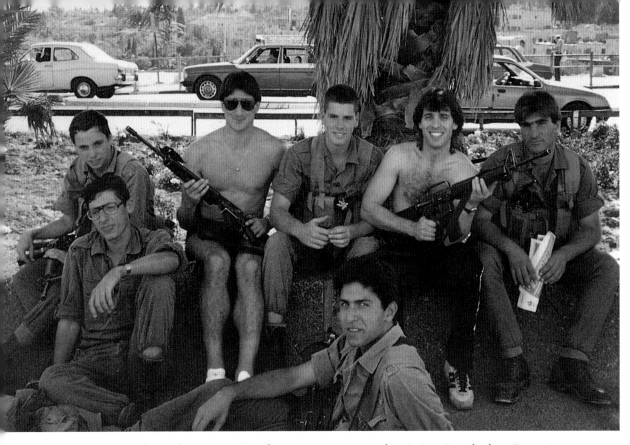

perhaps closest to it. 'Frank was a great motivator and thinker. He knew players and what he could get from them. He wanted players who were desperate to play for Australia and encouraged his team to believe in themselves. It was in the period between '83 and '85 that the confidence grew, and even though we lost to Scotland in '85 [during the '86 World Cup qualifying series], we played them off the park [at Melbourne's Olympic Park]. It's been said that it started a new era for Australian soccer, because we genuinely thought we could win every match from there on.'

The spirit developed by Arok began to break down in the late 1980s during the 1988 Seoul Olympics. 'I was honoured to be Australia's second Olympic captain after Bobby Bignell in '56. We had a great first-up win against Yugoslavia over there, then

lost 3–0 to Brazil where Romario tore us apart. We then beat Nigeria 1–0, then lost 3–0 to Russia in the quarters. Arok had always wanted to win – especially against top soccer nations – but in the lead-up to and during that tournament he became obsessed. He made some decisions that confused, and sometimes frustrated, the players and the harmony began to crack.'

By that time, opportunities for Socceroos to play overseas were becoming more attainable and Arok had to start managing the thorny new issue of club versus country. 'When I started with the national team in '83 – and especially for the guys earlier than that – our Aussie soccer heroes were all playing here. We could watch them, play alongside them and learn from them. The number one priority for young players was to join them in the national team. From the

late eighties into the nineties, and certainly these days, the priority for players is to play overseas. It's not that playing for Australia is not important, but individual career goals are now the number one priority. It means our domestic competition has suffered and we don't get to see the Socceroos play as often. But when they do, they are now a bunch of world-class players because of their involvement in world-class competitions.'

Charlie's final game in a Socceroo shirt was against Dinamo Zagreb in 1990. His representative career spanned seven years, two failed World Cup campaigns, one Olympic tournament and eighty-eight performances.

•••

Charlie may have closed his own soccer chapters, but this chapter is not complete without mentioning one of his defining features. Charlie has never been a tall person – but his legs are like tree trunks that used to spring him around the ground like a kid on a trampoline. If they were prime beef sold by the kilo, you would have to take out a loan to buy them. Legs Of Mass Destruction. And they have been responsible for a couple of the most memorable moments in Australian soccer. Take a bending piledriver with the outside of the boot from thirty-five metres against world champion, Argentina, on the way to the Socceroos 4–1 win in the 1988 Bicentennial

Gold Cup – a goal that almost caused Frank Arok to burst a blood vessel in excitement, as well as almost bursting the net. Then there was the thirty-metre strike on an angle, blasted around the near side of the wall into the top corner, in the pressure cooker Tel Aviv World Cup qualifier against Israel, to draw us level in 1985 – followed by near suffocation from teammates in the celebratory stacks-on.

Two goals don't make a player, but they are the signature of Charlie's career, and illustrate the skill, power, dedication and strength of conviction that have taken him to the top. But to Charlie, they are just two underlined sections in a series of well-written chapters that outline his distinguished career. The 'Vuno' sees greater value in his time in the game than goals scored and trophies won. *'I've learnt a lot about the complexities of people and personalities, and some important principles about how to deal with them. My soccer career was all on my terms, all about my goals, and was helped along with a great deal of good luck. I have travelled the world and experienced so many things. I have captained Australia in some good and some bad times, and on the occasion when I look back into the closed chapters, I don't regret a single thing.'*

Fair enough, too.

Ange POSTECOGLOU

Socceroo 1986–1986

'It wasn't cool to be Greek when I was at school. It wasn't cool to play soccer either. In fact, I didn't want to be Greek at the time; I wanted to be an "Aussie". I realise now that I was being an Aussie. We all were.'

Ange Postecoglou came to Australia with his family in 1970. He was just five years old and doesn't have many memories of the five-week boat trip. All he knew was that he was going to a new life. 'My parents decided that it would be a good idea to move from their village in Greece in search of opportunities in Canada, America or Australia. They decided on Australia, but the unusual thing was that we didn't know anyone out here and didn't travel with anyone but Mum, Dad, my sister and I. Usually, extended families went to join the rest of the family who were already there. We were sponsored by a family friend though, and slipped straight into the large Greek community.'

The Postecoglous settled in the Melbourne suburb of Prahran. They didn't speak a word of English, but it wasn't as big a problem as one might think, because of the tightknit community with which they surrounded themselves. The kids adapted more quickly. 'We spoke Greek at home and English at school. I guess we all got by, but I soon got sick of being a translator for my parents all the time. It's the last thing a kid wants.'

While Ange and many of his Greek-born school friends harboured ambitions to shun their heritage and be accepted by the wider Australian community, the lure of soccer ensured they still remained 'outsiders'. 'Our soccer team at Prahran High was pretty good – we won the State Championships one year and started to break down some social barriers, too. It was actually my first introduction to coaching as well, because none of the teachers wanted to take soccer and the one that was landed with it knew nothing about the game, so I

began to lead the way. Another indication of our standing was that the uniform we wore was the previous year's woollen, sleeveless footy jumpers. Tight footy shorts, too.'

It was from within this Greek community, however, that young Ange was introduced to his beloved South Melbourne Soccer Club. 'The Greek community would all go out to watch South Melbourne play. They used to wear suits, ties and caps to games. It was a day out and a great social occasion. I do remember there being big crowds – but that might have been just because I was small!'

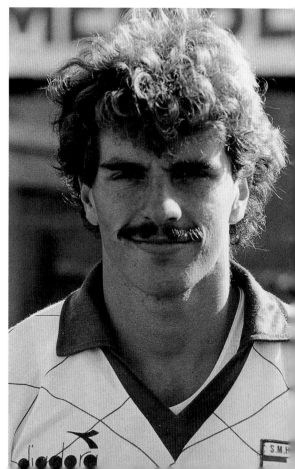

Footy top and Supernaut record,
an elite career was under way!

'**It wasn't cool** to be Greek **when I was at school.**'

Ange is one of the rare players who spent his entire career playing for one club. He started at South Melbourne with the Under-10s and made his senior debut as a 17-year-old in 1984 (a championship year for the club). '*My first senior game was against Sydney City at home. It was the game where [Socceroo] Alan Davidson swallowed his tongue and couldn't breathe – not long before he left to play for Forest. Someone in the crowd jumped the fence to help him. I was the bloke who came on to replace him. It wasn't too serious in the end, but it was pretty scary, and not the debut I had planned. You take your luck where you can find it, I guess.*' Ange's last game as a player was in 1993 after accumulating over 200 games for the club.

The 1984 Hellas team contained nine Socceroo internationals and proved a fantastic learning ground for the enthusiastic Postecoglou. '*There were so many good players at the club and at times I couldn't believe I was playing with them. Most of them were ex-pats from Britain and even though it was a Greek-backed club, by then I was the only player of Greek heritage.*'

His first national team experience was a year later in 1985 when he was the 'lucky last' player picked to play in the Australian team for the 1985 Youth World Cup in Russia. In a story he regularly recounts to his young charges when he selects the Joey and Young Socceroo squads in his role as

National Youth Teams coach these days, Ange illustrates the sensitivities and humility that are the hallmarks of top-level coaches. '*I was the last guy picked for the Youth World Cup and I was over the moon. The trouble was, when I was coming back from the camp, I was sitting on the plane next to a guy who didn't make the squad. He missed out and he was devastated. Of course, it tempered my excitement and made me feel quite uncomfortable. I remember wondering at the time what would become of the player and whether he would stick with it. It turned out that while I only played four times for the senior national team, the guy sitting next to me ended up playing more Socceroo games than anyone else in history, including many as captain. His name was Alex Tobin.*'

Ange made his full senior debut as a 20-year-old in 1986, and while he was obviously proud, playing for his country was not his main driving force at the time. '*My main ambition from when I was young was to play for South Melbourne. Perhaps it was because there was so many expats playing for Australia when I was growing up that the Socceroos didn't seem like a national team, or perhaps it was because soccer did not have the recognition and acceptance at a national level as it did among the various ethnic communities around the country. Or maybe it was because I had grown up with South Melbourne soccer and not so much*

Australian soccer. It is not that I didn't want to play for Australia, but whatever indifference I felt soon evaporated once I got involved.'

Ange made his debut against Czechoslovakia under the guidance of Frank Arok at Melbourne's Olympic Park. '*The whole thing was surreal. It wasn't until later that I realised how much it meant to me, because at the time everything happened so quickly and I was just concentrating on not doing anything wrong from the time the*

Champions 1990–91. Captain Postecoglou with the trophy and one of the biggest influences in his career – then-South coach and Hungarian legend, Ferenc Puskas.

team met through to the end of the match. Even when we were on the bus leaving the ground, I was waiting for someone to grab me by the collar and kick me off because they finally realised I shouldn't be there.'

One of the disappointments in Ange's career is that he did not make more than four appearances in a Socceroo shirt. *'I was in plenty of training squads, but regularly just missed out. I played two games against Czechoslovakia and two against New Zealand. I have loved every second of the Socceroo squads I've been involved with, but the feeling of satisfaction and pride was magnified during the matches I actually played. I knew at the time it was a huge honour, but I recognise it even more now. I injured my knee when I was just twenty-six and that ended my playing career at NSL and national level.'*

Injury is unfortunately a constant, unwelcome shadow in every athlete's career. Knees and ankles are soft spots for soccer players, and when Ange's knee finally gave

way, after progressive degeneration weakened the joint, he knew his time at the top was over. He attempted to play in the lower leagues for a short time before he decided to stop playing altogether. So began the coaching career of this mature, thoughtful player, and a new passion arose like a Phoenix from the ashes. *'Perhaps the injury was a blessing in disguise. I hit a real low when I realised what it meant, but then decided to get off my arse and make the most of it.'*

Make the most of it he did. At twenty-six he was coaching Western Suburbs in the Victorian State League. At twenty-seven, he returned to his beloved South Melbourne to become assistant to Frank Arok. At thirty, he became the senior coach of South Melbourne. Just two years later, in 1998, he led the club to championship glory, then backed it up in 1999 and took the club to the World Club Championships in Brazil. Upon his return, he was asked to apply for the vacant Socceroo coach position. *'I was honoured to be asked and the idea of being*

involved with the Socceroos again was exciting, but I was not that confident of assuming the role with my limited, albeit intense, coaching experience.'

Ultimately, Frank Farina was offered the senior job and Ange was offered the National Youth Teams coaching job. Both accepted and neither have looked back. *'The more I am involved with the Socceroos at senior and junior level, the more passionate I become. Frank, assistant senior coach Graham Arnold and I all have a driving ambition and passion to leave a mark on the game with our current roles. From a selfish point of view, it also provides me with the opportunity to still be involved with World Cups and big games, and I still get to wear the Australian tracksuit even if not the Australian shirt.'*

The role of National Youth Teams coach exposes Ange to the vast array of Australian talent from various backgrounds. *'The Greek community sometimes thinks that I should be doing more for the Greek kids, but I don't see the players like that. I see them as kids who can play for Australia, whatever their background. What does interest and intrigue me, however, is that kids who come from various backgrounds – even if they are born here and have had all their training here – often display traits of their ethnic heritage's playing style. What I can't wait to see is when Australian teams have their own signature. The best attributes* of the styles from all over the world. We're not there yet, but we are heading in that direction. And when we get there, look out!'

As the number of Asian and African immigrants making Australia their home increases, another dimension may be added to 'Australia's signature'. *'There aren't any players of Asian or African background in my teams at the moment, but it won't be long before there will be. Within the foreseeable future, I can't see why Asian and African communities won't be represented in the Socceroo squads as well.'*

As the proliferation of communication and ease of travel continues to make the world smaller, the future generation of players has an increasingly world-wide perspective. It's a double-edged sword for Aussie soccer. *'When the kids are asked to write down their ambitions in soccer, the overwhelming majority want to play overseas. Of course, they also see that as a stepping stone to playing for Australia, but I work to see that situation reversed. If they are playing for Australia then a career overseas with big money will take care of itself, and a positive cycle will be in place for them and for the Socceroos. It is almost the reverse situation to the sixties and seventies, where people came from overseas and rapidly developed the game and the history of the Socceroos. These days, the Aussie players are that good that they are going over there to take the Australian game back to them. The experience they are getting is also good for the national teams and that is still the priority. Our progress to international acceptance is well under way.'*

Ange is a believer that, after decades of battling, acceptance within the Australian community is also increasing. *'The game is a lot more obvious now at the top level than it has ever been. There are massive crowds at big games and a general understanding through the Australian community that soccer is the game of the world and that Australians are pretty damn good at it. These days it is cool to play soccer and these days it seems a lot cooler to be from an ethnic background. The world is getting smaller and the more people see the international impact of soccer, the greater foothold the game will continue to have in this country.'*

•••

Ange's Under-20s national team recently qualified for the World Youth Cup being held in the United Arab Emirates. Due to the war in Iraq, the Cup was postponed. Ange may passionately organise every small detail of his coaching plans for Australia's future stars, but some things are beyond the control of even the most motivated of national coaches. The world game indeed.

Happy times at South Melbourne.

Frank FARINA OAM

Socceroo 1984–1995

As coach of the Socceroos in the modern era, Frank Farina has at his disposal a collection of players of the highest pedigree, playing in leagues from across the world. It presents a set of logistical and management issues most other Socceroo coaches haven't had to endure, but it is also an indication of Australia's growing reputation as an exporter of world-class players.

Much of the early development of those top-class Aussies playing overseas can be attributed to the state-based programs and national championships run by the national Associations. There is an army of talent scouts scouring the countryside to find the best young players and help them along their way to stardom. As national coach, Frank Farina sits atop that coaching and development structure and moulds them into the finished Socceroo product. However, his own journey to the top as a player proves that it is not just the beaten path of elite junior programs that can turn a soccer player into a Socceroo.

Frank was born in Darwin in 1964. In 1965, his father's work took the family to Papua New Guinea. Just before Frank's tenth birthday the family moved back to Australia to escape growing tensions as Papua New Guinea gained independence. The family home became Cairns, which in 1974 was a far cry from the tourist heartland it is today.

'The big thing for us in New Guinea was going to the cinema after a game on a Saturday. No one had TVs and it was a big deal. It was strange going through a country's independence, and not something many people experience. We used to use Australian dollars and had all the Aussie heroes like [cricketers] Thommo and Lillie. Then the government changed, the money changed and a lot of the work was given to local business instead of the expat families and foreign investment. It became easier for families like ours to move back to Australia rather than stay, and that's what we did.

'After independence there were periods of martial law where you couldn't be on the streets after nine o'clock at night. It became quite a dangerous place, particularly around the time when Dad went back in 1977–78. He used to carry a gun in his car, after he had been held up once or twice. Early on, kids would wear kinas (local currency that had a hole in it) around their necks to school. At times I would wear thirty bucks around my neck, never thinking that I could easily get mugged for it.

'We did play soccer there, but most of the guys didn't wear boots. It was gym shoes or bare feet. It was a popular sport up there though, and very social. It wasn't until I moved to Cairns that I started playing a bit more seriously and ended up joining a club.'

Three years after moving to Cairns, Frank's parents split up. His mother moved to Darwin and his father returned to Papua New Guinea, so Frank's brothers and sisters went to boarding school. The mother of a friend in his soccer team suggested the 13-year-old should stay with them for four months to see out the school year. Four months quickly turned into three years.

Frank became independent during this period and developed a strong will and his trademark larrikin streak. He grew his hair because he wasn't supposed to and teetered on the edge of serious trouble. 'Teachers often thought I should have been going through a tough time in my teens, and I took advantage of the sympathy. It could've been a traumatic time for me, but really I was fine. I do remember Brother Peter at the Marist Brothers School in Cairns sitting me down after I'd got in some trouble and telling me to concentrate on what career path I was going to take. He told me there was no money in sport and no future in it. I wasn't thinking about a career path in sport then either, but I just loved it too much to stop. I still have a bit of a giggle about that when I look back on that and think of the career I've had.'

By the time Frank was sixteen, he was living in a house his dad had bought and was sharing the rent with a woman who had answered an ad in the local paper. He was

Plotting Our Socceroos' future.

'He told me there was **no money in sport** **and no future in it.**'

still playing soccer for love rather than as a career choice, but it was at this time that he got his first pay cheque as a sportsman.

'By then, I was in the Far North Queensland Schoolboys team, which, while a long way from the Queensland state team, was still a big deal for us. The two coaches played seniors for a state league side called

Mareeba and they suggested that I play for them. I used to go up to training in the back of their ute and one day they signed me on. I played for twenty minutes in the game the next week, then at the next training session – I'll never forget it – the boss came around and handed out envelopes. I opened mine up and there was thirty bucks in it. I said, "What's this for?" They told me there'd be

more if we won. I was freezing my arse off in the back of the ute on the way back, but I didn't care, because I was on top of the world. I ended up buying a rug for the house with it.'

'...there were 110,000 for the opening game of the Youth World Cup. The stadium is like a giant beehive and the noise was incredible.'

It was during a regional Schoolboys series that Ronny Smith, Assistant Coach at the AIS, initially asked Frank if he wanted to go to Brisbane and be a guinea pig for an AIS coaching course. *'It certainly wasn't a trial program for any players – it was all being done to help develop coaches.'* Frank figured he might as well go, and it is a good thing for Australia he did. During the course, his talent impressed the AIS coaching staff and he was asked to join the AIS in Canberra. *'I remember when Jimmy Shoulder asked me if I wanted to be a part of the AIS program. I said yes straightaway and knew at the time that it was pretty amazing that I'd been asked under those circumstances, even though I didn't really know what it all meant. When I rang Dad, the conversation went:*

> *"Where will you live?"*
> *"Don't know."*
> *"Do you still go to school?"*
> *"Don't know."*
> *"How long will you be there?"*
> *"Don't know."'*

Jimmy Shoulder persuaded Paolo Farina it was a good idea, though, and at the end of year eleven, Frank jumped in his old man's Sigma (which he had left for Frank when he went back to PNG) with his friend Ray Junna and made the journey to Canberra's 'big smoke'. From there, the real journey began.

'I knew school was important, but this was a great opportunity. We still went to school down there as a part of the program, but the focus was soccer. Everybody knew each other from National Championships, but I was a nobody when we got there and only knew Ray. We used to play up a bit but it was great being around so many athletes from so many sports, and I began to think from there that I wanted to make a career from the game.'

Partway through 1982, the National Championships were held and the players from the AIS program went home for training camps. Except Frank. *'I wasn't in the Queensland team, so I asked the AIS coaches what I should do for the week. Ronny Smith rang the Queensland coach to let him know he had another player at the AIS. The coach reluctantly agreed to let me train with them, but he couldn't say I'd play. In the end, the first-choice striker rolled his ankle and I was in. I ended up top scorer for the tournament and Queensland won.'*

In 1983, Frank left the AIS and joined the Canberra Arrows in the national league. *'It was just before the Youth World Cup. I scored on debut, then got injured in the second game. I was rushed back to fitness to make the trip to Mexico but wasn't at my best over there.'*

Things developed quickly from there and by the time qualification came around for the 1983 Youth World Cup in Mexico,

Frank was in the squad. A bonus was that the initial qualifying games were in Papua New Guinea and he was able to see his father for the first time in years. The Young Socceroos made it through after the second qualifying stage in Costa Rica, and Frank was about to experience one of the most memorable games in his entire career.

'Our first game in the Mexico finals was against Mexico in the Azteca Stadium. The biggest crowd I'd played in front of before then was 20,000 or so in Costa Rica for the qualifiers . . . but there were 110,000 for the opening game of the Youth World Cup. The stadium is like a giant beehive and the noise was incredible. We were battered, really, but we managed a 1–1 draw. I scored our goal and the deafening noise for most of the game turned into complete silence. It was bizarre, but it still remains one of my strongest memories.'

There was an even more bizarre incident leading up to the game. *'Going to the ground we were stuck in traffic that was made worse by a protest going on at the same time. The police escort basically told us we couldn't go any further, so we all got out, grabbed some gear and jogged the couple of kilometres to the stadium. When we got there, the security guards wouldn't let us in. The kick-off had already been delayed and [assistant coach] Raul Blanco spoke to them in Spanish and let them know we were the game and without us, there*

would be a riot. Two hours after leaving the hotel we finally got in and started preparations.'

While this tournament was being played, the senior Socceroos were playing a series of games against England in Australia. The Socceroo coach at the time was Les Scheinflug, and he decided that it was more important for him to go to the Youth World Cup instead. Frank Arok took charge of the Socceroos in his absence – a move that became permanent after a final disagreement between outspoken Soccer Federation President, Sir Arthur George, and Scheinflug while in Mexico. Frank Arok took charge of the Socceroos for a number of years from that point and was the man who made Frank Farina a Socceroo. *'I came back [from Mexico] and settled into the NSL well . . . and in 1984 I got a telegram to say I was in the Australia "A" squad to play a tournament against some touring international clubs. I had to go to the post office to get the telegram – I don't know why they didn't just call – but I couldn't believe it. I was nineteen and I was going to play for the Socceroos.'*

Frank played a couple of games off the bench in that tournament, then was selected for a world tour in late 1984. He was away for eight weeks and played a lot of games. He also met his grandparents for the first time when the tour took in Italy, and it was during this trip that his desire to play overseas began to take hold. By the time the Socceroos returned, Frank was maturing into a very dangerous attacking player and he made his first big move by joining Sydney City in 1985.

'Sydney City was the club that everyone loved to hate. We were successful and the club was very professional. I was already very competitive as a person, but Sydney City gave me the winning mentality and really toughened me up. There were nine internationals there before I joined and Eddie Thomson was coach. The standard of the NSL was pretty high back then, because all the best players were here. We are exporters of talent now, but back then things were different.'

The 1986 World Cup qualifying preparation began with a tournament against club sides in 1985, as well as a series against China. The actual qualifiers were against New Zealand, Israel and Taiwan. The next hurdle was Scotland and it proved too great for the Socceroos. 'We lost 2–0 in Glasgow, but it could've been more. We then drew 0–0 at Olympic Park in Melbourne, though we had our chances to win the game. I was a fringe player at that time, but I was still shattered. The team was like an extended family and we spent a lot of time together. We might not have been the best of teams throughout the 1980s, but the closeness and understanding got us through a lot of games.'

Farina's mullet and muscles, playing with Club Brugge in Belgium season 1989–90.

By 1987, one of the many stories of financial ruin in the NSL's history was unfolding at Sydney City. When the writing was on the wall for the club, Frank accepted an offer to move to another powerful club in Australia – Marconi. He would stay for two seasons and accumulate an NSL Championship, two Player of the Year awards, two Top Goalscorer awards and the 1988 Oceania Player of the Year title. His Italian heritage and explosive performances quickly won over the fans and officials of the large Italian community club, and Frank was flying. *'The transfer fee was $30,000 for Marconi and I was getting $45,000 in wages, which was pretty good at the time. I was playing well and the Italian community really accepted me. After my first year there I actually signed a contract worth $400,000 with Dutch club Roda JC, but it fell through. In some ways I am glad it did because I could concentrate on the Bicentennial Gold Cup, Olympics and getting more experience with Marconi.'*

The 1988 Bicentennial Gold Cup was a success for the Socceroos (including a 4–1 win against world champion Argentina) and the preparations for the Olympics were on track. Frank became one of the stars, however the qualifying series was the beginning of his frustration with Frank Arok's management methods. His frustration would grow steadily as the years passed. *'If you aren't playing well, you shouldn't have to ask why you have been dropped. When you are playing well and there are no explanations, you start to wonder what's going on.'*

The Olympic team had a great 1–0 win over Yugoslavia, were thumped 3–0 by Brazil, beat Nigeria 1–0 (minus Farina) then lost 3–0 to eventual Gold Medallists, Russia. *'It was the first time we had qualified for the Olympics. We were there as hosts in 1956, but this was a big deal. It was great to be among so many great athletes from around the world – even though the uniforms we had were horrible. The soccer team began to get a reputation for enjoying a party while in Korea, and it's true. We really enjoyed the experience and would often go to other sports as a group and cheer the Aussies on.'*

In the late 1980s, the only Socceroos playing overseas were Eddie Krncevic, Jimmy Patikas, David Mitchell and Chris Kalantzis. Craig Johnston and Tony Dorrigo were successful in England, but decided not to play for Australia in order to secure their club careers. Playing in Europe was not commonly discussed among the players in the NSL at that time, but Frank knew that's what he wanted to do. The 1988 Olympics helped his cause and a number of clubs began chasing his signature. *'Israel Maoz had become my agent and the offer he had that interested me most was from Club Brugge in Belgium. I went over for some trials, but tore my quad after a few days.*

I was really enjoying the club in that short time, but thought it was all over after that. Then, [Brugge Manager] Henk Houwaart came to the hotel and said the club had a contract for me to sign. I was over the moon. We went to see the President and I said yes to him before I had even seen the terms.'

Frank's quick response and enthusiasm immediately endeared him to the President, but his first game for the club was not so auspicious. *'My debut was in the Cup against a second division side, and unfortunately I got sent off for elbowing the thug who was marking me. I didn't mean it, but I was obviously very disappointed. The coach was good about it though and said he was happy to see some aggression. He was worried I might be too quiet!'*

Frank had joined the Belgian superclub halfway through the 1988–89 campaign. He played a number of games in the league, but at the end of the year a new coach was appointed who made it clear that Frank wasn't in his plans. Each club could only have six foreigners on their books, and name three for any one match. Frank could stay, but only as the fourth foreigner. While appreciating his new boss's honesty and enjoying his surroundings in Brugge, he considered leaving. *'In the end, I decided to stay and fight for a spot throughout pre-season. [The new coach] George would make me warm up for forty minutes at times*

during games, and then not put me on, and it got to me. One time I just said no and sat back down on the bench and he ripped into me. I told him where to go and we were toe-to-toe on the sidelines. I began to walk off, but he grabbed the back of my shirt and told me I was going on. I did well and began to play more regularly from there. Later he told me he liked my attitude.'

The 1989–90 season started poorly for Brugge, but they came back to win the league title. Frank began playing regularly, and won over the Brugge supporters when he finished the season as top scorer in Belgium and was voted by the media as the best foreign player. It was also a time when the club versus country debate, which currently consumes much of his time as Socceroo coach, began in earnest. In fact, it was a new era in the dynamic of the Socceroos. *'In the 1986 World Cup campaign, Dave Mitchell was the only overseas-based player. By the 1990 campaign there were a few of us and the luxury of team building was gone for Frank Arok. There was some unspoken resentment from the local-based players of the foreigners who only came back for the bigger games, and it wasn't managed particularly well. We lost to New Zealand, then drew with Israel and we were out.'*

It signalled the end for Arok and he was replaced by Farina's old Sydney City coach, Eddie Thomson. Even so, Frank did not play another game for Australia until the 1994 World Cup qualifying campaign in 1993. His bread and butter was in the cut-throat leagues of Europe and he couldn't just leave whenever he wanted. The Australian media and establishment frowned on such an attitude, but the fact is Eddie Thomson understood the predicament of the increasing number of Australian stars playing overseas – and they weren't asked back for small games. As Socceroo coach these days, Frank needs to go to Europe to play international games because his whole first-choice squad is there. The metamorphosis is complete.

At the end of the 1990–91 season, after some stellar years in Belgium, the knockabout Aussie kid transferred to Bari in Italy for $3 million and wages of $900,000. He would become the first Australian to play in the Serie A, but it was not the dream he had imagined. *'I was on a hospital bed in Brugge having knee surgery and feeling a bit down when Bari gave me a big offer. The lure of playing in Serie A and earning big money was strong and, a bit rashly, I agreed. I hadn't even been to Bari and that was my first mistake. I played the first five games, but we weren't doing well and they sacked the coach. The new coach brought a new foreigner, and in Italy you were only allowed three on your books. I had to make way and couldn't play. It was a tough time.'*

‘The lure of playing in Serie A and earning big money was strong…’

Sheffield Wednesday in England wanted to sign Frank, however the deal fell through and that signified the end of his relationship with Israel Maoz. Bari were still paying his wages, so Frank and his wife Julie decided to go back to Brugge where they felt comfortable and were among friends. Ultimately, he ended up playing five games in the English first division on loan to Notts County that year but was released when it was clear the club couldn't avoid relegation. He and Julie went back to their rented apartment in Brugge where Frank's professional disappointment was eclipsed by the birth of their first child.

•••

His new agent, Vladimir Pavcovic, was recommended to him by Eddie Krncevic – who helped Frank settle when he first arrived in Belgium. Vladimir asked Frank what he wanted to earn, then came back to him with a club in the French first division. *'I joined Strasbourg in the 1992–93 season. I injured my ankle in training just before the first game, though, when the massive lug of a reserve 'keeper fell on me. I struggled to get over it all year and didn't have the best of times on the ground. I came back to Australia for the World Cup qualifiers in '93 and made the injury worse, which didn't make me the most popular guy at the club when I got back. As far as they were concerned, Strasbourg were paying me good money and I should've been fit for them.'*

Frank returned for the World Cup qualifiers which once again ended in heartache for the Socceroos, when they were beaten by Argentina at the final hurdle. Frank was suspended for the first leg in Sydney, but played in the Argentinean cauldron in Buenos Aires. *'After three attempts and three near misses, I knew that it was my last chance to play in a World Cup. I retired after that game to give the young guys a chance, because I knew I wouldn't be around for the 1998 campaign. It was very sad for me.'*

Not long after he returned to Strasbourg, a new coach came in and Frank departed by mutual agreement. He had one year left on his lucrative contract and could've stayed getting minimal game time while earning good money, but he wanted to play. That's when Lille stepped in. They were another club in the French first division and while they were offering less money, Frank was keen for a change. Part of his agreement with the club was that Frank could be a free agent at the end of the 1994–95 season, resulting in a very handy negotiating position for future contracts. *'Lille was a great place for our young family to live. We enjoyed our time there, but for the first time I began to lose passion for the game. It was becoming a job.'*

Soccer Australia had begun to realise the drawing power of its overseas-based stars and decided to lure Frank out of international retirement in 1995 for a game against Ghana. Frank had been outspoken about a number of national team issues in his years as a Socceroo and had become disillusioned with Soccer Australia. He appreciated their gesture to give him a testimonial, though, and agreed to come back and take his Socceroo appearances to seventy. It gave him a chance to take a bow before the Australian public, but ironically, it was more of a welcome back than a farewell. *'I had been thinking about coming back to Australia and giving something back to the game here. It wasn't about the money, I just thought it might be time to come home. In saying that, before I left Europe to come back for the Ghana game, my agent was trying to sort out a new contract for me. He rang me when I was in Australia to tell me he had got what I had wanted with a new club . . . but I told him sorry, a few people in Australia had fired me up and I was going to stay and play for the Brisbane Strikers. Initially Julie wanted to stay in Lille or Brugge, but we had two young kids by then and coming back to Queensland was a good thing. People in Europe thought I was mad, but I was excited about it.'*

Once again, the Australian public was able to see Frank Farina back in the national league. He played with renewed enthusiasm and was glad to be home. The club did quite well that year, but still decided to sack the coach. Frank was as surprised as anyone

'After three attempts and three near misses, I knew it was my last chance to play in a World Cup.'

when they then asked if he would be player–coach for the 1996–97 season. The next door in his footballing life had opened. *'I was unsure at first and had to think about it. Ultimately, I'm very glad I took it. We won the championship that year and had 40,000 people at the grand final in Brisbane. There was a great build-up to the game that lasted for weeks. I really felt that soccer had arrived in Queensland and winning this game was one of the best moments in my career.'*

If 1996–97 was a party, then 1997–98 was the hangover. The club sold many of its quality players from under Frank's nose and struggled to be competitive. In 1998 he was offered the job of coaching Marconi and he returned to his old club to take charge for the 1998–99 season.

Then, in 1999, Soccer Australia began interviewing for the job of national coach. The huge expense of employing the internationally renowned Terry Venables for the failed 1998 World Cup campaign had taken its toll, so the focus had turned to employing a young, local talent for the role. Frank Farina was the chosen one. *'I was asked to apply, and I got the job in September 1999. I was honoured and excited and I have a driving ambition to be successful for the Socceroos.*

'The job is largely about managing players, which is sometimes difficult when they are all over the world. I am not in regular contact with them and I don't aim to make friends with them. I have to keep some distance because, in the end, I am their boss not their friend.'

Frank's ambition and strong will is as evident in the Socceroo coaching jacket as when he wore the playing strip. *'Everybody has opinions and it is one of the great things about this game. I can handle differences of opinion and as long as my personal life and family are kept out of it, I am glad people want to discuss the game. While I am in charge, though, I will do it my way. In my position, I am able to act on my opinions.'*

Frank Farina has a couple of nicknames in soccer circles. From the AIS, he picked up 'Fingerbone' or 'Bone', due to his apparent likeness to the character played by David Gulpilil in *Storm Boy*. Eddie Thomson named him 'Cranky Frankie' because of his short fuse and competitive nature. These days he is more likely to be known as 'Mr Farina', travelling the world as our national team's coach. He may never have dreamed of a lucrative career during his youth in Papua New Guinea and Far North Queensland, but that is where he has taken his life. He knows he will have a long future in the game, but his current planning doesn't go beyond taking the Socceroos to the 2006 World Cup finals. The rest can wait.

All action, versus Juventus in 1984.

Robbie SLATER

Socceroo 1984–1997

Robbie Slater was a European professional for eleven years. He won an English Premier League championship with Blackburn Rovers in 1995, collected two Oceania Player of the Year trophies in 1991 and 1993, and wore the Socceroo strip proudly for thirteen years. Each one of those achievements changed his life in some way, but it is the twists and turns along the way that made success possible.

'I guess there were some key moments in my career, but I didn't spend time stressing about them while they were happening. I can look back and spot them now, but I didn't really think about them then.

'I was born in England, near Liverpool, and came out to Australia in 1966 when I was about eighteen months old. Dad had a mate who emigrated to Australia and sent a postcard from Bondi saying how fantastic it was. We came out as £10 Poms like heaps of others, and my parents made a new home in a new country.'

It wasn't a bed of roses. The family was given accommodation in a migrant hostel in Sydney's west, a long way from Bondi's surf. The family had made some friends on the boat, but it wasn't enough. After six months, the Slaters went home. After six months back in Liverpool, they came back with renewed vigour – and this time they were here to stay. Robbie's appreciation of his parent's decision to become Australian was

patently obvious every time he pulled on the green and gold later in life.

Robbie enjoyed cricket and rugby league with his mates at Picnic Point, but soccer filled his time at home. 'My mates didn't even know I played soccer – right up until I was in the NSL and earning money while still at school. My brother is four years older, so he wasn't interested in playing with me either. It was the back wall of my house that kept me company. We all used to sit up and watch FA Cup finals at Wembley, and I would be wrapped up in a Liverpool scarf, hat and shirt sent over by relatives. Match of the Day was religious viewing every week, and I always dreamed of being a player in the introduction to that show.'

Robbie was an energetic, confident kid – some may have said he was a handful. But his personality lends itself to sport, and he

attacked every game with vigour – whether it was with Revesby Rovers as a kid, or with Blackburn Rovers winning an English championship. He wasn't deemed good enough to make any representative sides, though, and had to go to trials at Auburn SC to see if he could make their Under-14s team. He did (along with cricket legends Steve and Mark Waugh) and played the remainder of his junior days there.

At sixteen, Robbie began playing with Auburn's third-grade side. It was a team full of talented young players, but Robbie wasn't tagged for senior experience. Still, after the 1982 third-grade grand final, he got a visit from some St George Budapest officials on behalf of Frank Arok, coach of the NSL club. *'I didn't even know who St George was. I was more interested in Liverpool. Still, we went down to meet Frank Arok and I was impressed. We really didn't know what it all meant, though. I remember $500 being discussed as a signing-on fee and I was a bit downhearted – we couldn't really afford to pay them that. Then I was told, no, that is what he was going to pay me to join them. I would get wages on top of that as well, and even though it wouldn't break the bank, I was sixteen and I was loaded!'*

Third grade in the NSW State League to NSL powerhouse employee is a major leap in anyone's language – so Robbie bought an HT Holden to celebrate. The good news didn't stop there, either. *'Dad thought I would spend a bit of time in the St George youth team, but Frank made a point of telling us that he did not sign players to play in the youth team. After six games of the 1982 season, he told me I was going to play first grade. I was still trying to get used to thinking I was good enough for the youth team [at St George], then I was going to make my debut against Marconi! I didn't play overly well, to be honest, and some of the crowd got on my back. Still, Frank persevered, and I managed to set up our second goal. That's the bit people remembered, and the Daily Mirror ran the headline "Star of the Future". I admit that I had the clipping on my wall for quite a while. It was from there that I thought I could make something of the game.'*

In 1983 Robbie was selected to play for the Young Socceroos side that toured Mexico in a dry run for the upcoming World Youth Cup championships. By now, school had taken a back seat but he still had to sit his final exams – in the Australian Consulate in Mexico. Even a sneaky phone call to mates who had already completed the exams in Australia (the benefit of time differences around the world) didn't help the end result for a guy more interested in soccer than study. Things went a little better on the field, but when the team returned, Robbie was dropped. *'I was one of only a few guys playing in the NSL and the only one dropped. I still don't know why. It was tough to take, but I got on with it and helped St George win the NSL that year.'*

'My mates didn't even know I played soccer.'

139

' Third crack at going overseas down the toilet. '

Robbie's parents loved football and loved their son. Now that school had finished and all Robbie was interested in was soccer, they figured it might as well be all or nothing. Either he had to get a job, or he had to get serious and play overseas. He was wasting his time in Australia. Robbie couldn't have agreed more.

Concurrently, the President of St George was entertaining a business partner in Australia who happened to be a Director of Nottingham Forest in England. He took the Director to a game, and the player who stood out was the red-haired kid with all the energy. As soon as the 1983 NSL title was won by St George, Robbie shot off to an English Midlands winter on Forest's invitation and he revelled in it. *'I loved being in the big club atmosphere. I was staying with the apprentices and youth team players, and even though I had to do the crappy jobs like cleaning boots and toilets, I loved the whole thing. I was scoring goals for fun in the youth team, and after a while they wanted to sign me. St George were asking for $30,000, though, and Forest said they only wanted me for free. I had to come home. My parents were fuming.'*

Reality kicked in. Robbie tried, and failed, to hold down a number of jobs while sticking his head down training hard. He was teetering on the edge of bitterness after falling from the heights he had reached, and

although he managed to negotiate better terms with St George for 1984, things weren't quite the same.

In 1984, Frank Arok coached Australia as well as St George. That should have been a good thing for Robbie, but he could only muster four representative appearances for Australia 'B' that year. In the next couple of years he was consistently left out of international reckoning, even though he was winning plenty of admirers in the national league. Increasingly disillusioned, he moved to Blacktown City in 1986 for a change of scenery, and hopefully a change in fortunes. That lasted only one fruitless year, before he moved on to Sydney Croatia.

By now he was twenty-three and could have quite easily drifted into the big pile of 'almost' players. His hunger to play overseas and represent his country was becoming more habit than desire but then entered Bernie Mandic – unknown, ambitious soccer lover, but now world-renowned soccer manager to the stars – to stoke the flames. *'Bernie came up . . . and said that he would like to work with me, and help me to become a better player. We ended up spending a lot of one-on-one time together improving my fitness and getting my head right. He got me to write down my goals in the game, and I ended up achieving all of them except one . . . to play in the World Cup finals. He got me focused again.'*

Bernie also organised a deal with Dinamo Zagreb, which ultimately fell through, but it was a period that re-energised Robbie and gave him renewed confidence. So much so, that his improving NSL performances led Vedran Rosic – ex-Hadjuk Split player and then-Sydney Croatia coach – to recommend his Aussie charge to the Yugoslav superclub. Robbie and Split agreed terms, and it looked like third time lucky for Robbie's overseas ambitions. As sometimes happens though, life got in the way.

'I announced my deal with Split at the '88 NSL awards, during my acceptance speech for Most Entertaining Player. Thing is, it was the first my girlfriend had heard of it, and she wasn't particularly happy. I also picked up an injury at the '88 Olympics that put me out of action for three months. Third crack at going overseas down the toilet.'

• • •

Robbie had rejoined the international fray for the 1988 Olympics, and was also a part of the shambolic loss to New Zealand in 1989 that ultimately left the Socceroos watching the 1990 World Cup on TV. A low point, yes, but a turning point as well. *'Eddie Krncevic was playing for Anderlecht in Belgium and, in my eyes, was a superstar. I talked to him about wanting to play in Europe during a Socceroo camp, and how my previous three attempts had failed. He asked if I had a tape of me in action – which*

I didn't. He told me to get one and that he'd show it to a few people. I did, and a week or so later I got a call from his agent [Vladimir Pavkovic] saying he'd get me a club. Within two months Sydney Croatia had an offer on the table of $100,000 from Anderlecht and I was on my way.'

So, after years of frustration, Robbie finally became a European professional. At twenty-four, his ambitions were realised – almost too easily compared to his previous troubles. The excitement left him sleepless for days. Soon though, the harsh realities of professional football life deflated his enthusiasm. He made a grand total of zero first team appearances for Anderlecht that year, and was lucky to be kept on the books at all after an impulsive decision to come home over Christmas and not return until a month later. *'My girlfriend decided she didn't want to come over and join me, so I thought I'd better go back and sort everything out. I told the club I had to sort out some tax issues. I stayed in Australia far too long, and I was lucky to have a job when I got back, really.'*

The glamour which filled his childhood dreams about being a professional footballer didn't reflect his life in Belgium. He was living in a pokey flat that required more than a serious spring clean. It backed directly onto a major railway line, and the old chandelier clung wearily to the creaky ceiling every time a train rattled by. There was a dusty, old television blurting out shows in Flemish to keep him company, and usually a six-pack of beer and some earplugs to help him sleep. Something had to change.

So, after a forgettable first year in Europe, Robbie was looking forward to a holiday on the glorious Croatian coast with his visiting girlfriend and Eddie Krncevic's family. At the same time, his agent had been working behind the scenes and organised a trial with Lens, a team in a small mining town in the North of France, in the French second division. Robbie had never heard of them, and certainly didn't want to cut his holiday short to trial there. That is, until a senior pro at Anderlecht (Milan Jankovic), who befriended the young Aussie, force-fed him a dose of reality. *'There is very little difference between success and failure, and thankfully Milan made me listen . . . Everyone went on holidays to Croatia, including Milan, and I went with [my agent] Vladi to Lens.'*

Dusty streets, rubbish and mining slag heaps were their uninspiring companions as they entered the town. *'I had been really down over the last six months and I remember asking Vladi if he was trying to finish me off! Then we approached the*

'There is very little **difference** between **success** and **failure**...'

'I took the place to heart, and it was reflected in my performances.'

stadium and it was brilliant. It was massive and new, and my attitude changed completely. When we walked in, I knew I was going to play there. The trial game was on an outside pitch, and about 5,000 people still turned up. Afterwards, the Chairman said, "I will speak to your manager. You will play here." It was the only English he ever spoke to me.'

Robbie made a belated appearance at his Croatian holiday, but didn't want to rest. For the first time in a long time, his trademark enthusiasm was bursting at the seams. Within a few days he got the call he was waiting for, so he borrowed Milan's Mercedes and drove for twenty-eight hours straight to sign for his new club. The episode snapped his priorities into perspective and signified the end of a tumultuous relationship with his long-term Australian girlfriend.

'Lens benefited from the years of pent-up determination and desire. I was grateful for the chance, and I was flying. We were training twice a day and I loved it. I used to do extra training in the carpark of the hotel as well. The people were fantastic and quickly became like an extended family.'

The club was coming last after twelve games in the first year, and pressure was building. Robbie had not learnt enough French by then to fully comprehend the newspapers, but seeing your club at the foot of the ladder is pretty clear in any language. From game thirteen onwards, though, Lens could do no wrong and made the playoffs – only to miss out due to a loss in the final game of the series. Still, the club was satisfied and sent the players off to Morocco for a holiday. 'We were all shattered, but we were about to get some good news. There had been some financial irregularities in the French game, and Nice were dropped from the first division in the wash-up. We were the next best-placed team so we took their place. A good year turned into a great year, and the holiday turned into a massive party.'

By this stage Robbie was working hard to pick up the language, earning significantly more money than in Belgium, winning the affections of the fans and driving his first Porsche. This was more like it. 'Lens are a big club and the fans are nuts. There are 35,000 people in the town, but the ground regularly fills its 55,000 capacity. I took the place to heart, and it was reflected in my performances.'

It wasn't just the club and town Robbie took to heart. In April 1993, he married Nathalie, who was born and bred in the area. Her father was one of the few non-soccer fans in the town, but Robbie eventually won the family over. Their wedding was overrun by Lens fans, so Robbie threw on a keg in the carpark for the uninvited guests and the party continued inside and out.

No wonder the Lens fans loved him!

'...but then there's the
English Premier League.'

A couple of months later, in late October 1993, Australia's final hurdle to qualify for the 1994 World Cup was a home-and-away fixture against Argentina, with a returning Diego Maradona set to play. The first game was in Sydney, and Robbie was outstanding in a 1–1 draw. In fact, Maradona was moved to invite Robbie into the Argentinean change rooms and give him his shirt. A few favourable comments to the press by the footballing God soon reverberated around the world. The return leg was always going to be an uphill battle in the Buenos Aires cauldron, and a courageous Socceroo outfit was unlucky to go down 1–0. Once again Robbie was a standout in the Australian side, and once more Maradona sung his praises.

'It was obviously very disappointing to be knocked out, but we did so well against one of the best teams in the world. The Sydney game in particular was one of those rare moments when things seemed so surreal. Like time wasn't there. The kid from Picnic Point playing against Maradona's Argentina in Sydney. Although we ultimately lost, it was one of my greatest moments. Everyone wanted to know me after Maradona's comments. I was known as "El Colarado" [The Red] in South America.'

When Maradona spoke, the soccer world listened. The extra attention and Robbie's ongoing form at Lens meant that, when it became known his contract would expire at

Robbie 'El Colorado' Slater and Diego Armando Maradona.

> ' That championship is something
> # no one can take away from me,
> no matter what happens. '

the end of 1994, there was no shortage of suitors. Blackburn won the race and paid A$1.5 million for the red-haired flyer. After four successful seasons with Lens, it was with mixed emotions that he left. *'After I had signed for Blackburn in '94, I went to watch one final [Lens] game. The President said I could farewell the crowd, so before the match I had the chance to tell the fans what they meant to me – that I came to Lens with nothing, and left with everything. After the post-match function, I snuck down to the ground and said my own private goodbye. I still get chills thinking about it.*

'I was obviously happy at Lens, but then there's the English Premier League. I mean, I watched it when I was a kid. It was my dream. My boyhood hero, Kenny Dalglish, wanted to meet me [as manager] at Blackburn Rovers. Aston Villa were interested too, but Kenny was the difference. They had also just signed Alan Shearer, had done well the year before and were very ambitious. I couldn't not sign, really.'

Robbie's first game for Blackburn was in the Charity Shield against Manchester United. At twenty-nine years of age, his youthful fantasies were about to become a reality. *'It was the first time I'd ever seen Wembley other than on telly. I remember how much smaller it seemed in real life.'*

Blackburn lost 2–0, but Robbie was still proud to be able to walk up the famous Wembley steps. As he received his medal, he waved to his visiting parents in the stands as a gesture of thanks. And there was more. *'Not only did I play at Wembley, but Match of the Day used a snippet of footage from that game where I was tackling Ryan Giggs.'* An immediate rendition of the show's theme music by Robbie illustrated how symbolic, even now, that moment was for the young dreamer-made-good.

Blackburn went on to win the title that year (1994–95) proving that Robbie had joined a group of 'super-elite' players. *'It was a much more relaxed, old-school attitude in England than in France. Much more beer drinking and less attention to the finer points of diet. Still, the players were incredibly fit and incredibly competitive at all times. That championship is something no one can take away from me, no matter what happens. Not many people have had that privilege – but the hard work and patience paid off, and I became one of them.'*

Kenny Dalglish left Blackburn after the championship that year and things weren't the same. Robbie was made aware by the club that West Ham were interested in him for the 1995–96 season, and his experience

On the way to a premiership winners' medal with Blackburn, 1995.

'There is nothing better as a sportsman than to represent your country.'

told him he should consider it. *'Clubs don't tell you about offers if you are firmly in their plans, so when Blackburn told me West Ham were interested, I thought I'd make the most of it.'*

Robbie's one year as a Hammer in London was punctuated by some club versus country arguments (in which country always won) that made his employer a little hot under the collar. Another of his boyhood Liverpool idols, Graeme Souness, then began chasing his signature. Souness was managing Southampton, and it didn't take much persuasion to sign Robbie for the Saints. After a while, though, Dave Jones took the reins and it became clear that Robbie was not going to be first on his team sheet. Taking the bull by the horns, he accepted an offer to drop into Division One with Wolverhampton Wanderers. The move lasted one month.

Another Socceroo, Graham Arnold, had finished his European career slightly earlier than Robbie and returned to coach the fledgling Northern Spirit in the NSL. A 'team for mainstream Australia', the new organisation held high hopes. And so, it must be said, did Soccer Australia. *'Arnie rang and asked if I'd like to come back and play for him at Spirit. I told him to piss off. But he kept ringing, and the idea grew. After eleven years away, I was missing Australia a bit and while Nathalie wasn't very keen, I thought it would be good for the kids.'*

Arnie is one of Robbie's best friends, and he managed to wrangle Bulldog (as Robbie is known in Socceroo circles) out of the contract he had just signed at the Wolves in England, and bring him back on a significantly reduced income. Robbie was happy to be putting something back into the Australian game, but struggled to settle back into a country where soccer didn't equal life. Still, he captained the team in front of crowds of 12,000–15,000 throughout 1998. *'It was fantastic at Spirit early on, and everyone thought it was the start of something new for the game here. It's what kept me going. I even invested $250,000 into the club in the second year, but things dropped away pretty quickly after that, and I found out later that my money went straight to paying off debts.'*

Within a couple of years, Spirit was playing in front of small crowds, and was in serious financial trouble. *'I still believe the game has so much potential here, and while I lost $250,000 due to some ill advice, at least I put my money where my mouth is.'*

As Spirit's fortunes spiralled downwards, so did Robbie's enthusiasm. He had retired from the international scene in late 1997, and in 2001 decided to completely retire and chase his growing children around, instead of a ball. *'Family is such an important influence. Most players are tough to live with after a loss or bad performance, and I was certainly no different. The wives in particular put up with a lot and Nathalie has been great. Getting married puts things into perspective and, as I am sure any parent will agree, having kids is the best thing in life.'*

• • •

While it was Frank Arok who gave Robbie his break at club level, it was Eddie Thomson who really set Robbie's international career in motion. Arok's reluctance to use his St George star in many Socceroo fixtures was the cause of immense frustration in the 1980s, but when Thomson took over in the early 1990s it was a different story. Thomson organised training camps in Europe, and reassured the European-based

'The best and worst experience

as a Socceroo all wrapped up in one.'

players with a more liberal and understanding attitude. It was Thomson who gave Robbie his first 'A' start for Australia – amazingly, after sixteen other substitute or 'B' international performances in the green and gold. He was twenty-eight years of age, and the game was the 1993 World Cup qualifier against New Zealand. The Socceroos overcame the 'All-Whites' in that series, beat Canada in the next round of fixtures, then fell against Maradona's Argentina.

'Eddie was a huge influence on my career. He fired me up again and helped me feel incredibly passionate about playing for Australia. There is nothing better as a sportsman than to represent your country – and that feeling can give you the highest of highs and, unfortunately, the lowest of lows.'

The lowest of all lows was the 1997 World Cup campaign that ended in heartbreak when the Socceroos were disposed of by Iran. Australia was leading 2–0 with eleven minutes to go, when a spectator ran on to the field and tore down the net, causing lengthy delays. Robbie couldn't help but take a moment to reflect on the symbolic match and crowd. *'When that nugget tore down the net, I looked around [the Stadium] and said to Craig Moore, "How good is this!" We were killing them. Right from that rendition of the national anthem in front of 90,000 at the MCG, to being 2–0 up. It was one of the*

best moments in my life. Eleven minutes later there were grown men on the ground crying. The harshest thing is, we were on planes back to Europe the next day. You have to sit in solitude on the plane and deal with it in your own way. Fans can deal with it together, but the players have to go back to their clubs in a foreign country and play. In club football there is always next week, but that was my last chance to make a World Cup. The last thing to tick off on my goals list. The psychology of something like that isn't well handled by the clubs, and you can usually see a dip in form from the players involved when it happens. Especially after being knocked out like that. The best and worst experience as a Socceroo all wrapped up in one.'

Eddie Thomson's favourable attitude towards overseas-based players was refreshing for the growing number of players involved, but by the time Terry Venables had taken over for the 1997 games, it was a necessity. In Robbie's eyes, however, there were still sections of the soccer community who weren't as accepting. *'It always upset me when the European-based players were branded as being "less Australian" than the local players. It is such a load of rubbish –*

we are away from home doing what we can to improve ourselves and we have to leave family, friends and the country we love to do it. That's what our chosen career demands. Being involved in Socceroo squads gives us a slice of home, and we all love being together. Coming home to play matches is something very special, and to say that it doesn't mean as much to us is just plain wrong. The idea that at least the captain should be a home-based player is also ridiculous.'

●●●

Robbie is currently the anchor of Fox Sports' soccer show – and therefore holds down one of the few reasonably secure jobs in the Australian game. He has also set up a website to inform people about all things football – from home and abroad – and runs clinics for kids. While he doesn't discount the possibility of living in France once again, he will always remain a proud Australian. He is a fine example of how patience, determination and enthusiasm play such a vital role in sculpting a successful, professional sports career.

'How good is this!' Australia versus Iran at the MCG, 1997.

Milan IVANOVIC

Socceroo 1991–1998

When Milan Ivanovic finished his playing career at the top level in Yugoslavia, he figured he would play out his last few years as a professional in Australia. But, just like a team that's had a rousing address from an emotional coach, Milan got more out of the second half of his career than he could ever have imagined. He still shakes his head in disbelief when thinking about the second wind that enabled him to play international football across the globe. In fact, after playing against Australia four times with Red Star Belgrade in 1985, he went on to accumulate sixty 'A' international appearances for Australia, in what he considers a far more memorable half of his career. *'The feeling that I should come to Australia certainly paid off. My career was extended beyond what I could've imagined and I have had some great experiences. I celebrated my thirty-seventh birthday in Saudi Arabia with the Socceroos during the 1998 Confederations Cup. I was playing against Ronaldo of Brazil and Zidane of France years into what I thought would be my retirement. It is just fantastic. Unbelievable. Beautiful.'*

•••

Milan Ivanovic was born and grew up in Yugoslavia, in a golden era for the country. The 1960s and 1970s were a time of peace and ethnic harmony. There was soccer in the streets and, from Milan's perspective, people were happy. *'I had a good childhood. Sivac*

[my birthplace in Serbia] was a nice place and life was pretty easy.'

His time with a soccer ball was also pretty easy. There were, and still are, thousands of talented youngsters playing in Yugoslav streets and schools, however Milan was identified as one of the most talented on the rich production line. *'People in the area begin to know who can play that bit better than the others. Most of the time we played in the streets, but I also played for a school team and that is where I was officially spotted.'* From there, Milan played in what was the equivalent of Australia's National Titles for juniors, where he represented his state against others in Yugoslavia.

Since World War II, Yugoslavia's former states have gained independence as their own countries. *'After [World War II] finished in 1945, Yugoslavia was made up of six states: Croatia, Macedonia, Slovenia, Bosnia, Montenegro and Serbia . . . Yugoslavia stayed that way until around 1990, when some of the states wanted to be their own countries. That is when the fighting and other problems began, and in the end only Serbia and Montenegro were left as Yugoslavia.'* It was not until early in the new millennium that Yugoslavia ceased to exist on the soccer field. Serbia and Montenegro now compete as one in the old blue, white and red of Yugoslavia – in what is the only international team to have an 'and' in its name.

That said, Milan entered the junior system in the old Yugoslavia with Polet in 1974 – a lower division club near where he lived. It was the start of what seemed an effortless journey to the top. *'I was with Polet for two or three years and it was easy, to be honest. By 1978, I was in the Yugoslavian youth team without really knowing what was going on and without putting in any real effort. In the same year, I joined the senior side of a third division club [Crvenka] where there were crowds of a couple of thousand. I was still living at home and my life as a 17-year-old was pretty simple.'*

Although in a time of peace, Yugoslavia was one of many European countries that required its young men to complete compulsory army training. It didn't matter if you were a professional footballer, academic or doctor – before you were twenty-seven years of age, you had to spend thirteen months in army boots and combat fatigues. It may sound daunting, however Milan took it in his elegant stride. *'The idea, I guess, was to help boys become men. We did the training, but there was never really a thought of having to fight anyone. We didn't get paid anything, but it didn't cost us anything either. To be honest, it was quite a good time.*

'I chose to do my training when I was still young. You get the opportunity to choose when you would like to do it when

you are seen as a success at something, and I wanted to do it before I reached the peak of my career. Some players kept putting it off, then had to do it at, say, twenty-six, and they never quite got their career back. As it was, I was nineteen and played almost every day in the army anyway. Lots of small games with some good players.'

When Milan came out of the army, he joined another third division club and continued to get noticed. His spell away from organised football did him no harm and 1981 was another good year on the field. 'Again, it was still quite easy and I don't remember having to try very hard. Everything just fell into place and I guess it could've been that way for any number of good young players at the time.'

By 1982, the pressures of one of the most competitive domestic competitions in Europe came knocking. The first division club OFK Belgrade decided they wanted the talented 21-year-old, and he decided to go. He floated straight into the first team and, in time, onto more and more newspaper pages. 'OFK are the third-biggest club in Belgrade and with a great tradition. It is seen as basically a training ground for the two big clubs, Partisan and Red Star, and it has a lot of good, young players. We would have crowds of 15,000–20,000 and I really enjoyed it.'

The attention Milan began to receive by the end of 1983 included being touted for full international honours and being actively pursued by Belgrade's big two. His career was on fast forward, but things stopped being so simple. The ease of his youth was over. 'I was a Partisan supporter and people knew that. Of course I was thinking of joining them, however Red Star were very persuasive and kept at me. In the end, I joined Red Star and it caused a lot of tension. It made so much news and was more controversial than I expected. I began to feel the pressure and it was decided that, while I had officially become a Red Star player, I would have another season with OFK.'

'I don't **remember** having to **try** very hard.'

Relaxing in Adelaide.

'I was playing with some of the world's great players

at Red Star, and in big games in front of 80,000 and 100,000 people.'

So in 1984 the Red Star player turned out on loan for the club that had just sold him. He began to lose momentum a little, but was still one of the more accomplished defenders in the competition. The next year he began pre-season training with Red Star. The controversy of his decision to join them had now abated, he was ready for the big-time. *'I played in all the big games [in 1985] for what is one of Europe's bigger clubs – the derby [against Partisan] and the big league games, as well as the Champions League against the likes of Athletico Madrid. I liked the coach, the club was good to me and I should've been happy, but for some reason things didn't click. Maybe I should've just played for Red Star in 1984, and looking back I do regret staying with OFK for that extra year. Even though I was doing what most boys only dreamt of doing, something wasn't right.'*

In 1985 Milan had his first experience of Australia. Red Star came Down Under for two games in Sydney, and two in Melbourne. Milan remembers scoring at Olympic Park in Melbourne and also that he had a notion he would be back at some stage, though only for a holiday. *'We weren't in Australia for long, but the place had a good feeling to it, and while coming back wasn't something discussed by the players in general, I somehow knew I would at some point.'*

In 1986, Milan asked to leave Red Star and people were shocked. Perhaps the pressure of being at a big club and the fierce competition for places had diminished his joy of the game. Whatever it was, things were definitely not so easy any more. *'I joined another first division club for a couple of years. The game by now was a routine. A job. A fantastic job, yes, but still a job. I still enjoyed the game, but there were things that didn't feel right. I wanted to leave Red Star, which I guess was seen as strange, but for some reason that I still don't really understand I wasn't enjoying myself.'*

Milan performed consistently well for the next two years at his new club and even though he didn't get back the full momentum he had before joining Red Star, life was okay. His confidence grew with experience but he admits to thinking that maybe it was a mistake to leave Red Star when he did. *'I was playing with some of the world's great players at Red Star, and in big games in front of 80,000 and 100,000 people. Perhaps if I had stuck it out a little longer I may have felt more settled and enjoyed it.'*

Soon, however, Milan would get the chance to answer his 'what if'. Red Star had every right to never consider Milan again – after all, he was the one that left them. However, in 1988 his former club wanted him back. *'I thought it was a good chance to give it another go. Back to a big club, but this time more experienced. I was a little anxious, but I had to give it another go.'*

It only lasted six months. *'There was a different coach to last time and he treated me well. We had a good team with some great, world-class players and I was once again playing in the Champions League against the likes of AC Milan. Unfortunately though, I had the same feelings about being at Red Star as I did the first time. I still don't know what was troubling me there, but once again I didn't want to stay.'*

Up until 1990, the Yugoslav Association did not allow its players to transfer to clubs outside Yugoslavia until they were twenty-eight. With so much talent in the country, the league was a strong one and the pressure for places in the big two clubs in Belgrade was intense. The career path for Yugoslav professionals became quite defined. *'You would play in Yugoslavia and earn enough to own a flat in Belgrade, and maybe a nice car. You could live a good life, but not really put money away for the future. When most good players turned twenty-eight, they would then go into the other leagues of Europe and try to earn some good money for three to four years before they retired from the game. There weren't many players still in Yugoslavia over twenty-eight.'* By the end of 1990, the 'departure age' was dropped to twenty-four, then by the end of 1991 it was abolished altogether and the world began to get a real look at the quality this part of the world was producing.

Milan turned twenty-eight in December 1988. He was married that year, and his desire to leave Red Star – and Yugoslavia – was strong. *'I could've gone to Sweden or France, but I wasn't too keen. It was then that I had an offer from Zoran [Matic] in Australia and I immediately said "No way."'* Soccer in Australia was a long way from offering the good money and the status of soccer in Europe. In fact, for Milan, it was a long way from anywhere.

Zoran Matic was the coach of Adelaide City. He was friendly with the ex-assistant coach at Red Star and the then-coach of Melbourne J.U.S.T, a club formed by Yugoslav migrants. *'Zoran had come over to Yugoslavia to look for players and he wanted me. I was not interested at first and thought I would never hear from him again. He was persistent, though, and called again in January '89. I began to get more interested, then somehow the idea grew on me. Something was telling me it was the right thing to do.'*

It was Milan's gut feeling that swayed his decision to continue his career on the other side of the planet. He had not followed his instincts previously when he joined Red Star (twice!) and this time he thought he would try something different. By 24 February 1989, he had landed in Adelaide.

Congratulating his adopted country-men.

'We did not know one word of English and I just remember it was so hot.'

'People thought it was crazy to continue my career in Australia where soccer is not a big sport. But when you immigrate to Australia you have to have full commitment – whether you are a soccer player or not. We did keep the apartment in Belgrade (which was rented by Red Star to use when new players came to the club) but I had a two-year contract in Adelaide and that's what we were going to commit to.'

•••

It was minus-twenty degrees in Belgrade when Milan kicked off the second half of his career. It was thirty-five degrees when he and his wife landed in Adelaide. 'We did not know one word of English and I just remember it was so hot. We were both in a daze.'

He may have been in a daze, but the new star recruit could not be kept under wraps. 'There was quite a bit of media coverage about my arrival. Who was I, and what was I like? I arrived on the Friday and on the Saturday was in the team to play Marconi in Adelaide. I was still jet-lagged and really had no idea what was going on in the heat that day. I played the second half and Zoran played me in midfield. We lost 3–2, but that's about all I can remember from that game. The season had already played seven rounds and Adelaide were not doing well. I was quite fit due to the training I had been doing with Red Star before I came, but I am not sure I should count that game against Marconi as my debut!'

The next game was against Wollongong. Milan was the best player on the ground and the team began to win games. 'My first thought was that this was quite easy again, like when I was young in Yugoslavia. We only trained three times a week, but the standard was actually pretty good, I fitted in quite easily.'

There were no full-time professionals in Australia, but Milan was earning enough money from playing and running clinics that he did not have to work. The standard and cost of living in Australia was excellent, but it was a far cry from the serious money other 28-year-old Yugoslavs were earning in Europe. Still, he had made his bed and he was committed to lying in it.

Adelaide missed the finals that season, but the team was taking shape. Even though more South Australian players were making Australian squads and Adelaide City were doing well, Milan once again began to wonder if he had made the right decision. 'I was slowly learning English and meeting

Serbian-born Socceroo Ivanovic tackles English-born Socceroo Awaritefe in the NSL. Adelaide versus Marconi.

people through soccer, but it wasn't easy. My wife and I split up, and she went home. It was hard on both of us in a foreign place, but even harder on her. As I was approaching the end of my two-year contract in 1990, I was seriously considering going home. It probably would've meant retirement from the game, though, because not many good European clubs would take a 30-year-old. You could come to Australia and play well, but it was very difficult to go back.'

Then, in late 1990, there was talk of Milan playing in the national team. He did not pay much attention until Eddie Thomson called him and asked if he would play against Czechoslovakia in the January 1991 series. It was like a shot in the arm. 'I was shocked. To play for a national team! I mean, it gave me a whole new lease on life. I became enthusiastic again and excited about training and playing. I thought I would play in Australia for a year or two, then go home. Playing for Australia extended my career so much and I am forever grateful to Eddie Thomson.'

So, in just under two years since arriving in Australia, Milan made his debut for his adopted country. 'I guess I did not feel the same pride in the Australian shirt as most of the other guys. It did not mean as much to me at first. After a while, though, the boys all became very close in the squad and we

would do anything for each other on, or off, the field. I was a part of that and it is probably what made me feel more and more Australian.'

In an interesting twist, 1991 was also the year Red Star won the European Champions League. 'I began playing national team soccer in my new country, while seven or eight of my old teammates went on to win the Champions League with Red Star. I really don't know if I would have still been in the team by then if I had stayed, because for their standards I was getting on in age. I didn't feel jealous – I was playing international soccer.'

His initial Socceroo games were friendlies and he didn't need to be an Australian citizen to play. When it came to the World Cup qualifying campaign for USA 1994, though, he had to make a decision. 'I needed to be naturalised to play in the World Cup qualifiers. Eddie wanted me to be involved, so that was all I needed. In May '92 I officially became Australian, even though I had already played for the country.'

The Socceroo squad toured South America before playing the Oceania qualifiers against the island minnows. '"What's going on here?" was all I could think of when we played those games. Poor pitches and a bad standard. I had to remind myself that I was playing in the World Cup qualifiers.'

153

Earning his money for Adelaide City against the Melbourne Knights.

The 1993 series against Argentina removed any of those doubts. It didn't get much bigger than that series – the last hurdle before the World Cup finals. *'The biggest game of my career was against Argentina in Buenos Aires. Who would've ever thought? I had played in front of 100,000 people a few times before that, but the 70,000 that were there for that game were the noisiest and the most intimidating. It also meant the most because there was so much at stake.'*

Australia didn't make it after conceding a one-in-a-million own goal in Argentina, and nor did they succeed in the 1997 campaign. *'I played all the lead-up games in that campaign – even when Terry [Venables] was coach from 1997. I didn't play against Iran at the MCG, though, and was on the bench. Of course I wanted to play and many people said I should've gone on when we were 2–0 up, but I grew up where the coach is the boss. You jump off bridges for him and you respect his decisions. I have no hard feelings for Terry and the only thing I am upset about is that we didn't go through. That game was almost too easy. We were so much better that we naturally kept getting in positions going forward, and that exposed us more than it otherwise would've. The atmosphere was just unbelievable that night and we just could not imagine it could go wrong. The rest is history.'*

• • •

Milan still waits for someone to pinch him when he is reminded that he has played sixty 'A' internationals (and seventy-one matches) for his adopted country in an international career that spanned seven years. In fact, he is sixth on Australia's list of most 'A' internationals played and has also amassed 301 NSL games at Adelaide City – at the same time as mastering a new language. He still owns his apartment in Belgrade and enjoys going back from time to time. Favourable property prices and the low cost of living in Australia have enabled him to put some money away for the future, even though he didn't bank the big bucks in Europe. He enjoys many aspects of European life and occasionally wonders if he'll move back. Or maybe to Melbourne where he sees life as more cosmopolitan. His old homeland may still hold some appeal, but he is more than happy with his decision to have become Australian. And that will be the case wherever he lives.

Alex TOBIN

Alex Tobin had not seen a National Soccer League game until he was eighteen. It was in the 1984 season when South Melbourne hosted Adelaide City and he remembers it vividly – he was making his debut for the South Australian club.

'My progression to the national league happened quickly and there was no real time for me to think about what was going on. I was playing in the local state league and in our third or fourth game we played the Adelaide City second team, who were playing in our competition. The senior coach was there and he asked me to join them. I pretty much went straight into the first team after I had signed, then travelled to Melbourne to make my debut. It was the first game I saw, and I was in it!'

That game was the start of an NSL career comprising an Australian record of 522 appearances. It is a career that has also seen Alex amass 113 Socceroo appearances, including eighty-seven 'A' international games for Australia – the most of any player in Socceroo history. He has won awards and accolades for being a polished, consistent defender, and his leadership skills made him the natural choice to captain the Socceroos from 1996 until his international retirement in 1999. In 2004, at thirty-eight years of age, Alex retired from professional football completely. His involvement in the game extends to the presidency of the Professional Footballer's Association (the player's union), and as everyone who speaks of him will assure you, Alex Tobin is a fine ambassador for the sport.

•••

Soccer began for Alex as an 8-year-old at school in Glenelg, Adelaide. His older brothers were also showing some interest and the three of them were in the same team. Their neighbour's wall got a heavy workout as they passed time kicking the ball. Alex joined the senior team at school, then in his final year was called into the senior team at his local club side. 'I am not from what you'd say is a traditional soccer background. My father is third- or fourth-generation Australian and is a history professor with no interest in the game. My three brothers and sisters and I all have degrees, but I am the one that somehow stuck with sport as well. I didn't ever really think about a career in the game, though. I just did what I did and things happened.'

It was in the 1984 Under-18s State Championships that things started to get more serious for Alex. He played a good tournament and was selected in the Australian squad preparing for the Youth World Cup in Russia. Add to that his NSL debut in the same year and 1984 would seem to be a year from heaven. Not quite. 'I got dropped from the Youth World Cup squad after playing all the practice games and I was crushed. In some ways it was good that my dad wasn't into the politics of the game. We both didn't know enough about the system to blame the system, and he encouraged me to keep at it, just as he would my studies or anything else. It was a simple, yet positive, attitude and it didn't give me an excuse for not making it. I just had to do my best to make it next time.'

By 1986, Alex was making a name for himself with Adelaide City, and Adelaide City had made a name for itself by winning the NSL championship. South Australian soccer was getting a lot of attention and the players began receiving increased exposure. By late 1987, Alex joined a number of his Adelaide City teammates in the national squad. They were preparing for the upcoming Olympic tournament and Alex was thrilled. 'I guess by then I wasn't too surprised to be asked into the squad. It had been rumoured for a little while. That didn't detract from the excitement, though.'

Alex was selected to be on the bench against Gothenburg of Sweden in January 1988, in the build-up to the Olympics. He was quietly happy to be able to gain experience from the bench and get used to being an international player. That comfort zone was soon shattered though, when coach Frank Arok gestured to him with about thirty minutes left to play. 'I went over to Frank to ask what he wanted, as if he wanted me to get him a hot dog or something. He looked a bit confused as to

why I went right over to him, but he told me to warm up. I was going to play. My nerves pretty much disappeared as soon as I got on the field. I did okay, and was pretty satisfied. I was now an Australian international.'

Alex made his full debut as a starting player in an 'A' international shortly after, against Chinese Taipei in a qualifying match for the 1988 Seoul Olympics. The game was in his home town of Adelaide just two months after his Gothenburg appearance. *'It was a great thrill to be able to walk out with the team and hear the anthem from the centre. I had a good game and even scored. I hadn't scored in my four years in the NSL to that point, and in front of my home crowd I scored on my full debut for Australia. I think the crowd were cheering and shaking their heads at 5the same time.'*

The 1988 Olympics were the last time that a full Socceroo team was selected before a rule change stipulated that only players under twenty-three years of age could play in national teams contesting the Olympics. Alex travelled with the squad, but remained a fringe player throughout the tournament, and during the next two years. However, under the guidance of Eddie Thomson as the new national coach in 1990, Alex made nine full appearances and was on his way to collecting more 'A' international Socceroo appearances than any other player in the green and gold.

Through the 1980s and early 1990s, most of the players in the national team were still locally based. It meant that a lot of games could be organised and most of the players spent more time together. Part of the reason the overseas exodus of our best players had not begun in earnest was that FIFA had stipulated European clubs could not play any more than three foreign players at one time. Clubs had to be very choosy about the overseas players they bought. *'If you have a look at it, the first group of players that went to Europe around that time were strikers or attacking midfielders. The fans wanted their imports to be the match winners and goal scorers and it was the likes of Eddie Krncevic, Frank Farina, Graham Arnold, and later Aurelio Vidmar and Robbie Slater, who went over.'*

Although Alex would like to have played for a European club if the offer was right, he did not have a burning motivation to prove to himself that he was good enough. *'I had a couple of offers but they weren't really worth leaving Australia for. I believe that if you are good enough to play regularly for Australia, then you are good enough to play in professional European leagues. It was therefore never a question of proving myself and I hold the same opinion of other Australian internationals. I didn't push hard to go, but that doesn't mean I wouldn't have if the right offer came through.'*

In 1993 about half of the Australian squad were still playing in Australia. Once again, the Socceroos just missed out on World Cup qualification, when they faced Diego Maradona's Argentina at the final hurdle. *'It was 1–1 in the Sydney leg, and we knew it was going to be tough over there. [Argentinean-born member of the Australian coaching staff] Raul Blanco had warned us that we wouldn't be able to speak to each other during the game. We wouldn't be able to hear instructions like "man on" and the crowd would be deafening. We didn't really understand what he meant until we experienced first-hand that noise. There*

was no pre-match entertainment before the game – the crowd took care of that. We went out to warm up and I yelled at Aurelio [Vidmar] from about four metres away. He didn't hear me at all.'

The Aussies were narrowly beaten 1–0 in the Buenos Aires cauldron, courtesy of an unfortunate own goal – by Alex Tobin. *'I have the dubious honour of scoring the last goal of the entire 1994 World Cup qualifying campaign. Too bad it was at the wrong end. I stuck my leg out to block a Gabriel Batistuta cross and the ball clipped my knee or shin, then looped into the*

swirling wind. There were people getting back onto the goal line but somehow it bounced in. What a way to lose it – but it's not something I beat myself up over. These things happen.'

By the time the 1998 World Cup campaign came around, Alex was the only locally-based player to face Iran in front of 90,000 people at the MCG. He had been captain for a couple of years and it was his one-hundredth appearance for Australia in all games. It is a night he and the Australian sporting public will never forget. *'The arena was spectacular. The build-up had been massive all week and soccer was on everyone's lips. The noise was incredible when I led the team out, and the national anthem was like nothing else. You definitely don't want your first game to be a game like that, because your head would just be spinning. Playing the first leg of that [qualifying] series in Iran in front of 130,000 people was intimidating, but in some ways that MCG atmosphere on such a big night for Australian soccer was even more so.'*

History tells us that the Socceroos pummelled the Iranians for most of the game and were 2–0 up with half an hour to go. It should've been more, and in the end it needed to be. The Iranians scored twice in three minutes to level the game and level the series at 3–3, after the 1–1 result in Iran. International rules stipulate that to break such a deadlock, the team who has scored more goals away from home in the two-game tie will advance. Iran's two goals in Melbourne meant they would go on to play in the 1998 France World Cup – and Australia was left to ponder another heartbreak. The Socceroos did not lose a game throughout the entire campaign, yet in the end it wasn't enough. Grown men wept and thousands of soccer supporters in Australia were silent for weeks. Many will still not discuss that night.

One of the more uplifting footnotes from that series was an illustration of Australian cheekiness. '*Women are not allowed into soccer games in Iran, so the 130,000 people that were there in the first leg were men, and were very loud. Well, make that 129,998 men because we had been told that two women were in the arena. One was [Soccer Australia Chairman] David Hill's partner who had to be fully robed and was in one of the VIP areas, and the other was a backpacker who dressed up like a guy so that she could get in. That takes some courage!*'

It is difficult for Alex to put his finger on what it meant to him to play for Australia. Being captain of his country for so long means a number of things in itself. There is

Against Manchester United in 1999.

the fact that playing at an international level was good for his career and provided a chance to play all over the world against the best players. There was also the honour of representing all those people who play and love the game in Australia. *'Whenever I played, I just made sure that I did my best and did what was required. Playing for Australia is obviously more intense than playing in front of a couple of thousand in the NSL, but in the end you do the same things. Being captain also did not change my game. It was a great honour and the* *memories magnify with time, but there should be eleven leaders out there, and I didn't have to make an extra effort when captain.'*

•••

Alex's productive and successful time at Adelaide City drew to an untimely close in 2000, after sixteen seasons with the club where he was captain, development officer and stalwart. *'I wanted to spend my career at that club. There were some strange things going on there at the time and for some* *reason that I still don't really understand, two of the board members didn't want me there any more. The coach did, I did and the players did, but that wasn't enough. There was public and private confusion and I am still disappointed, but in the end you have to move on.'*

Parramatta Power quickly swooped to grab the prized player for the 2000–01 season. That lasted two years before Northern Spirit secured his services until the 2003–04 season and Alex's thirty-eighth

Opening the 'Captain's Bar' at Aussie Stadium; Tobin (Soccer), Lewis (League), Meninga (League), Johns (League), Farina (Soccer), Farr-Jones (Union), Wade (Soccer), Yankos (Soccer).

Train as you would play; Tobin doing what he does best against Kewell.

Tobin rushes in to celebrate Vidmar's goal against Iran at the MCG, 1997.

> **'** Players might have come here for a **well-paid holiday** in the past, but thankfully **those days are gone. '**

year. He is not sure about coaching in the future, but is interested in the administration of the game – something he enjoys in his role as president of the player's union. *'The PFA has done some great things for the players and for the game since it was formed in 1993. Clubs used to railroad players and provided no secure future. The PFA has worked hard to rectify that, as well as try to assist in the development of the game in general. To that end we have probably gone beyond our mandate slightly, but we have had to.'*

Having spent a career in the NSL and travelling the world with the national team, Alex is a firm believer that the standard here is higher than people give it credit. *'If you put most NSL games in front of big crowds and packaged them well for television, then the NSL would be comparable to some overseas leagues. Some of the stuff played here is excellent, but it gets no media coverage and the crowds are not coming to see it. Gone are the days when the odd overseas player would come here and be streets ahead. In fact, many of the highly paid guest players that come here do the game an injustice. They earn big money and do nothing for the league and the players – but our quality has matured and no longer is it an easy ride. Some players who have been successful in Europe still come here near the*

end of their careers, but they come to play and know they have to be fit and ready to go if they are going to make an impact. Players might have come here for a well-paid holiday in the past, but thankfully those days are gone.'

During the years in which he has seen the standard of the NSL improve on the field, Alex has also seen the ethnic rivalries between clubs soften. Adelaide City is a club backed by the Italian community of Adelaide. The other major Adelaide club is the Greek-backed West Adelaide. From Alex's point of view, however, that is where the ethnic divide stops. *'It really didn't mean much to the players that we were Italian, they were Greek or another club was Croatian or whatever. The players from all those clubs were from all over the place and while some of the committee and the older fans let us know the importance of certain games due to ethnic backgrounds, it really didn't matter to the players. In many ways, the actual game has evolved more in a multicultural sense than the clubs and some of the fans, but as the older generation move on, I think things will catch up off the park as well.'*

Alex now resides in Sydney and thinks it is the best place to be if he is to continue in the game in some form. He has never lived in England, France, Scotland, Uruguay, Iran, Colombia or Argentina – although they are just some of the footballing nations where he has plied the trade. He has played the most 'A' internationals of any Australian player and he has done it all from home. He has provided outstanding service to Australian soccer, and Australian soccer should hope that once his boots have been framed, his plans to continue that service off the field are made a reality.

Mehmet DURAKOVIC

Socceroo 1989–2002

Mehmet Durakovic was born in Montenegro into an Albanian family that was one of thousands living in the Yugoslav state. *'When people ask me where I was born I say Montenegro. When they ask about the nationality of my family I say I am Albanian. It was a beautiful place to be young and there were no problems back then. We moved to Melbourne when I was six, though, so we are Australian really.'*

The Durakovic family left Yugoslavia in search of better work and opportunities for their growing children. They went to Italy for three months to decide whether to go to America or Australia. *'We had relatives in both countries and obviously Australia was chosen. I am not sure why. The family here sponsored us in case things went wrong and*

I think we came out with [Australian] Government assistance. We didn't speak any English, but knew some Italian after being there for a couple of months.'

The family settled within the migrant communities of St Albans, western Melbourne, and began to adapt to life in Australia reasonably well. *'We stayed with my aunt, uncle and cousins for four months. They helped Mum and Dad get jobs in a factory, showed them where to shop and helped them with the language. It is easier for kids to pick up the language at school, and there were a lot of other migrant kids also trying to adapt. There were people from all over the world where we lived and everyone got along well. Soccer was the most popular sport at school because of all*

the migrant kids, and I always had a ball with me. I guess it helped me fit in. My grades weren't the best, but I loved it here and settled quickly.'

Mehmet's official playing days began at Footscray juniors, then he moved on to Port Melbourne juniors when the family moved to the inner-city suburb. *'I was with Port Melbourne from Under-10s to Under-16s and they were great times. We had some great players who went on to play for Australia and overseas. We always wanted to beat South Melbourne juniors, but most of the guys wanted to play for South Melbourne Hellas in the national league as seniors. I certainly did.'*

Mehmet's plans for Hellas had to be placed on hold, however, because his parents decided they were going 'home'. Life was good in Australia, but they were missing family, friends and the language in Montenegro after ten years away. So they sold up and left. *'I wasn't happy about going, but what can you do at fifteen or sixteen and your family moves?'*

Back in Yugoslavia Mehmet began to take his soccer more seriously. He played with a local club in the lower divisions. However, in just over a year the first division club Budchnost asked him to trial with them. *'Budchnost were over an hour away from our home so they put me up in a hotel. It was a good introduction to professional soccer, but I found it strange that the senior players would pull my shirt and kick me a lot. I mean, we were all at the same club after all. I was young and didn't understand that I was a threat to their jobs. An enthusiastic young Australian (I told everyone I was Australian) that the club was keeping in a nice hotel. I took it as a compliment when I realised later.*

'It was a good experience and it really helped my development, but I was lonely in the hotel after training. [Future Yugoslav international] Dejan Savicevic was another young player at the club and we were friendly, but that was it. After a month or so, I decided I had had enough. I simply packed my bags and left the hotel. I didn't

even tell anyone – I just shot through. I wonder if they are still waiting for me at training . . .'

Not long after, Mehmet also decided he had had enough of Montenegro. At seventeen years of age he felt he was old enough to make the significant choice to, not only leave Budchnost, but bid Yugoslavia farewell too. *'My friends and I constantly wrote to each other and I missed Australia. It wasn't that life in Montenegro was bad, but life in Australia was better. Six months after I returned, Mum and Dad*

came back too. They had to start from scratch again, but it shows they thought Australia was worth it.'

It was 1984 when Mehmet returned from Montenegro and he went straight into the Port Melbourne senior team. After one month, he had been signed by NSL club Brunswick Juventus. *'I came back not really knowing what I would do. I had finished*

'I was young and didn't understand that I was a threat to their jobs.'

'...but I was walking on clouds from my debut onwards and had goose bumps all over.'

my schooling and I went back to living with my cousins. Then, all of a sudden I was at a national league club.'

He spent most of his first year at Brunswick in the reserves or on the bench for the seniors. He came off the bench a couple of times in 1985, but did not make his full debut until late that season. *'I made my first full appearance in the '85 preliminary final and my second game was the grand final against Sydney City. Not a bad place to start – we won and I was having a great time.'*

In 1987, however, Brunswick began a downhill slide and were relegated from the NSL by 1988. Mehmet was loaned out to Footscray J.U.S.T in 1988 and stayed just one year before his boyhood idols, South Melbourne, asked him to play for them. *'I have never worked with an agent. I have always looked after myself, and Hellas came to me to see if I wanted to play for them. Of course the answer was yes – I had always wanted to play for them. I used to run down to watch South Melbourne train as a kid, after I had finished my training as a Port Melbourne junior. I joined in the 1989–90 season and stayed until '94–95.'*

The 1989–90 season was also the year of Mehmet's Socceroo debut. He had been in squads before while he was at Brunswick, but this was the real thing. Mehmet's face still fills with light when he talks about what playing for Australia meant to him. *'My debut was against Moscow Torpedo and when I got the letter to say I was playing, it was just amazing. It took me back to a Socceroo squad training session at Port Melbourne when I was a young fan. I took a camera down there and I was in awe. I remember taking photos of John Kosmina and thinking "I want to be like him". I also remember Jimmy Rooney encouraging me, when I was even younger, that I should stick at it. Even from those early days I wanted to be a Socceroo. I didn't tell anyone, but it is what I always wanted – I never wanted to play for Albania or Yugoslavia. Every time I put the shirt on before a Socceroo game, it was just something else. I can't really explain it . . . but I was walking on clouds from my debut onwards and had goosebumps all over.'*

Life was good at South Melbourne and with the Socceroos, but in 1995 Mehmet was presented with the opportunity to do something different. *'[Australian] Ken Worden was the coach of Selangor in Malaysia and the club was having a tournament to open their brilliant new stadium. Vasco de Gama, Dundee United, Bayern Munich, Leeds and Selangor were all to play and Ken wanted to strengthen his squad for the tournament. In the end, Eddie Krncevic, Bruce Grobbelar [Liverpool's legendary goalkeeper] and I were asked to play a couple of games. I didn't get match payments, but they paid my airfare to Malaysia and then on to Montenegro to see family and that suited me fine. They must have liked what they saw, because at the start of the next year, they offered South [Melbourne] $130,000 and me a one-year contract.'* His Asian adventure began.

At that time, each Malaysian club was only allowed three foreigners per squad. They had to be careful to select the right type of character as well as the right type of player. *'My wife and I had recently had a daughter, but we thought it couldn't hurt to go for a year. We treated it as a working holiday and a learning experience, and if you go with that attitude you can't fail. We were able to see a lot of Asia and could come home quite regularly as well. We were treated so well over there and had everything we could have wanted.'*

Tradition, respect and honour are the backbone of many Asian cultures. Malaysia has a current population of over twenty-two million, and although it has been occupied by a range of countries in its long history, there is a fierce pride in being Malay. Selangor is one of the most powerful states in Malaysia and its soccer club has the respect of the whole country. It has a 120,000-seat stadium and the team attracts the best players in the region.

There was a lot of pressure to perform, as the foreigners were usually paid much more handsomely than the locals and were therefore expected to play well. *'Money was no object. If a foreigner did not do well for a few weeks, then you would just have your contract paid out and you would be replaced. Also, if the locals didn't like you, they would rally around and get you sacked. Foreigners who didn't show respect and didn't play well didn't last.'*

The highlight of Mehmet's playing career with Selangor was lifting the prestigious Malaysia Cup as captain of the club. Not long after, he was awarded the highly distinguished PJK Medal for *'Services to the State'* by the King of Malaysia – an honour virtually unheard of for foreigners. *It takes a unique type of person to achieve that level of acceptance in Asia, and it is something that gives Mehmet a strong sense of pride.*

'It was a great experience just to play in Malaysia, but to be the first foreign captain of Selangor, to lift the Malaysia Cup on their behalf in front of 120,000 people, then to be presented the State Award by the King is something beyond normal soccer experiences. Respect is a big thing in Asia, and it is important to have an understanding that they operate very differently to what we are used to in Europe or Australia. On a personal level, my acceptance there is something I am very proud of.

'The top teams in Malaysia were of a good standard, but there wasn't the depth. We had a brilliant stadium and most of the good players, but we went to some tinpot places to play against some ordinary teams. It was interesting, though, when we would play touring club teams like Manchester United. They were amazed at our stadium. They were used to playing in front of 50,000 people because that's what their stadiums held – but we had 120,000. They were still the millionaires, though.'*

Mehmet would have liked to play in Europe with those millionaires, however he was never one to push his own barrow and ask for favours from the Socceroos playing in the big leagues. *'It wasn't about the money in Europe, it was about playing at the highest level. The money was good at Selangor, but everyone wants to play in Europe. I didn't feel comfortable asking for recommendations in Europe when we were in Socceroo camps, and there are so many good players out there.'*

'**Money** was no object.'

'Yeeessss . . .' Celebrating his goal against Canada.

' That's a good thing about Australia;
it depends on the person,
not where the
person is from. '

Asian soccer was plagued by bribery and corruption in the early 1990s, but a government inquiry seemed to have put a stop to that by the time Mehmet arrived. *'I had heard a lot of stories, but they were before my time there. They were cracking down on it and I didn't see any first-hand. They didn't target foreigners, anyway, because foreigners were well paid and didn't need bribes. At Selangor, most of the locals were in the national team and were well looked after as well, so they probably didn't need bribes, either. That's as far as I know, anyway . . .'*

Mehmet's Asian experience finished prematurely in 1998 due to the Asian economic crisis – another impact of making a living from the world game. *'The club could not afford to keep the foreigners when the Asian economies crashed. I was getting paid in Australian dollars, so when the value of the Malaysian currency fell so steeply, it was the same as them paying three, four or five times as much. They couldn't afford it and all the foreigners had to go. I was gutted.'*

Mehmet didn't have many options other than returning to Australian soccer, but didn't go back to South Melbourne because Selangor wanted a transfer fee. Selangor were happy for him to go to another club for a nominal amount, and he ended up at Sydney Olympic. *'I didn't particularly want to go to Sydney, but it was a good offer and*

I couldn't go back to South. It was tough to come back to the national league after the big crowds and life in Malaysia and, to be honest, it took a little while to settle. The soccer is good here, but there just wasn't the atmosphere. I had a two-year deal, but my dad was sick in Melbourne after a year and I told the club I had to be with him. They agreed and said they'd fly me to Sydney three times a week to train, but I didn't feel that was right on the other boys. In the end, they let me go – as long as I didn't sign for South. At that time, I really thought I wouldn't play anywhere. I thought that was going to be it.'

Mehmet spent as much time as he needed to with his father, and as the new year approached he still didn't know what the future would hold. But he did know the boots he thought he had hung up were starting to look appealing again. *'Jeff Hopkins was one of the foreigners at Selangor with me, and when he had to leave like I did, I spoke to Gippsland Falcons on his behalf. [The coach] Stuart Munro took him in a flash. Jeff and I are good friends and by the time I had left Olympic, he was coaching Gippsland. I went there to play for him and become assistant coach . . . I had a good time.'*

It wasn't long before South Melbourne came knocking again, however. *'They*

needed some experience and I was happy to go back. I didn't go straight there from Olympic, so I guess I did as they asked. I didn't hear of any problems anyway, and was with South until my retirement after the 2004 NSL finals.'

•••

One constant in Mehmet's career has been his desire to play for his country. He has managed sixty-four appearances in games that have taken him all over the world. He enjoys travelling, but it isn't the countries he's seen that provide the fondest memories – it's the mateship. *'We didn't get much culture in other countries, even though we have played all over the place. It's really just hotels and soccer grounds. It brings teams closer when you travel together, though, and the Australian squads have always been great. All the players got along well no matter where they were from. That's a good thing about Australia; it depends on the person, not where the person is from. The atmosphere in Socceroo camps was always great and something I really enjoyed.'*

One of Mehmet's best memories on the field is not of turning some of the world's best strikers into insignificant bystanders as he is paid to do, but of scoring against Canada to keep the Socceroos in the 1994 World Cup qualifiers. *'I played that game with more than twenty stitches in my forehead after copping an elbow in the NSL. I wore a headband and kept it quiet . . . but it split again and it wasn't pretty. There was quite a bit of blood. We were losing against Canada, but I managed to pop up and score a good header to send it to penalties. Mark Schwarzer won us the game from there, but I was pretty happy with my contribution.'*

That win sent the Socceroos to the next stage – playing Argentina, home and away. *'We did so well against Argentina. They scored one-in-a-million goals in both legs, and when that ball looped over my head on the line after Alex Tobin's deflection in Buenos Aires . . . well, they say God is Argentinean, and at that moment I thought they were right. It was so intense over there; it is a matter of life and death. "May the best team win" is irrelevant to them.*

'I was also shattered after the Iran game at the MCG. I couldn't play one of the lead-up games for Terry Venables because I had to stay at Selangor . . . I [therefore] didn't make the squad and was in Malaysia

watching it on TV. It was heartbreaking watching it, but to see my mates so upset on the ground afterwards – I just wanted to smash the TV. I was crying with them.

'In the end, though, the positives of my career far outweigh the negatives. Two championships in Australia and plenty of success in Malaysia. South Melbourne's Team of the Century and a lot of games for Australia. I am not one of the millionaires, but I have met so many good people, and I certainly can't complain.'

Now on the forty side of thirty-five, and with four years of experience in Malaysia and 360 NSL games under his belt, Mehmet's enthusiasm for the game still burns brightly, even after retirement. *'I could've earnt more money being a sales rep or something, but I wanted to keep playing in the NSL as long as the club wanted me. It's not about the*

money, it's about helping the young kids along and helping the club out. I kept playing as long as I had my pace, but in the end injuries took over. It was an emotional farewell at Bob Jane Stadium [South's ground] but I was happy to have the chance to say thanks to the fans.'*

So, an Albanian born in Montenegro who found cultural acceptance in Asia and takes immense pride in being an Australian. Mehmet will leave as his legacy a Socceroo career filled with great moments on the field. But, of course, it wouldn't be Mehmet to agree. *'In the end, I'll go quietly and the sport will move on . . . but I managed to hold off slipping away as long as possible because I love the game so much.'*

'I am not one of the **millionaires,** but I have met so **many good people,** and I certainly can't complain… I love the game so much.'

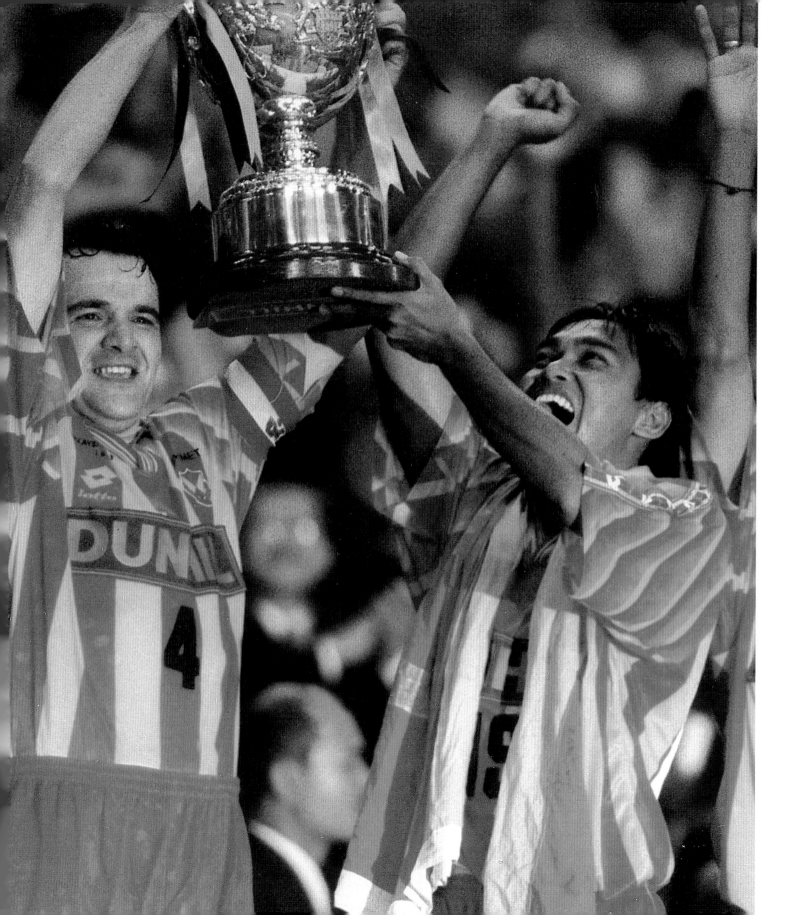

Paul OKON

Socceroo 1990–current

Paul Okon is a winner, but after years playing in the top European competitions and captaining his country, he has developed the maturity to know when to switch on the winning focus, and when to put the bigger things in life into perspective. It's an attitude that means wherever he is, and whoever he is playing for, he can't lose. *'I have never been interested in the stardom and fame associated with the game. For me, it's all about always aiming to get the best out of myself every time I step on a field, whether it's at training, or a game in front of a packed stadium. The rest will look after itself. I have never been worried about going to new places where I didn't know people either, because it is all about the football. And in the end, I view these years away as a vacation. It's all an experience and it has helped develop me as a player and as a person. Sooner or later, I'll go home, but for now there are still more things to experience.'*

•••

Paul Okon was born and bred in Sydney. When he moved out of home at the age of nineteen, he didn't just move into a flat with mates down the street – he moved to Belgium. It was the start of an ongoing adventure in which he has called places like Brugge, Rome, London, northern England, Florence and Vicenza (near Venice) home, and has seen him accumulate more stamps

in his passport than the most travelled holiday makers. And even though he views the experience as a vacation, it is definitely 99.9 parts working holiday to 0.1 part sightseeing jaunt.

Instead of picking up trinkets, photos of tourist havens and perhaps some sunburn on his travels, Paul has collected two Belgian championships, two Belgian Cup titles, Belgian Player of the Year and Oceania Player of the Year Awards, as well as an accumulated thirty-seven Socceroo appearances; many as captain. *'I didn't really think about playing overseas until about a month before the transfer to Brugge was finalised. It was a big deal to be playing in the NSL back then, and overseas wasn't really considered. I used to tape World Soccer on SBS and watch it over and over after school, but I spent a lot of time watching Australian soccer on the hill behind the goal at Marconi Stadium as well. That's what I associated with.'*

The young Marconi fan was also a young Marconi player. He was born in Parramatta, not far from the NSL superclub, and went to school just down the street. He began playing at the age of seven, and continued through the junior ranks up to sixteen. During the 1989–90 season the 17-year-old made his NSL debut, and promptly went on to win the Under-21 Player of the Year award. Marconi finished Minor Premiers

that year, but lost the grand final 2–0 to Sydney Olympic. Paul won the Under-21 Player of the Year award again the next year, but the club was knocked out at the semi-final stage of the competition. But it wasn't just the location and perennial success that drew Paul to the club. *'Dad played for Marconi years ago, and he coached me all the way through from Under-7s. It was a very close-knit community club, more like a family . . . I had some great times there.'*

Paul's dad, Klaus, is German, and came here as part of a small family in the 1950s. His mother, Cleo, is Italian, and arrived with a huge family around the same time. They met a couple of years later, got married and started an Australian family of their own. Paul is the second son. While he tried his hand at all sorts of sports in his youth, he was only ever going to end up a soccer player. He left school after year eleven to concentrate on his game, and while there were plenty of tears at the airport before the trip that signified the start of his European adventure, his parents have always been supportive and understanding of their son's ambition. *'I think I would've been a school teacher if I wasn't a footballer. But I was in love with the game from the first time I played it, and never really wanted to do anything else. I can thank my parents for that.'*

•••

The commencement of Paul's NSL career in 1989–90 also signified the start of his international career. His first Socceroo appearance was in 1990 against Hadjuk Split, Eddie Thomson's first game in charge. He came on in the eighty-seventh minute, and relished every one of those 180 seconds. *'Your first game for the national team is something that you cherish forever. Forget about the thrill of putting on the Socceroo shirt . . . it was special to even be able to put on the Socceroo tracksuit!'* He made his full Socceroo debut in 1991 as a bright-eyed 18-year-old, in an 'A' international against Czechoslovakia in Sydney. He was also an integral cog in the 1991 Youth World Cup squad that made the semi-finals in Portugal.

After two successful years in the NSL, a couple of Socceroo appearances under his belt and with the Youth World Cup finals approaching, Club Brugge of Belgium came knocking. A month or two later, he became a full-time European professional.

'Belgium and Holland have always been a good pathway for Australian players. Although I didn't know it at the time, Brugge is a great city, and it wasn't difficult to settle. [Another Aussie player] Lawrence Kitner went over at the same time, and eighty percent of Belgians speak English, so that helped. I spent the first year in the reserves, and from there it was really just a case of proving to the coaches that I could do it in the first team. I knew I could . . . I just had to prove it to them.'

Captaining the Socceroos is serious business.

'In Italy, you are not excused if you lose.'

Proving his worth took until almost halfway through Paul's second season at Brugge, when he played five games straight for the defending champions. Injury then stalled his progress and relegated him to the sidelines for the remainder of the season. He had made a solid, if unspectacular, contribution in the games he played, but although he found relative international success at the 1991 Youth World Cup and 1992 Barcelona Olympics, club life wasn't outstanding. '*After eighteen months or so in Belgium I wasn't really playing, had been injured, and the coach didn't really seem interested. When I came back to Australia for two weeks over the Christmas break, I decided to really look after myself and trained pretty hard. When I got back [to Belgium], I was the only player to have lost weight, and it really helped my game. I was in the team the first game back, and was never out afterwards. It proved to me that it wasn't only about having the skills . . . and I never looked back.*'

By the 1993–94 season Paul was fit, focused and flying. He played the full season in the first team and became an increasing influence on the park. In 1994–95 he helped the club win the Belgian Cup, and played to all sorts of acclaim. The next year, Club Brugge won the Cup once again, but this time added the coveted league title as well. Paul was voted the best player in the entire competition, and therefore became the first foreigner to win Belgium's Golden Shoe award. He was also voted Oceania Player of the Year, and topped off a memorable season by transferring to one of the biggest clubs in arguably the world's toughest competition. He became a Lazio player in Italy's Serie A. '*I was happy at Brugge, but when the likes of Lazio come in for you when you are only twenty-four and playing well . . . you don't say no. It all happened very quickly, and while it was a bit sad to be leaving, I was looking forward to another challenge.*'

Paul's Italian heritage, combined with his formative years immersed in the Italian traditions of Marconi, meant that he could communicate with his new teammates and settle quickly into his new surroundings. Lazio is the region of Italy that contains the eternal city of Rome. Both the Lazio and Roma clubs share the same massive stadium in the heart of Rome, but the rivalry between them is immense. There are three sets of change rooms in Stadio Olympico – one for Roma, one for Lazio and one for the away team. Derby games are anticipated around the world like few other Serie A fixtures. In fact, the fans' battle to win over the terraces with song and colour adds as much spark to the occasion as the players' fight for the three points. '*When I joined Lazio, I was told it didn't matter what happened all year, as long as we beat Roma. Those games are massive occasions. The build-up is intense, and in the week leading up to the game, the climate gets very warm!*'

It was impossible for Paul to live in the centre of Rome, and the hills surrounding the great city were somewhat of a refuge for the players. He could still venture into town when he needed to, but had to be careful not to draw unwanted attention to himself. He enjoyed the surroundings and settled well into the team under the management of Sven Goran-Erickson. He played fourteen games that first year, then was sidelined by a knee injury for eighteen cruel months. Three operations and so much time out of action made it difficult to break back into such a powerful team. '*I missed all of '97–98, and there were times when I got to the stage of asking if it was all worth it. Every time I did, though, it didn't take me long to answer yes. I was determined to get back into action.*'

The injury also meant he had to sit in the stands along with the other 90,000 Australians at the MCG when the Socceroos had their hearts broken by Iran's escape act to qualify for the 1998 World Cup finals. Paul's helplessness in the Australian cause was difficult to take, but galvanised his mission to recover. Near the end of season 1998–99 he managed five games for Lazio, but could see that if he wanted to prove he was truly back, he would have to move to get more game time. Goodbye Rome, and hello Florence. '*It was important for me to*

be back, and fit, for the year. I needed the season to prove that I could do it again in the Serie A.'

Unfortunately, Fiorentina coach Giovanni Trappatoni ultimately decided that Paul and another team member weren't suited to play on the field together, and only selected him for eleven games. Still, Paul's main aim of proving his worth was achieved, and clubs in the English Premier League began to show interest. Middlesbrough won the graceful Australian's signature, and Paul played twenty-four games in the 2000–01 season to help stave off relegation. He enjoyed the move to northern England, but noticed English professionals went about their business differently to Italians. *'The training facilities in England have now caught up, but in many cases the attitude is still behind. It is changing as more and more foreign players and coaches go to England, but there has traditionally been far less attention to nutrition and fitness techniques. There is still a bit of the "English drinking culture" in the game there as well, but it is slowly changing. Also, the fans in both countries are very passionate, but the English tend to support the players, win or lose. In Italy, you are not excused if you lose.'*

The fickle nature of Paul's chosen profession was highlighted by the next stage of his career. Steve McClaren took over as Middlesbrough boss from Bryan Robson, and Paul was forced to get comfortable on

Australia 1, Uruguay 0. First Leg, 2002 World Cup qualifier at the MCG. We lost the second leg 3–0 in Uruguay to be bundled out once again.

the bench. He was only selected in four matches before club and player agreed he could look for employment elsewhere. As the end of the 2001–02 season approached, Watford of London were vying for promotion from Division One, and wanted the Socceroo captain to help them. He joined for the remaining four months of the campaign and played fifteen games, but the club was ultimately unsuccessful. *'The four months at Watford flew by and I really enjoyed it. It was great being in London – we didn't get promotion, but mark it up as another fantastic experience.'*

Paul's talents couldn't remain outside the Premier League for long. Ex-Socceroo coach Terry Venables already had Aussies Harry Kewell and Mark Viduka (among others) at Leeds United, and persuaded Paul to join his green and gold charges. So he moved back north, and played fifteen games for the whites in the 2002–03 season. Peter Reid then took over from Venables and Paul was given the cold shoulder once again. Time for his agent, Leo Karis, to go to work.

What better way to showcase your talents than to captain your country against the nation that invented Association Football – England? What's more, why not do it in front of a packed house in London as well as a massive television audience? As is Paul's way, in 2003 he led his team from the front with a commanding midfield display. The Socceroos played the Poms off the park and were resounding 3–1 winners. The years of ignorance, when the Socceroos were known as 'The SoccerWhos?' around the world, had been worn away gradually over time, but this result punched holes right through it. It also made Paul's agent's job that little bit easier. But while the result was great and indicated the Socceroo's development, it was a friendly nonetheless. *'True respect comes from qualifying for the World Cup, not beating England in a friendly. We have had fantastic results in friendlies over the years, but when it comes down to it we have failed at World Cup level, and people don't look at what doesn't count.'*

Next stop was back to Italy. As it happened, Paul ended up in another one of the better parts of the world when he moved to Vicenza, just outside Venice. Things started well, but took a disappointing U-turn just months later when he fell out of favour with the coach.

With national coach Frank Farina's mantra of only selecting players that perform regularly at club level at the front of his mind, and with the World Cup 2006 looming, Paul decided to cut his losses and make a 'home coming' to Belgium. He joined table-topping second division club AK Oostende mid-season 2003–04, with the target of getting enough game time to retain his Socceroo shirt. *'I can only imagine how good it would be to play in the World Cup finals. The disappointments of Iran in '97*

and Uruguay in '01 were massive, but they don't make me want to get to the World Cup more. I mean, it's the World Cup, and it is not possible for me to want it more, whatever happens. Moving to Vicenza and then AK Oostende so soon after was all about that. I will have been in Europe for fifteen or sixteen years after the 2006 World Cup, and more than likely will want to come home by then. My career is now totally directed towards the World Cup.'

•••

Paul captained the Socceroos in 1996, prior to his crippling knee injury. He next wore the captain's armband against Brazil in 1999 and it hasn't been removed since. He is honoured every time he leads the green and gold onto the pitch. *'I love every game I play in, and big club games are great. But when you get to lead your country, it is something else. The joy of playing is the same when you are captain, but there are extra responsibilities too. You have to show extra commitment and try to get that little bit of extra commitment from your team, but everyone should be doing that anyway, not just the captain. We have a great, tightly knit Socceroo squad, and we all love going into camp and catching up with our mates. We all want to do whatever we can to play for Australia whenever we can. Australians have an edge, or a different spirit, when we play any sport because it's "us versus the rest of the world", and we want to prove*

that our small country that is so far away can still do well. I would hate to think of a career where I didn't play for my country.'

Nerves play a part in any elite athlete's career, and the swelling masses of passionate soccer supporters around the globe place footballers under an intense spotlight. Some players buckle, and some thrive under the pressure. Others place little stock in outside influences over performance. Whatever the approach, all top players have to learn to cope. *'I remember my debut as a 17-year-old for Marconi. I guess I had every right to be nervous because the NSL was important to me, but when I was young I didn't know the pressures of failure. The older guys helped me out, and it was more about fun. I sometimes wish I could go back to those times, but really the only pressure now is to keep reaching the standards that I set earlier in my career. And in the end, that is only up to me.'*

Of course, pressures off the pitch have hamstrung plenty of players over the years. Media, money, adulation, public scrutiny and unwanted attention are part and parcel of a professional's life in Europe. *'It's important that players learn to cope with the life of a [professional] footballer. You can only get so much guidance from experienced people, though in the end it is up to each individual to keep out of trouble. What's the saying – you can lead a horse to water, but you can't make it drink. It's important that*

'Gym work is just as important as skill work, and players need to be **great athletes, too.'**

players learn how to deal with both the highs and lows, because this game can give extremes in both, and both can be pitfalls. I don't stress over things like the media any more. I have realised how unimportant it is to performance.'

Other off-field pressures the Socceroos have had to deal with is their relationship with Soccer Australia, which was strained at times. With the recent formation of the Australian Soccer Association (ASA), Paul is one player who looks forward to focusing on more positive aspects of the game. *'Lots of things have happened over the years that shouldn't have happened, and we all hope that now the ASA has been formed everyone can pull together in the same direction. When you go into an international competition, you don't want to have to be negotiating for the Socceroos two days before games. It does affect us, and it is something we can do without. Hopefully people won't speak about that side of the game now, because there'll be nothing to speak about. We just want to get on with playing for Australia and making the World Cup.'*

After so many years at the top of his profession, Paul can put the developments he has witnessed in the game into perspective. *'It is no longer just about turning up for the game. Technology now plays a part and training is more specific and tailored. No longer are good skills*

enough, and only those who prepare can succeed. Gym work is just as important as skill work, and players need to be great athletes, too. Nutrition is also important, but as long as I am eating fresh and healthy food then I am happy. In the end, I try not to take it to extremes. Life is all about balance.'

Those years at the highest level of the game have also seen him play with, for and against some great footballers. *'The most influential coaches would have to be Zemen, who signed me for Lazio, and Venables for both club and country. He is the complete coach. A master. The best players are Roberto Mancini at Lazio, and probably Batistuta for his goals at Fiorentina. My hero when I was young was Frank Farina – and we ended up following similar career paths, and now he's my Socceroo coach. I think the best Socceroo I've played with would have to be Harry Kewell, but overall, the most influential guy would have to be my dad. It starts with natural talent, and I got that from him. He also gave me the enthusiasm and taught me the basic skills.'*

Paul has a huge memory bank of the game. Sure, the big matches with a thick atmosphere and boisterous crowd will be squared away forever inside his head. And moments when he has led the Socceroos into cavernous stadiums around the world take pride of place upstairs, too. That part is easy to appreciate. But Paul maintains a detailed collection of the specifics of every performance – no matter how big or small – and is a firm believer that he can learn from each and every one. And that includes his time as a 7-year-old Marconi junior, and the countless hours spent on the training pitch. Professional achievement lives on a knife's edge, where everyone is talented and everyone craves success. Top professionals need something extra, and in Paul's case it is his acute attentiveness that has helped him develop into a man who many say is the most complete player to have ever pulled on the green and gold.

Let me at 'em! Okon shows Michael Owen he means business in Australia's 3–1 victory, 2003.

Mark SCHWARZER

Socceroo 1993–current

Mark Schwarzer is the longest-serving member of Middlesbrough Football Club in the English Premier League. It is obviously a reflection of his outstanding ability, but it is also a sign of the times for Australia's soccer stars. The start to his European adventure may have coughed and spluttered, but the big goalkeeper has since secured a reputation as not only one of Australia's best ever, but an equal in company with the world's best.

Mark grew up in Sydney's far-western suburb of Richmond, the son of German migrants. He owes the opportunity to represent Australia to his father's enthusiasm and persuasive abilities – in keeping Mark's mother in Australia when they first arrived from Germany in 1967. In fact, Doris

Schwarzer wanted to go home to family and friends for fifteen years after arriving. *'Dad had apparently wanted to try somewhere other than Germany for quite a while. There were ads in the German newspapers from South Africa, Australia and Argentina for people with a trade, and Dad applied to them all. He proposed to Mum around the same time, and made sure she knew that was what he was going to do. He told her that the first one to reply would be the country they would be going to, and that was Australia. The Australian Government paid for their boat trip, found them jobs and got them accommodation in a complex with other migrants. The boat trip out here doubled as their honeymoon, because they married just before they left. They didn't*

know any English, but were given visas for two years and had to stay for that period before they could decide if they wanted to stay permanently or go home. Mum wanted to go home for fifteen years, but they both feel like Australians now. In fact, Dad didn't go back to Germany for twenty-seven years.'

Mark played juniors for a local club. When his dad took over the coaching reins the ten-year-old Mark played in goals for the first time. He began to make it into regional representative sides and when he was fifteen he joined the youth development program at Marconi. Four years later he made his senior debut, and in the 1992–93 season he won the Goalkeeper of the Year award as well as the NSL Championship.

'My two years in the NSL with Marconi were probably the most enjoyable in football – both on and off the pitch. I wasn't a commodity back then, and my mind was a lot freer. I could still enjoy my youth and the pressures were less intense. Of course, the fact that it was in Australia helped as well.'

Mark made his Socceroo debut against Canada in 1993 as part of the 1994 World Cup campaign. *'I wasn't a part of the squad until Mark Bosnich pulled out. Robbie Zabica became the number 1 and I became the number 2. I was just back from holidays and had to leave on short notice. I wasn't expecting the call-up at all from Eddie Thomson, but of course I was happy to go.*

Schwarzer's close-knit Marconi team.

I didn't think I'd be playing anyway. After sixteen minutes though, Robbie got sent off and I had to go on and an on-field player was sacrificed. I don't care what anyone says, it is not possible to be as prepared for a game when you are on the bench, and Paul Wade and I were still looking around the stadium and getting settled into our seats. I just remember thinking, "Uh oh, here we go," and running on. I did quite well, and even though we lost, I was pretty happy to have played. The thing is, once you get a taste, you want more, and I began to get nervous about whether I was still going to be in the squad for the return leg in Sydney.'

With Zabica suspended and Bosnich still unavailable, Mark's debut performance earned him a second go at being a Socceroo. This time he could walk on with the team from the start, in front of his home-town crowd, and stand in the middle for the national anthem. *'My home debut was tremendous and it was great to scrape through that game. I made a bit of a mistake for the goal we conceded, but Mem Durakovic made up for it by scoring a header that sent us to penalties. I managed to save two of them, and that is how the game is remembered – not for the mistake. I am pretty happy about that!'*

Bosnich was back for the next 1994 World Cup qualification stage against Argentina, and this time Schwarzer could do nothing but get comfortable on the bench and experience another of Australian soccer's near successes against the South American giants. Although Mark had done his bit to help the Socceroos reach the final stage, he was helpless to do any more.

His next appearance for the Socceroos was in June 1994 against the touring South Africans – the first game between the two nations since the lifting of sanctions against South Africa, in line with the abolition of apartheid. Mark came off the bench for the first game in Adelaide, then played from the start for the second game in Sydney. Both games resulted in 1–0 victories to the Socceroos.

It was the last Australia saw of Mark for quite a while, as he then took advantage of his German heritage to commence what has become a lucrative European career.

•••

By the mid-1990s, the doors to top-class European competitions were well and truly open for talented and ambitious Aussies. If you are going to do something, you may as well do it well, and for top soccer players that equals Italy, Spain or England. Times were good for Mark in Sydney, but the 21-year-old had some dreams to fulfil. *'Ever since I was in the Under-17s for the [1989] Youth World Cup squad in Scotland I knew that I wanted to play soccer in Europe. It was as simple as that. My family knew what*

Secure as ever for Marconi.

I wanted to do and I began to work towards it. I also knew that, because of my heritage, the only place I could go to play, and not have problems with work permits, was Germany.'

One of Mark's Marconi teammates had a Swedish friend who was playing in Germany and had a German agent. After a few international phone calls, Mark went with the same agent and, with plenty of excitement but not a great deal of surprise, he signed with Dinamo Dresden's Bundesliga (German first division) squad. 'Agents are a necessity these days, really. You need them

to help keep a bit of distance from the clubs when it comes to negotiation, and they help you avoid getting caught up in a lot of rubbish that will take your attention away from playing. It is a sinister world out there, though, and you can't trust people one hundred percent. In the end, if you're playing well the agent's job is easy. It is when you're playing badly that you really need your agent to open doors.'

The first two-and-a-half years of Mark's European career in Germany only yielded six first-team games. The only upside was that it didn't leave him much opportunity to

make mistakes – but of course, thoughts like that wouldn't even come close to a professional athlete's mind. Every top athlete sweats a river for a chance to prove their worth, and not getting it can lead to immense frustration. 'The first year in Germany was pretty tough, both in terms of settling in and also because I wasn't playing much. I wanted a chance to prove myself. It was tough to be patient but it was a sacrifice I had to make. I could speak German, but the dialect in Dresden was so different I couldn't really understand people. Five years or so before I arrived, the Berlin Wall had come down which meant Dresden [near the

The big fella training before the Socceroos 2003 clash against England.

182

> **'** There were definitely times when I thought about **calling it quits** and putting those years **down to experience.'**

border of the old East and West Germany] had become open all of a sudden. Even without the wall, though, it was still very much a case of the haves in the West and the have nots in the East, and it was quite a culture shock. I was there by myself for the first six months before my girlfriend [Paloma] came over from Australia, and that definitely helped. These days there is a better support network around the world because there seems to be at least one Aussie at every club.'

Another different aspect of life as a professional player in Germany was the lack of team spirit among the players and clubs. Mark had left a close-knit group of players at Marconi who were backed by a supportive administration to enter a more selfish, bitchy environment. 'The way things are done in Germany is unbelievable. There is no real rapport between the players and the club, and the backstabbing is amazing. The vast majority of players are paid by appearance money – sometimes up to sixty percent of their wage – so if they aren't playing, they are obviously not going to be very happy. It creates a lot of instability, and sometimes even intimidation among the players.'

Needless to say, if your payments are based on appearances, two games in your first year won't fill your garage with fast cars and line your wardrobe with Armani suits. But irrespective of money, Mark

simply wanted a chance to prove himself. Dresden was relegated in 1995, and it was time for Mark's agent to go to work. The club that signed the big Aussie to their books was another Bundesliga club, Kaiserslautern. It didn't quite go to plan, however, and in the next eighteen months, Mark only mustered four games. Once again, not really the reality he had dreamed of. 'There were definitely times when I thought about calling it quits and putting those years down to experience. I was sick of the intimidating environment and of people putting each other down. I wanted to play, and as time passed I could see that it didn't look like I was going to get a chance. I began to wonder if it was all worth it, but Paloma [my fiancée by this point] was very supportive and reassuring and helped me to stick at it. In the end, though, we knew we had to leave Germany. A lot of good can come from bad experiences and it was a great grounding, but we had just had enough.'

It was late 1996 by then, and the European Union had been formed. It made border crossings easier for Europeans and visas for employment within EU nations a thing of the past. For example, an Australian international soccer professional playing in Germany on a German passport could now play in other European countries without the need for a work permit. Mark and Paloma could make the most of the cut red tape and move on.

Of course, a player who has only appeared six times in two-and-a-half years is not going to have his door battered down with offers. Soccer is a fickle industry, though, and sometimes the darkness can turn to light with just the flick of an unsuspecting switch or by the surprise re-call for a national team game. 'I had been on and off the bench [for Kaiserslautern] in '95–96, and we also got relegated. Not the best of times, but then I got a call up for the national team to play Saudi Arabia that October. The call-up was totally out of the blue. I had to ask if they were sure! I was absolutely delighted and surprised to be involved again because I hadn't been playing much, and it gave me a good chance to have a break from Germany. It was brilliant to be able to catch up with my mates in that squad and it really started to give me my confidence back. I only played the last fifteen minutes of the game, and it was the most nervous I have ever been playing for Australia. I hadn't seen the guys in a long time, and I didn't want to play badly in front of them.'

While in camp, Mark took the opportunity to talk to some of the other Socceroos about his desire to leave Germany. Lucas Neill, who was playing with Millwall at the time, put Mark on to his English-based agent, Barry Silkman.

By the time Mark returned to Germany, Kaiserslautern had appointed a new coach

'I became a
premiership player...'

for the 1996–97 season and he brought a 37-year-old 'keeper with him. The coach didn't mess about in telling Mark that he would now be on the bench as the third-choice 'keeper. The door that had been threatening to close slammed shut, but another one soon edged open. *'I wasn't really getting along with the new coach, and I basically told him what I thought. It was then that I knew it was time to go. I took that surprise Socceroo call-up against Saudi as a sign. My German-based agents didn't have contacts in England, but since I was allowed to play elsewhere in Europe by then, England is where I wanted to go. After getting around some legal issues, I ultimately went with Barry Silkman on Lucas' and Eddie Thomson's recommendation.'*

Trials with Manchester City were promptly organised, and Mark did well, both at training and in a game behind closed doors. The club wanted to test him in a competitive environment, though, so asked him to play in a reserves game against Bradford City in Bradford. *'As the story goes, [Manchester City's Assistant Manager] Phil Neal mentioned to [Bradford Manager] Chris Kamara that he hoped Bradford were playing a strong team because he wanted a test for me. Little did he know that Bradford were also looking for a 'keeper, and he was in there talking me up! The funny thing was, I immediately felt at ease when I entered Bradford's ground to play*

for Man City. I liked it there, and I played well. Chris Kamara was on the phone to Barry almost immediately after the game to try and get me on loan. I wasn't interested in a loan deal, though, and wanted to give Man City first priority seeing as they had given me a chance. I went back to Germany thinking that I would become a Man City player, but when the contract came through it had spelling mistakes, and a zero missing in the most important section! Phil Neal had also left during the negotiations, so I became a bit uncomfortable with [Manchester] City. Bradford felt right and were still keen, so ... that's where I went.'

Bradford recognised Mark's talent and drive so paid Kaiserslautern £155,000 (approximately A$350,000) for his services. A pittance for a goalkeeper in England, but a nice return for the German club for an under-used 'keeper.

'Bradford were in the first division and were a selling club at the time. They wanted to get players in cheaply then hopefully sell them for a nice profit in a short time frame. If I did well, I expected not to stay too long, but even I was a bit surprised that I only stayed for thirteen games before I signed for Middlesbrough. It was great to be given the opportunity to play regularly and I was enjoying myself again.'

When Mark signed for Bradford, there was a clause in his contract that would

allow him to go to any club that was willing to pay £1 million (approximately A$2.5 million) for him. An ambitious target for his potential market worth, considering his lack of games to that point, but a clause Bradford couldn't lose by. Ultimately, the clause enabled Mark's rapid rise to the big-time when Middlesbrough offered £1.5 million for his services after his thirteen-straight games for Bradford. *'It only took twenty minutes of discussion with [Middlesbrough Manager] Bryan Robson for me to decide. I became a premiership player, and I must admit it felt good to think about what the people in charge at Kaiserslautern and Dresden must have thought. In German terms, that was huge money for a goalkeeper, and they missed out on it.'*

Mark made an accomplished debut for Middlesbrough in a victory against Stockport in the League Cup semi-finals. Then there were a number of league games, before he walked into a packed Wembley Stadium to face Leicester City in the 1997 League Cup final. Amid the pulsating atmosphere, he was a world away from being a third-choice Bundesliga benchwarmer.

The final went to a replay to break the 1–1 deadlock in the first game. 'Boro lost the second leg 0–1, but Mark didn't take part. In fact, he couldn't use his own second leg for quite a while. *'We played West Ham*

in the league just days after the first game at Wembley, and unfortunately I broke my leg and was out for the rest of the season. The club made the FA Cup final that year, too, but lost to Chelsea. We also got relegated, so it was a rollercoaster start to life in England, to say the least. I played eleven games, though, and despite the disappointments with our results and my injury, I was still happy with my move there.'

After a long and frustrating recovery, Mark became a regular starter for Middlesbrough in the 1997–98 first division. The club was promoted straight back into the Premier League the next year, and Mark's German experience got tucked away in the far recesses of his mind. Middlesbrough has threatened success for a long time, tinkering with the purchase of star players from all over the world to create a winning blend that would finally bring home some silverware for the club's barren trophy cabinet. Seven years after their League Cup final appearance and in Mark's second game for the club, 'Boro secured the 2003 League Cup against Bolton, in front of 72,500 fans at the Millennium Stadium in Wales. In between those two League Cup finals, Mark has toiled to become Australia's number one choice goalkeeper – although his international path was almost as rocky as his club career's.

•••

2003 League Cup winners, Middlesbrough. German frustration is a distant memory.

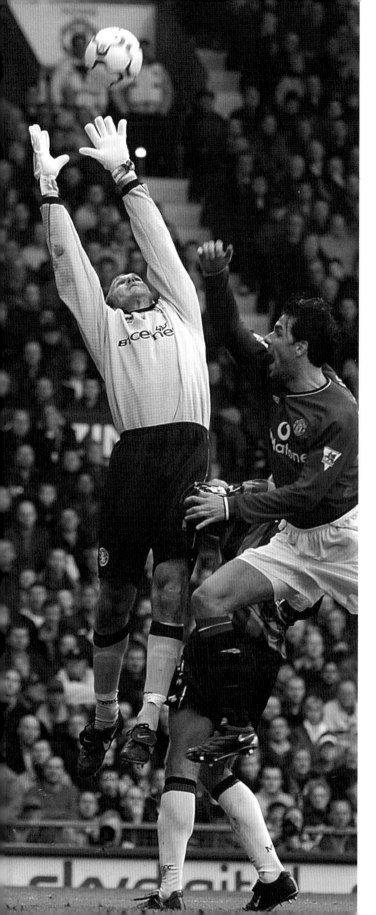

Mark was overlooked for the 1998 World Cup qualifying campaign by then-Socceroo coach Terry Venables, and was disappointed enough to announce his resignation from international duties. In an ironic twist, Venables became Mark's boss at Middlesbrough not long after his failed stint at the helm of the Socceroos. 'Obviously I had my reservations when Terry was first appointed as 'Boro boss, but as soon as I had spoken to him I knew that things would be okay. We got on really well and even managed to joke about what had happened in the past with the [Australian] national team . . . I got to really know what he was like as a person and as a manager, and was really impressed. I consider him one of the best managers I have ever worked with.'

Mark's self-imposed international retirement came to a close in 2000 upon Frank Farina's request that he play, and since that time he has helped the green and gold earn valuable respect among his Australian professional peers playing in Europe in the top leagues. The overpowering in 2000 of Scotland in Scotland, the defeat of France and Brazil in the 2001 Confederations Cup, strong early results in recent World Cup qualifiers and of course the 3–1 defeat in 2003 of England in England gave the European-based Aussies enhanced bragging rights and showed the world our potential. 'The players are desperate to make the World Cup and really show how good we are. We missed out against Uruguay qualifying for the 2002 World Cup and really didn't do ourselves justice over there after a decent 1–0 victory in Melbourne [in front of 90,000 at the MCG]. It is difficult to compare eras, but surely this team is the best we have ever had. We have a team of guys playing well every week in Europe's biggest competitions, and we are hungry for success. We want to make sure the '74 team won't be the only Aussie team in a World Cup finals, and we all want to play for Australia on the world's biggest stage.'

And so, the next big international tournament Mark hopes to play in is the 2006 World Cup, in Germany. The significance of the location for the world's biggest soccer event is not lost on Mark, however being able to prove a point to some knockers in Germany takes more of his focus than his ethnic heritage. 'The fact that the 2006 World Cup is in Germany is an added bonus. Not just because of my family background, but more because I would love to go back there and show a few people where I have got to now.'

•••

Playing regularly in a top European competition has plenty of perks, but it also has its downside. Whether they like it or not, the players are public commodities, and the passion of the fans can mean the players

The kid from Western Sydney stretching to collect against Manchester United.

are showered with praise or heaped with derision depending on the team's fortunes. 'Paloma and I made a conscious choice not to live in Middlesbrough, to give us some privacy. We lived right in the middle of Kaiserslautern when I played for them, and we had people come up to our flat all the time. You do sometimes get people who have the bollocks to come up and have a go at you when you are just walking the streets – even in front of the kids. The only time Paloma and I speak German these days is if we are out and don't want anyone to know what we are talking about. I look forward to when we come back to Australia, so the kids can be treated as their own people at school, and not the kids of a professional footballer. It's great when we come back with the Socceroos. Australian fans are passionate, but in a fun way. It's different, and a lot more enjoyable.'

A professional soccer player's life is full of sacrifice and dedication, however there is also plenty of spare time after training and games. Some players get bored, others become brilliant at Playstation and some become horse racing pundits. Some may study or pursue outside interests, and some, like Mark, find stimulation from family and business interests. For other players, money, fame and time can make for an unruly mix. 'Most of the kids coming through are arrogant to the extreme. They have been told they are good from when they are young, and it often goes to their heads. They are under a lot of pressure from a young age and their youth can just pass on by in that environment. As they get a little older and they have money and fame, they can easily get themselves into trouble. I had my youth in Australia and now I have my family to keep me busy. I rarely go out on the town, because you put one foot out of place and you can be in trouble.'

While time may be on the soccer player's side, when they go to work it is time to work hard. Each player is under intense scrutiny and constant pressure, and if you don't perform, you are out. Move on, next one please.

The typical off-season lasts seven weeks, with an intense five-week pre-season to prepare the players for the upcoming year. Where, just a few years ago, you could report back for a new season in almost any condition expecting pre-season to get you fit, times have changed. 'These days, you have to meet certain weight and skin fold targets when you return, or face heavy fines. I usually take three weeks to put my feet up, then run four or five times a week for a month to keep my fitness levels before I go back.'

While Mark has cultivated a distinct English accent in his time away, he certainly hasn't lost the love for his home country. He and his family will definitely return, it is just

A WEEK AT THE OFFICE...

A typical week for Mark is as follows:

Monday	9.30 am, training. Weights for forty-five minutes with the team until 1 pm. Back into the gym for some abdominal work.
Tuesday	Two sessions. Physical work in the morning, and more tactical/goalkeeper-specific activities in the afternoon. Weights and abdominal work as well.
Wednesday	Rest day (unless injured, when players are required to report for treatment and extra training).
Thursday	9.30 am to noon, training including weights and goalkeeper-specific work.
Friday	9.30 am to noon, training with minimal weights.
Saturday	Let the game begin . . .
Sunday	Day off. Check up on how the Sydney property market is faring, spend time with family.

a matter of when. He may well even play in Australia again to complete his journey, but it would have to be in a Sydney-based team. 'We really miss Sydney. The beaches, the lifestyle, the food, the coffees and being close to everything are huge pluses. I have been away for over ten years, and while I would prefer to live in Sydney, living in England for twelve to fifteen years is a small sacrifice to be doing what I am doing. I can come back in my mid-thirties and if I don't want to, I won't have to work again.'

In the end, elite football in the modern era is a job, and like any other job it has its good and bad points. But Mark Schwarzer knows that if you were to lay all the jobs in the world out in front of him, he wouldn't choose any other. Not many people would.

Lucas NEILL

Socceroo 1996–current

There are approximately 1,400 registered football players at Wakehurst Soccer Club in the Manly district of New South Wales, hundreds and thousands playing all over the state, and recent statistics show there are more than 1.2 million players across Australia – a figure that moves into multiple millions when you include Asia. Add millions more when you enter South and North America, and then consider the millions of European players. All told, FIFA report 250 million people playing organised football – one in every twenty-five people on the planet.

Even though many of those 250 million players may dream of life in the big-time, playing at the pinnacle of their sport, it is a vast understatement to say that most of them will not experience it. For example, there are only 220 players in any given round of the English Premier League, and if you try to figure that out as a percentage of people playing the game worldwide, it's enough to send your calculator haywire. Therefore, the chances of a teenager from Australia breaking into that elite circle are, well, infinitesimal. But while even the slightest chance remains, there will always be hardy and talented players who are willing to give their heart and soul to make it into such elite company.

Lucas Neill is one of those talented and willing players. He became a European professional at seventeen years of age with Millwall, in the English first division. In 2000, he became one of the precious 220 in the English Premier League, when Blackburn Rovers bought him for £1 million (approximately A$2.5 million). In 2003, he had the honour of being selected in the Premier League's 'Best Eleven' by the respected Opta Index, which accumulates statistics throughout the entire season. He was in the company of players such as Ruud Van Nistelrooy, Thierry Henry, Paul Scholes, Patrick Viera and Roy Keane. The kid from Wakehurst Soccer Club had hit the big time. *'From when I was about eight or nine I knew I wanted to play soccer in England. By the time I was ten or eleven I was taking it seriously. I played a lot of sports with my mates, but to make it to the top in soccer was always my dream.'*

In 1969, Lucas' father, Ed, came to Australia as a 21-year-old to get away from the fighting and social tensions in his native Northern Ireland. *'Dad is a smart guy, and saw the opportunities in Australia. He paid the £10 fee to get here by himself, and began working right away in the computer industry. Mum was born here, but had a large family from an Irish background. Dad is Protestant and Mum is Catholic, so it caused a few problems with the respective families when they decided to get married.'*

Lucas was born in Sydney in 1978, and began kicking a ball around from a young age. The Wakehurst Under-7s outfit was his first team and he loved it. Then, when he was eight, Ed's work took the family to England for eighteen months and a key part of Lucas' footballing development took place. *'There didn't seem to be any junior teams in England for me to join, so I had to join the Takeley Cubs to play. Cubs wasn't really my thing, but I loved the football. Just being in England gave me a taste for the game that has never left me. I watched it all the time on TV, and mixed with all the passionate supporters of the game. I became hooked in that environment. Of course, I took heaps of scarves, shirts and the best boots with me when we came back to Australia, but by then I knew I wanted to go back there to play one day.'*

By the time the Neills returned to Australia, Lucas was a 10-year-old with the beginnings of an English accent. He rejoined Wakehurst and became part of one of the most successful junior teams in the state. He wasn't shy, and on school casual clothes days he wore his prized English soccer uniforms (including shorts and socks) instead of the usual board shorts and thongs. He slept in a room covered by posters of Dalglish, Rush, Souness and Johnston from his beloved Liverpool FC. But daring to dream is one thing – deciding to turn those dreams into reality is an entirely different matter. *'We had a perfect backyard for soccer and cricket. Then, Mum and Dad decided they wanted a pool so the*

Socceroos 3, England 1. Lucas, Craig Moore and Stan Lazaridis show what it means.

'…I had to pick out different sections of brick and aim for them for hours on end.'

soccer games had to move to the street. Not long after, a wall was built as a part of the yard, and it happened to be about the same size as a goal. I remember hearing that Craig Johnston used to mark targets on a wall for practise when he first got to England, so that's what I did. I got in trouble for marking the wall, so I had to pick out different sections of brick and aim for them for hours on end. Dad always said to practise my left foot too, and it made a big difference to my game. I didn't just do it because it was fun, though, I did it to get better. I did it because I knew I had to.'

He started building a reputation in his area as a talented, energetic midfielder who was a great passer of the ball, and it was no surprise when he was selected in the Manly Warringah Under-11s representative team. Not long after that, he was picked in the New South Wales Under-13s team, and began his steady progression up the hierarchy. *'I played well in the first game at the Under-13s national championships, and scored to top it off. There was a write-up in the paper the next day, and I began to think that, just maybe, I could achieve my dream. Mum and Dad did a great job of keeping me grounded though, and didn't let any of it go to my head. Those lessons helped later in my career.'*

He continued to impress at national championships each year up until the Under-15s titles in Brisbane. After that tournament he was asked by AIS Head Coach Ron Smith to spend a week in Canberra, to see if he liked the idea of training there. Lucas liked what he saw, and eagerly accepted a two-year scholarship. *'I didn't really know what to expect from that week, and had no idea how good the set-up was. It didn't take long to realise how good the opportunity was, though. Ron Smith was great right from the start, and remains probably the biggest influence on my career.'*

Lucas' family had always stressed the importance of an education, and the AIS scholarship program paid attention to that aspect of a young soccer player's life. In truth, for the players, school studies came a distant second to soccer. *'We only had to do four subjects, and most of the soccer players chose to study Children's Books because it basically gave us Friday off and we could go and play soccer instead. The whole thing was very relaxed. It was casual dress, and [the soccer players] stood out in our sponsored, AIS tracksuits. The girls loved us, but the boys hated us.'*

Lucas is the big kid in the back row, third from the left. Jimmy 'The Jet' Trevener (L) remains one of his bigger coaching influences.

Rubbing shoulders with Pelé.

Team training was held every day at 5 pm, for at least two hours, coupled with weight sessions on Tuesday and Thursday at 6.30 am. There were also frequent games and tours, and Lucas couldn't get enough. *'Training was always intense and all we seemed to do, but for me it could never go long enough. We were learning every day and it was brilliant. The facilities, the education – in terms of how to look after yourself and handle things off the pitch – were fantastic. In fact, the AIS program was untouched by anything I saw when I got to England. Only a few English clubs even come close now, and more and more of them are starting to study how things are done in Australia.'*

Another aspect that prepared Lucas for a professional life in England was developing maturity and independence, vital for sticking it out by yourself in a foreign country. He was only fifteen when he moved to Canberra, and developing as an adult in the positive environment constructed by Ron Smith and assistant coach Tom Sermanni was hugely beneficial. So too were the

international tours that introduced the young players to different cultures, as well as the experience of playing the game out of a suitcase. It also did quite a bit for their confidence. *'I remember a tour to Hong Kong and Malaysia, and another to South America. Even in South America we would win games against the next lot of Brazilian stars. While I was in the AIS I knew I was getting closer to my dream, and by the time we began winning games overseas, I could start to smell it.'*

Just as Lucas' two-year AIS scholarship came to an end, Tom Sermanni organised a trial for he and Andy McDermott with Queens Park Rangers of London. QPR signed Andy and wanted Lucas too, but the 17-year-old's parents wanted him to come home and finish school first. *'I wasn't too annoyed about having to come back, because after seeing what I did while I was there, I knew I would go back again and make it. Andy and I were both way ahead of the kids [in England], and I just knew I would be able to do it.'*

In 1995, with Children's Books and his other subjects out of the way, Lucas unwrapped his passport for another trip to the UK. QPR wanted to have another look over a week, but Lucas felt he had done enough previously to not have to trial again. Millwall had seen him in trial games for

QPR and agreed with this sentiment. His agent, Barry Silkman, negotiated on his behalf, and Lucas became a Millwall player without a trial – and without even meeting the coach or committee. He boarded the plane to England with his school leaving certificate and a four-year contract as a professional soccer player in the English first division.

•••

Lucas arrived at Millwall in early November 1995, and played in a youth team game two days later. He did well, and immediately earned respect from his peers. He tested a few nerves, though, when he refused to clean boots and toilets with the other young players at the club. *'I didn't sign as a youth player, I signed as a pro. I wasn't there to clean boots.'* He was soon playing regularly in the reserve team, and then early in 1996 Mick McCarthy was replaced as coach by Jimmy Nichol. On 17 February 1996, Lucas' dreams began to materialise when he was selected to play on the right of midfield against Luton. *'I began to think, "I've made*

'The AIS program was untouched by anything I saw when I got to England.'

'It took years, really, to get back to my best.'

it." I wasn't nervous though, because I knew I was good enough, and my parents reminded me that it was what I had been waiting for and to make the most of it. I was a bit in awe of the crowd when we started, but I soon settled. We lost by a last-minute goal, but I did well and was pretty happy.'

Millwall were on top of the table for much of the 1995–96 season, but they slipped alarmingly throughout the year and ended up in the relegation places. 'It was a weird feeling because I was doing quite well and playing regularly, but we went down. It was a good lesson, actually, because I saw how much it meant to the players and the fans to be tagged as losers. It was a pretty harsh introduction to life as a professional.'

The 1996–97 season was spent in Division Two, but Lucas stood out in the lower league and played thirty-nine games. He missed Australia, but was comfortable in his life overseas and knew his career would develop further – a belief echoed by his first Socceroo appearance. 'I made my debut against Saudi Arabia during Eddie Thomson's last game as coach, in October of 1996. When I came on at half-time, I was over the moon. I hadn't even played in Aussie youth teams before I became a Socceroo. The two things I had wanted when I was a kid were to play professionally in England and to play for Australia. I was still eighteen and I was doing both.'

If a professional sportsman hasn't experienced hardship on their journey to success, then they are about to. Lucas learned the truth of that old adage in the 1997 Under-20s Youth World Cup in Malaysia. The rigours of professional football were placing repeated strain on his feet, resulting in stress fractures. The problems were exacerbated in the first game of the tournament against Hungary, but Lucas was determined to play the next match against Argentina. 'I had a cortisone injection for the cause. I mean, we were playing Argentina at the Youth World Cup. [The cortisone] took the pain away, but it put a lot of fluid into the area and gave me no flexibility. I came on with fifteen minutes to go, and as I turned I snapped it. We won 4–3 and everyone was buzzing, but I was gutted. My foot was gone and I was out for months.'

As fate would have it, the injury took place while some off-field issues were also causing stress. Millwall were experiencing major financial difficulties, and not long before the Youth World Cup, Glasgow Rangers came in with an exciting offer to buy Lucas for £800,000, with £5,000 a week in wages. The offer suited Lucas' growing ambitions, but Millwall demanded double that fee. This soured Lucas' relationship with the Board, and to make matters worse, he now had to come back from Malaysia and spend four soul-

destroying months in the gym. 'It's a cranky environment in the gym. No one wants to be there and everyone is frustrated. Sometimes it boils over, too. I was in there for what seemed like forever after an operation on my foot, then when I started playing again I had the same problem with the other one, and was back in the gym again. There were times I thought about going home and packing it in, but when life bites you on the arse, you just have to be strong. It made me hungrier, and while it took years, really, to get back to my best, I did it and now I am playing in the Premier .League.'

The 1997–98 season was basically a write-off, but in his comeback season of 1998–99, Lucas managed thirty-five games and scored six goals. He backed it up with thirty-three appearances in 1999–2000 and was playing near his best, but was experiencing more trouble with the Millwall Board. 'They wanted me to re-sign but I knew I needed to move on. I enjoyed being with the players and coaches, but I didn't get on with the Board and I told them so. It came to a bit of a head when I told them I'd been selected to play in the 2000 Olympic team and that I wanted to go. They said no and told me I had to choose between Millwall or the Olympics. If I went, I would never play for them again. I told them to stick it, that they could fire me if they wanted because I was going. In the end, they said they wouldn't pay me while I was gone – but it wasn't about the money, it was about playing for your country. We stuffed up in the Olympics, which is something I am still bitterly disappointed about, but at least I got to play for Australia again.'

He returned from the Olympics with a distinct feeling he wouldn't be a Millwall player for much longer. The team of maturing young players did well that year though, and won promotion back to Division One. It left a sweet taste, but by now Lucas knew he wanted more. He felt that his new agent had too many personal connections at Millwall so took matters into his own hands. His strong relationship with the coaching staff meant he could lay his cards on the table with them, and after the coach reluctantly agreed to put him on the transfer list, Ray Harford (Millwall Assistant Coach) organised a three-day trial at Blackburn Rovers. '[Blackburn coach] Graham Souness picked me up from the airport, and on the way to training said that the pace would be quick and would take some getting used to. It happened to be an international week [a designated time for international matches] and all of Blackburn's international players were away. So there were only 10 to 12 first team players at my first session. I did enough to hold my own, but the next day was one where everything I did came off. By the Thursday, the international players were back, and I did well again. That same day, the regular right-back got injured, and so did the guy who

would've taken his place. Unlucky for them, but lucky for me, because Souness decided I would fill that spot. That's football.'

Souness was so keen that he wanted Lucas to play two days later against Sunderland in front of 45,000 people. To make that happen, the transfer had to be completed by noon on the Friday, and until Thursday evening Lucas' agent and the Millwall Board didn't even know he was there. 'I told my agent to be in Blackburn on Friday morning to negotiate for me, then to sort out Millwall. Blackburn was offering £600,000 plus another £400,000 after I played thirty games. In the end, everything was agreed ten minutes before the deadline and I became a Blackburn player. I rang

Mum and Dad immediately and they starting crying. Dad got on the first plane he could to get over and watch the game.

'My debut was everything that I thought it would be, and more. There were times during the game that I thought "How good is this?" This was the real deal. I was a Premier League player. I had done it. My second game was live on TV against Ipswich, and the third was at home versus Bolton, and I managed to score. It was the last game Dad saw before he had to go home which made it even more special. The feeling was incredible. I got Man of the Match, and was a regular in the side for the rest of the season.'

Scoring goals sometimes makes people do funny things!

'My debut was everything that I thought it would be, and more.'

Most people who are even remotely interested in the English Premier League have marvelled at the skill of Scholes, the goalscoring ability of Van Nistelrooy, or the dynamic, creative influence of Giggs. Most people have shaken their heads in awe at Thierry Henry's devastating pace, guile and technique, or Alan Shearer's power and strength. Lucas Neill is just as impressed by these players, but he doesn't have the luxury of admiring them from a distance – he is paid to stop them in their tracks. *'There are some great players in the English game, and I love the challenge of playing against them. It's a good test and I love it when I come*

out on top, because it shows I belong in the Premier League. Harry Kewell would be up there, but the toughest three to play against would be Shearer, Van Nistelrooy and Henry at number 1. You really need him to have an off day and defend in numbers, because he can expose anybody. He is so fast, even when he has the ball.'

•••

Due to his family heritage, Lucas could have played for the Northern Ireland national team, and therefore spent more of his professional career in Europe. But there was no way anything was going to stop him playing for Australia. *'There is no prouder moment than singing the national anthem with all the Aussie boys. Everyone gets tingles, and everyone is willing to do anything for each other. It is great to catch up when we are together in camp, too. There are stories from guys playing in all corners of the globe, and it is always a good laugh. It's also great for a change of scenery, from training at your club every day, and to have everybody pulling the same rope. At club level you are in it for yourself, but with the national team everyone will fight for the common cause. At club level you want to make one position your own, and not let anyone take it from you. With the national team you don't care what position you play, as long as you can do your bit.'*

The Australian media feeds off the club versus country issue and likes to suggest a lack of national pride among Australia's elite players. It's an attitude that bemuses Lucas. *'Of course everyone wants to play for Australia, but it's a dog eat dog world out there and sometimes you can't have everything you want. Everybody's goal now is to make the World Cup finals, and I have to make sure I play in every game I can to make sure I am a part of the team that*

qualifies. I am not going to throw this chance away, and I know the other guys feel the same way.'

Lucas may only be a recent Socceroo, but he is a young player who will form the backbone of the team for years to come. And the more times he can pull on that shirt, the happier he will be. *'I know guys who have played 100 times for their country, but that won't happen for this generation of Aussies. There are simply not enough games played, but I want to make the most of each of them. Hopefully it's quality over quantity.'*

It is obvious that Lucas is a proud Australian, even if he has lived in England since he was seventeen, and has developed a distinctly English accent. He has no desire to play football in a country other than England because, in his view, the English Premier League is the most exciting competition in the world, and it suits his attitude to the game. He will return to Australia one day, but he hopes for the sake of his career that day is far, far away. There is still a lot more to do. *'I want to win things in England. I want to earn double the money and be bombarded by accolades. It's not that the money and attention is what it is all about, but they come with the territory of a successful, respected player in the world's toughest competition – and that's what I am after.'*

A dream come true. At Blackburn's Premier League home.

Make every pass count.

Of course, there is pressure associated with being a highly paid sportsperson. On-field pressure is something that most people at the top level thrive on, but off-field pressures can often be more problematic. For example, Lucas came under the international media spotlight after a tackle that broke the leg of Liverpool's Jamie Carragher in 2003, and had to deal with all manner of misquoting and innuendo. They were tough times, but sometimes the positive reports can be just as difficult to handle. *'You can't place much stock in what people outside the club say and think. For the first three or four years in England I used to pay attention to transfer speculation surrounding me and it affected my game. You often see young players who are supposed to be the "next big thing" talking the talk, but then they don't walk the walk and they get found out. I would rather my performances do the talking than my mouth, because performances are real and talk can be anything. I usually tell the media in the tunnel after games that the manager has banned me from speaking publicly, and it works pretty well I have to say!'*

•••

Right from his early days in the New South Wales junior state teams and at the AIS Lucas knew players exist in a funnel where their talent, determination, ambition and luck govern where they will settle. At the top of the funnel are the millions of players around the globe, and towards the tip of the funnel are the players with the talent to go all the way. *'We were told regularly at the AIS that only a few players would be able to squeeze out the bottom of the funnel and make it to the highest level. I haven't played in the World Cup yet, but I am playing in the Premier League, so I guess I am one of the lucky few.'*

As a kid, he used to have to wait for birthday presents or buy the soccer strips that he would wear to school or around the house. Now, Lucas has earned the right to wear them in front of a television audience of millions each week. And the enormity of that fact still excites him. *'I came to England as a little boy in a big man's world, and I guess in some ways that's still true. I still pinch myself every now and then to make sure it's real. The whole thing sometimes feels like a board game that someone else is playing, but this life exceeds my dreams. I wouldn't swap this job for the world.'*

'Of course everyone wants to play for Australia.'

Vince GRELLA

Socceroo 1999–current

When Antonio Grella was twenty, he left Italy with hopes and dreams of starting a new life Down Under. His future wife was also Italian, though she arrived in Australia when she was eight. They had three sons and one daughter in their adopted homeland, and spent most of their spare time at sporting grounds around Victoria. From a young age, one of the sons decided he wanted to be a professional soccer player. He went to the Victorian Institute of Sport (VIS) and Australian Institute of Sport (AIS), then played in the national league. When the boy turned twenty, he packed up to return on the path of opportunity his father had beaten from Italy, to play soccer in the land of his heritage. Vince Grella was about to fulfil his dreams. *'It was always my dream to play in Italy. I guess it was partly because of my background, but it was also because it is the best league in the world. My dad left Italy and went to Australia when he was twenty because of the opportunities and I did the same in reverse.'*

Frank Farina had spent a short spell in the Italian top flight, and injury had meant that Paul Okon was in and out of the first team at Lazio for a number of years. That was the history of Australia's influence in the Serie A and Vince knew the path wouldn't be simple. He was prepared to be patient and do the right things, though. He knew his time would come.

•••

Vince's journey began at Springvale City Soccer Club – an outer-suburban club in Melbourne, pretty much like any other club in suburban Australia. His brothers played at the same club and his parents were coach, kit washer, orange peeler, canteen assistant, amateur psychologist, line marker and taxi service. The Grella boys all showed great talent and quickly made the local representative teams. Vince, the youngest, developed a reputation as the most tenacious. He began to take up the most time in 'Dad's taxi' as the Toyota Lite Ace van began to clock up kilometres driving around the state.

'I guess it is the same for most young players all over the country, but no amount of money or presents could ever repay what my parents have done for me. The whole time, they didn't put much emphasis on results and even when I started to progress, they never bragged or pushed me. They kept me grounded and still do.'

The offer of a VIS scholarship came just after Vince's fourteenth birthday and he eagerly accepted. The program introduced him to sports science, a professional approach to skill development and what is required to 'make it'. *'I don't just say this to win points, but the VIS and AIS programs are well ahead of anything I have seen in Italy, and the other boys playing overseas say the same. [VIS Head Coach] Ernie Merrick is fantastic at running that program*

and he is also a gentleman in a bad man's game . . . Ernie and [former AIS Head Coach] Ronny Smith are the real people in this game – not the Vince Grellas getting their one second of fame.'

By the time Vince turned sixteen, the AIS offered him a scholarship to live in Canberra and take his training to an even higher level. *'I just made it into the AIS program after missing out on the Under-17s Joey's tour of South America [playing] under Les Scheinflug. Les also had an influence in picking the AIS squad, so I thought I would be in trouble. In the end, [AIS coaches] Ronny Smith and Steve O'Connor had faith in me and I made it. It was my first experience of the harsh side of soccer, but the respect Ronny and Steve gave me when I was just sixteen did wonders for my confidence. They said I wouldn't need the Under-17s to progress to the Socceroos one day, and that I should just keep my head down and get on with it.'*

Scholarships to the VIS and AIS are not automatic passports to fame, fortune and a Socceroo shirt, and the players were reminded of the need for something special that only they could provide. *'We were constantly reminded that, out of the twenty players in the AIS, only two or three were likely to kick on. We had to make the decision to work extra hard to be one of them. There was Brett Emerton, Marco Bresciano and me from my year, and I don't know what the other guys are doing now. While we were all ambitious to make it overseas, the coaches made sure to encourage us to be passionate about playing for Australia as well. We didn't see a future playing in Australia, but we certainly saw a future playing for Australia.'*

The first experience Vince had playing for Australia was in the Under-20s squad that played in the 1997 Malaysian Youth World Cup. He was only seventeen, and revelled in the opportunity. *'I travelled with the squad, then one of the players got injured and I was in. I played every game and loved the challenge. I was younger than most of the guys in that tournament, but I didn't care and just got stuck in anyway.'*

He had also finished his first year in the NSL with Canberra Cosmos by this stage. The relatively weak team provided a good introduction to senior soccer, but Vince decided not to leave the AIS behind right away. *'I was still living and training at the AIS, but also playing in the NSL. Sometimes I trained with the AIS in the morning before playing for Canberra in the afternoon. I was doing well . . . and didn't feel out of place.'*

As the 1996–97 NSL season closed, it was time for Vince to break his ties with the AIS and Cosmos and throw his lot in as a

full-time, professional player. The ambitious new NSL club Carlton had entered the fray, and they persuaded the young terrier to join their ranks for the 1997–98 season. It was a talented team under the management of first-time coach Eddie Krncevic and they made the grand final that year. Vince made twenty-two appearances and, while he was doing well, he wasn't billed as the star of the team, or as the 'next big thing' in Australian soccer. There weren't too many people willing to suggest he would create a lucrative European career at that point, but fortunately Vince wasn't one of them.

He was with Carlton for the 1998–99 season, but played only one game before being placed on the bench. In the meantime, however, he had a friend in Italy who was promoting his abilities. *'My agent called me and said that Empoli needed a young midfielder, so I went over for a week's trial. They were interested, but didn't want to pay for me, so I ended up going on loan for a year from Carlton in what was basically an extended trial. They offered me a professional contract after that year.'*

Carlton paid nothing to Springvale City, even though they made $200,000 when he was signed on to professional forms at Empoli. *'It is a shame that Springvale didn't get any money, I think they deserved it. In my opinion, Carlton was run by the wrong people, and should never have gone bankrupt. In saying that, I was enjoying it at first. Then they signed [NSL stalwart] Andrew Marth for season '98–99 and I could see the club's attitude was a short-term focus on the NSL instead of promoting the young players. It was from there that I started talking with Empoli.'* Carlton may have pocketed $200,000 for the young Victorian, but when recent talk from AC

'...no amount of money or presents could ever repay what my parents have done for me.'

Milan and Fiorentina placed Vince's market value at A$14 million, the club officials must have wondered what could have been.

From the day he arrived in Italy he had a job to do. Coming off the bench against the mighty Juventus at the Del Alpi stadium in his first Serie A game, playing against the World Footballer of the Year and World Cup winner, Zinadine Zidane, was just part of it. *'I do remember getting selected for the game. We always travelled with twenty players, but only eighteen would make the team sheet. I wasn't expecting to be in the eighteen, but one of the players got sick and I was in. I was doing cartwheels inside but had to keep a lid on it. I couldn't go jumping around the room or anything at the team meeting, because it is all about respect in Italy, and you have to keep cool. A lot of good things are played down in a career, and you have to keep your concentration – especially when things are written about you in the papers. As it turned out, someone got injured, and on I went. From there I just did what I was paid to do . . . words don't do it justice. All the emotions get put in a bottle. Maybe one day I'll open it and it will explode, but for now, it all gets tucked away.'*

Vince played five Serie A games that first season with Empoli, and although the club finished firmly at the foot of the ladder, he had done enough to be selected in the Australian 1999 Youth World Cup team in Nigeria. He was starting to experience – and excel under – increasing pressure. *'There is always pressure when you make those sides, because there are always people who think you shouldn't be there . . . or that you aren't good enough. They can talk as much as they like, though, because I was there and they were just watching. I use that as motivation because I know I have to take my chances.'*

Being a Serie A player did not equal a swollen bank account that first year in Italy. Because Vince was effectively on loan from Carlton, he was earning the same money as he was in Australia – and living in a country with a much higher cost of living to boot. But he was training and playing every day and he was determined to see it through. *'It wasn't easy in the first year. I could speak Italian, which helped, but I was still the outsider and basically by myself. There are not huge friendships in the game, and not too many people go out of their way to help you. I should've bought shares in Telstra when I first arrived, I was calling home so often.'*

Of course, it isn't just loneliness that can break an aspiring career. The consistently high standard, the huge number of high-quality players and the intense pressure to perform can only be withstood by the strongest of wills. *'It was a big shock when I arrived. The quality and the intensity is so high every day and at every training session. You can't drop off for even one second. All you do is play soccer . . . and it is all most of the guys there have ever done, so of course the standard is amazing. You just have to work extra hard and be ready for every session.'*

At the end of that first season, Vince and Empoli were relegated to Serie B for 1999–2000. Vince spent the first half of that second season frustrated on the bench, and his European career was at risk of stalling. Still, it was better than being on the bench in the NSL. *'We didn't tell Empoli that they basically bought me off the bench at Carlton. There is no way they would've let me trial if they knew! We have a laugh about it now, but it just goes to show how much opinions differ in this game. That second year was frustrating, but I was still glad to be there and learning about the game.'*

Vince's development would continue in Serie B for a couple more years, but not with Empoli. The club decided to loan him out to rival club Ternana, and it wasn't really a surprise. *'I arrived back to pre-season ten days late after the '99 Youth World Cup and too much partying back in Australia afterwards. I was taking too many things for granted and didn't have the right attitude. I was in bad shape when I got back and picked up injuries I couldn't shake. It is*

'overnight success' is an oxymoron. 'You have to be patient. The ages of nineteen to twenty-three are important development years. I spent time in the Serie B, which was perfect because I could get first-team experience. I knew the whole time that it was helping me prepare for the Serie A. No one makes it overnight. Harry Kewell, for example, went to what was then an unfashionable club [Leeds] at sixteen and paid his dues in the youth and reserve side before getting his chance. He was then able to develop in the first team because Leeds weren't a top club.'

Big clubs usually don't have the time to develop young players. They need success – and often they need to buy success in the form of proven performers. Therefore, playing in the lower leagues gave Vince the breathing space he needed. 'The pressure is on to perform. The clubs help you improve because it increases the chances of them getting a better financial reward from you. It is not like the coaches in Australia, where they do it for you and hopefully for the development of the game. In Italy, they coach you for their own interests – but that's okay because it helps my interests, too. In the end, though, if you aren't improving and adding value to yourself, you're out. And it can happen at any time.'

There is always an element of chance in an elite athlete's career, but it is those who make the most of their chances who find

lucky I have a good manager, and he got me out on loan for a change of scenery. I ended up living in Terni for eighteen months before Empoli decided they wanted me back. I knew they were keen to push for Serie A and had a good coach, because Marco [Bresciano] was playing there by then. We are great friends and he helped persuade me to go back. I had a new attitude by then, put in a great pre-season, then played every game [in 2001–02] on the way to promotion.'

It is a fallacy that talented young players can walk straight into the big-time of European soccer. Everyone has to pay their dues and prove their worth. The term success. *'You have to be ready to take your chance. That is what you train for. I got mine going to Empoli from Carlton, but ever since the day I arrived I knew I couldn't relax for a minute. All sorts of players get different opportunities, but not many see them through. It's like jumping the gun in a 100-metre sprint. They might be out in front for thirty metres or so, but then they'll do a hammy and won't last the 100 metres. You have to be prepared to take your chance, but also to last the 100 metres. And beyond. Just getting there is not making it, and there are lots of ups and downs if you want to stick it out.'*

And so, it took Vince three long and patient years of hard work and discipline to learn how to play at the top level, and for Empoli to see that he might just have a long-term future. It is not an unusual situation, but it is one that many aspiring players don't have the willpower to withstand. Vince does, though, and he played thirty-two Serie A games in season 2001–02, after the club won promotion, and confirmed himself as an equal adversary at that level every week. He backed up with thirty-one games in the 2002–03 season, and is no longer a player who had 'some' Serie A game time; he is a respected Serie A competitor.

Life in Serie A is life under a microscope. Privacy is at a premium, and the media are quick to take any word out of context. Fans have short, unforgiving memories. Players

have to be on guard at all times and friendships within clubs are rare. You have to look after yourself physically, and have to forego the natural social urges of young people across the globe. Players are quick to remind people of the harsh realities of the job, but most will also be quick to appreciate the upside as well – big crowds, pulsating atmosphere, adoration, fancy cars, expensive clothes and wages that can set up a family for life. But most importantly, every single day is spent kicking a beautiful, brand

'Life as a professional is tough, but can also be very rewarding.'

new, top-of-the-range ball around on a pristine, gorgeous piece of grass. That is the reason why thousands of young Australians will risk everything to turn themselves into a European professional and Socceroo. *'Life as a professional is tough, but can also be very rewarding. Everybody's experience is*

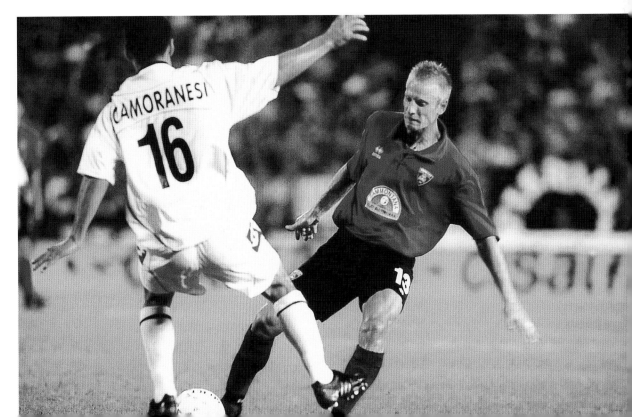

Tenacity and determination are hallmarks of Grella's game.

different, though, and there is no right or wrong way to do things. Some young Aussies are at Empoli now, and while we speak about how everything is going, I try not to give advice. It's just like if I see a good movie – I'll tell people it's worth seeing and let them experience it for themselves. I don't say why it was good because that's just my opinion. Sometimes you have to let your baby fall on its arse.'

•••

Vince, as a professional, may feel he needs to keep a lid on his emotions concerning ongoing achievements in Serie A, but he wears his heart on his sleeve when it comes to being a Socceroo. 'I made my Socceroo debut when I came off the bench against the FIFA XI, to open Stadium Australia in '99. I started against Manchester United a month later when I had just gone to Italy. Both times Raul Blanco was the coach, as he was for the 2000 Olympics when I also played. Other than that, I was out of sight for a while, so it was great to be asked into Frank [Farina's] squad in 2003 and get to wear the green and gold again.'

The 2000 Sydney Olympic tournament had been a huge disappointment, particularly considering the grand scale of the event. The first-up loss to Italy in front of over 90,000 at Vince's home-town MCG was particularly emotional. 'It was such a big occasion and I had all my family there watching. The crowd was huge and it was the Olympics, against Italy, of all things. People ask who my family was supporting, but every one of them, including my grandparents, were 100 percent behind us. Australia has given them so much.'

In 2003, he came off the bench in the historic victory over England, the narrow loss to Ireland and the victory over Jamaica. He is thrilled to have forced his way into the international picture pre-2006 World Cup, but knows that he will have to once again be patient to get his chance in his favoured midfield position – occupied by captain Paul Okon and coveted by a host of other top-quality Aussies. But when he does, he won't look back. 'Coaches make their decisions and you live by them. I am looking forward to playing a lot more games for Australia, and I am just going to be ready to take my chance when it comes. The spirit in the Socceroo camp was fantastic when I came back, and it was great to catch up with everybody in that environment. Of course it is competitive, but it is more relaxed than the club environment because there is a different sort of pressure, and the problems with clubs disappear. We are there to represent our country together.'

Considering the spirited, tenacious and considered way in which he plays the game, his attitude to the honour of being a Socceroo should come as no surprise. 'I can't get enough of that national anthem before a game and I want to be out there for it every time I can. I will bite, scratch and kick . . . whatever I have to if it helps get us to the 2006 World Cup. And when we get there, we will really show people what Australian soccer is all about.

'I can tell you it is complete rubbish if people think that we want to get there because it is good for our careers and will put more money in our pay packets. Playing for Australia has never been about the money. If it was we wouldn't do it. I add value to Empoli by my performances each week in the Serie A, not by a couple of games for Australia.'

•••

On one of the occasions I spoke with Vince on the telephone, he was preparing for a day at the office. For many people that might mean making a sandwich and ironing a shirt before heading off to write reports, pack boxes, conduct research, or paint houses. Vince, on the other hand, was in a plush hotel before a home game against AC Milan. 'We always stay in a hotel before games, whether it's home or away. It starts us getting ready for the match, and gets us away from other influences. The club can make sure we eat properly, and they can look after everybody. Everyone has breakfast together, then goes off for a light training session and practises set pieces before the game in the evening. I think it's a

Showing poise at the 2000 Olympics, against Italy.

'I am the kid from Springvale.'

good *way to do it.'* Our conversation was interrupted by a knock on his hotel door at exactly 10.30 pm. Vince excused himself, then neatly slipped into a brief Italian conversation. 'That was the masseur,' he told me afterwards. *'He always comes around at 10.30 to see if I want anything. I don't know if he'd actually give a massage then, though, to be honest – I have never thought to say yes.'* A minute later, we followed the same process as the doctor made sure Vince was okay. *'Si, si,'* Vince replied seriously before laughing down the phone, *'I reckon they only come around to make sure everyone is in their rooms alone.'*

Vince knows well enough that he has a dream job, and that most people don't get offered a massage or clinical check once a week before they head off to the factory. *'I still get excited about playing games against the big players and the big clubs like Juve, Inter, Roma and Milan. Bloody oath I do. I am the kid from Springvale!'*

Vince married an Italian and became a father to precious twins at twenty-four years of age. Their support has been a major boost in his career and has given him a new perspective on life's priorities. *'I can come home from the stress of training and see Barbara and the girls and be immediately relaxed. For the first two years in Italy, I ate every meal at a restaurant near my place (after making sure it was in my contract), and it is so much better to have a home life*

now. *Barbara and I met in Empoli, then I was loaned out to Ternana and we were apart for a while. I really enjoy living in Tuscany with her and the girls and while I do still think of Australia as home, I can definitely see us living in Italy for a long time to come.'*

His years battling to break into the toughest league in the world have allowed him to quietly appreciate his achievements and strengthened his belief that hurdles can be overcome. His million-dollar feet have not floated off the ground, and he knows that he is merely there to play his small part in the bigger story of world football. He has cultivated a maturity beyond his years, and is well aware that there aren't many people he can trust, that the pressure of the massive amounts of money that run the game are not conducive to the selfless acts experienced in his youth. But that's okay, because he has a grander master. *'Some people will like me and some won't. More than my fair share of people have said I don't have what it takes to play at the top level, but that's only their opinion. In the end, the green rectangle will be my judge.'*

'In the end,

the green rectangle

will be my judge.'

Eyes on the prize; his Serie A dream comes true.

ACKNOWLEDGEMENTS

Thanks must go to Random House for taking on this project, and to Leonard Montagnana and Woof Creative Solutions (www.woof.com.au) – a job bloody well done, and all for a couple of cans of Coke! The support of the ASA (and in particular Gary Moretti) has been invaluable, as has the support of Jimmy Tansey at Adidas, and the Australian Professional Footballer's Association.

Cheers to my mates around the country for accepting my freeloading ways on my travels – Steve and Be, Jase and Michelle, Jasp and Ang, Jodie and Christian, Ben and Jacinta. And cheers as well to Mike Edgley at Meaesh Marketing for lending me his ears from day one.

I am indebted to Neil Jameson, Craig Johnston, Matt Hall, Leo Karis at Management and Media, Sam Ayoub at Ultra Management, Ed Neill, Pas and the Grella family, Bonnie Mersiades, Joe Janko, Dean Hennessey, Jeff Hopkins and Ian Greener. Thank you for your enthusiasm and assistance in opening those doors.

Hats off to Val for tirelessly letting me know where apostrophes go and where commas don't. And also for making sure this book would appeal beyond the soccer world.

Thanks also have to go to the hundreds and thousands of people in clubs around the country who have quietly marked the lines and set up the nets over the years, played taxi service, cut the oranges, served in the canteen, raised funds and encouraged the kids. There would be no Socceroos without you.

And finally, thanks to the superstar who invented coffee.

'And thanks
to all the
soccer fans!'

PICTURE CREDITS

The author would like to acknowledge the following for reproducing photographs used in *Our Socceroos*:

Page ix, taken from *Walk Alone* by Neil Jameson and Craig Johnston.

Page 2, courtesy of Jimmy Rooney.

Pages 56, 59, 69, 70, 71, 72 (left) and 73, courtesy of Johnny Warren.

Page 105, taken from *Anderlecht Unique*, published by Roularta Books, Belgium.

Page 125, 131 and 159, courtesy of the Victorian Soccer Federation (VSF).

Pages 129, 151, 153, 161, 162, 173, 175, 176, 179, 182, 185 and 186, courtesy of Getty Images.

Pages 132 and 134, taken from *My World is Round* by Bonnie Mersiades.

Page 137, 152, 154, 155, 157, 158, 180 and 181, courtesy of Joe Janko, Double-J Photographics.

Page 143, courtesy of Action Images, UK.

Page 160, courtesy of Charlie Yankos.

Page 197, courtesy of Ian Greener, Victorian Soccer Federation.

All other photographs are courtesy of the players interviewed.

If you would like to contact the author or the designer directly, please visit their website, www.oursocceroos.com, or email to neil@oursocceroos.com.

REFERENCES

www.ozfootball.net.au
(I can't believe the amount of info on this site)

www.ak-tsc.de
(Andre the German Aussie's site)

www.australiansoccer.com.au
(the national team player statistics
are fantastic)

www.robbieslater.com
(for local and overseas information)

Baumgartner, Leo, *The Little Professor of Soccer*, Marketing Productions, Sydney, 1968.

Farina, Frank and Mersiades, Bonnie, *My World Is Round*, Vox Peritus, Queensland, 1998.

Olivier-Scerri, Gino E., *Encyclopedia of Australian Soccer 1922–88*, Showcase Productions, Sydney, 1988.

Schwab, Laurie, *The Socceroos and Their Opponents*, A Soccer Action publication, Newspress Pty Ltd (The Age), Melbourne, 1980.

Slater, Robbie and Hall, Matt, *The Hard Way*, Harper Sports, Sydney, 1999.

Warren, Johnny with Harper, Andy and Whittington, Josh, *Sheilas, Wogs & Poofters*, Random House Australia, Sydney, 2002. (Thanks Woody!!)